SPEAK FOR SUCCESS
&
SPEAK WITH AUTHORITY

Whether you have a cause to promote or a product to sell, whether you want to get ahead in your career, in school or in your personal life, *Speak for Success* will help you speak up and speak out—with confidence!

With a comprehensive series of exercises and rehearsal techniques, this book makes it easy to speak well—in every situation, every single time. Personally and professionally, you can speak your mind with...

SPEAK FOR SUCCESS

D0845172

SPEAK
FOR SUCCESS

Eugene Ehrlich
Columbia University

Gene R. Hawes

A HUDSON GROUP BOOK

BANTAM BOOKS
TORONTO · NEW YORK · LONDON · SYDNEY · AUCKLAND

SPEAK FOR SUCCESS
A Bantam Book / March 1984

ISBN 0-553-24005-6

Published simultaneously in the United States and Canada

Bantam Books are published by Bantam Books, Inc. Its trademark, consisting of the words ''Bantam Books'' and the por-
trayal of a rooster, is Registered in U.S. Patent and Trademark
Office and in other countries. Marca Registrada. Bantam
Books, Inc., 666 Fifth Avenue, New York, New York 10103.

PRINTED IN THE UNITED STATES OF AMERICA

H   0 9 8 7 6 5 4 3 2

ACKNOWLEDGMENTS

The authors wish to thank Emma Dally, Henry Ehrlich, Fran Hawthorne, Mary Racette, and Barbara Veals for their help with this book.

CONTENTS

CHAPTER 1

Five Key Secrets to Mastering Successful Speech

Fifty years of combined experience and training have gone into this book. That's right, fifty years. The writers of this book spend their professional lives as authors, editors, teachers, and communications consultants to industry, foundations, and government. Everything they do in these roles emphasizes real communication between people.

We speak to you, therefore, from practical experience. In speaking before large groups. In teaching. In coaching reluctant and hesitant speakers. In explaining. In convincing. In persuading. In improving speakers' mannerisms. In making shrinking violets bloom into leaders.

Nothing we tell you in this book is mere textbook advice. Everything we tell you has succeeded in turning thousands of ordinary people into successful speakers.

Want to join the club?

Knowing how to speak well can benefit you more than you can imagine. Good speech can help you earn high marks in any course you take. It is important for landing the job you want. For promotions. For making more money. For impressing friends and audiences large and small. Or even for your private life (yes, that too). And you won't find it hard to improve the way you speak. In fact, we promise that you will find your program of improvement fascinating, exciting, and immediately productive.

What you do is this: you improve in easy steps—one step

at a time. And each step brings you a big, lasting payoff. You need only minutes to start on any one step. And once you take that step, you will be that much better at speaking with everyone you talk *with*—and *to*.

For instance, in this chapter we want to offer you five key secrets to successful speech that, when mastered, will easily double the power of everything you say. Yes, double. And that will happen even if you do nothing else to improve your speech. See for yourself.

Secret I. Eye Contact— Make It and Keep It

Except for your voice, your eyes are the most important tools you use in speaking.

And this is true whether you are addressing a roomful of people or an employment manager. Whether you are accepting your party's nomination for President of the United States or demanding a refund at your local discount department store. Whether you are proposing marriage or summing up the facts of your case as lawyer for the defense.

People trust you.

People care about what you say.

People believe you . . .

IF THEY CAN SEE YOUR EYES LOOKING DIRECTLY AT THEM. This is known as *eye contact*.

We said that, except for your voice, your eyes are your most important tools in *speaking*. Well, except for your ears, your eyes are also your most important tools in *listening*.

Eye contact works both ways in opening up real communication.

Yes, people respond positively to what you have to say when they have eye contact with you. But eye contact also gives you a quick and reliable way to read your listeners' minds. Just as listeners look inside you when they read *your* eyes, you look inside them when you read *their* eyes. Without eye contact, you have no idea of whether you are making the impression you want to make. You lose the greatest opportunity you'll ever have to get your message across.

Reading your listeners' minds through eye contact gives you a chance to clarify a muddled message you have just sent. It gives you a chance to reemphasize a point that is scoring for you. It gives you a chance to supply examples that will convince your listener. It gives you a chance to change your entire sales approach. It gives you a chance to stop and wait for your listener to tell you the good news. The sale is made. The job is yours. The promotion is yours. Beginning Monday, you are vice-president of marketing.

The list of benefits of eye contact goes on and on. Let's take a moment to follow the story of a young man one of us knew more than ten years ago.

After six months as factory manager for a small North Carolina textile firm, Bill had to face facts. As a result of inflation, the cost of living there was not as low as he had been led to believe. He liked his job and wanted to keep it. The future looked good. But how could he make ends meet on his salary?

Bill and his wife had talked the problem through many times. Because Mary had to stay at home with the children, there was no chance she could take a job to help out. There seemed to be no other way than to make an appointment with Jack Ellsworth, the company president, and raise The Big Question.

Ellsworth was known as a stern man with only one interest in life—his company. He worked at least as hard as anyone he employed and was on the road working long days for weeks at a time. Because Ellsworth was on the road so much, Bill had spent little time with him. Mostly they had worked together on production plans and ways to raise company profits. Bill had no idea what he could expect as he waited for the president's secretary to call him.

Bill was frightened.

He kept his hands together in his lap and looked hard— right at the big cigar humidor on the president's desk. Just before he began to speak, he sneaked a glance at Ellsworth's face—no sign there—and quickly looked back again at the humidor.

"I know I'm not due for a raise until after the first of the year. . . ." He stopped. There was a long pause. Bill could not go on. The boss said nothing.

The silence seemed to go on forever.

Bill finally looked up. What he saw surprised him. Instead of the expected grim look saying NO, he saw a sympathetic smile.

"I know you wouldn't have come in," Ellsworth said, "unless you thought you deserved a raise. I've been keeping track of your work and I know you've solved more than your share of problems since you joined us. You've got the raise. Let's not waste any more time. Let's talk about next season's line. I'm looking to you for. . . ."

That night, at home, Bill filled Mary in on the good news he had already hinted at on the telephone.

"I could have saved myself a lot of handwringing if I'd just had the nerve to look at him while I was talking. I had thought he was one of those tough types I've never been able to look in the eye. My head was full of figures I had rehearsed fourteen times to justify asking for a raise, but I wasn't sure of myself. That's what made me tongue-tied. My father used to tell me that the eyes are the mirror of the soul, and he was right. If I'd looked Ellsworth in the eye right from the start, I would have known exactly how to present my case. I think he would have put me at ease right away. . . ."

Now let's see how *you* can benefit from eye contact.

Three Ways to Use Eye Contact

1. LOOK ALERT AND RIGHT INTO YOUR LISTENER'S EYES.

This doesn't mean you have to stare constantly without blinking or looking away from time to time. You are a human being and it is only natural to blink your eyes every few seconds.

But when you look at someone you're talking with, it is vital to look into his eyes.

Not at your listener's forehead. That's a sure way to make anyone uncomfortable. (Try looking at a friend's forehead while you are talking with him or her. You'll soon find you are not being listened to. Instead, your friend will be wondering what's wrong. If you don't believe this, ask someone to look at your forehead while you are speaking. You'll soon see how uncomfortable this trick can make you.)

Not at your listener's neck or chin. Same reaction.

The place to look is *right into the eyes of your listener.* That's real eye contact. And real eye contact is the most direct way of getting someone's attention and keeping it.

As long as you are looking someone right in the eye, there is no way that person can avoid listening to you intently. Real eye contact almost guarantees that your listener will understand exactly what you are trying to say. The direct communication you open up makes speaking easy and listening easy.

Avoiding eye contact kills communication. Anyone who looks off into the distance while he is talking invites the listener's mind to go off into the distance.

Anyone whose eyes follow a person walking by during a conversation tells his listener that the speaker is uninterested in the listener. You can verify this easily the next time you have a conversation with a friend. After you have allowed yourself to appear distracted two or three times, ask your friend whether your behavior was noticed.

Anyone who *looks* over a listener's head might just as well *talk* over the listener's head. Communication dies when the eyes do their own thing.

A person who will not look into another person's eyes while speaking is universally distrusted. The old barroom line "Look me in the eye when you say that!" is the final test. It warns of real trouble ahead. It's one thing to say something nasty about another person. It's quite another to look him in the eye—that is, prove you mean it.

The eyes give the final sign of intention. The listener finds out by looking at the speaker's eyes. If the speaker is not looking the listener right in the eye, the message is lost.

Did you know that Arabs are taught early in life that the eyes are a sure giveaway when someone is telling a lie? Students of Arab culture tell us that the pupils of a speaker's eyes dilate when he or she is telling a lie, so anyone who doesn't want to be fooled will look instantly into the speaker's eyes. It is for this reason that many politicians in the Arab world will wear sunglasses even when they are indoors. They want to hide their eyes!

2. USE EYE CONTACT EVEN WHEN YOU ARE SPEAKING TO A GROUP.

When you speak before a group, each listener must feel that he or she is the one person you're really interestea in How can you do this?

The trick is to address one person at a time and give that person your undivided attention for that moment.

This means you must deliver an entire sentence to one person, making eye contact all the while. When you've finished that sentence, you move on to the next, again making eye contact. By moving about the group, giving one person at a time your entire attention, you will maintain eye contact with the entire group. Each listener will know that he or she is important to you.

Don't think you'll be able to do this without practice. In a group of five listeners, for example, here is the way to move about the group with your eyes. First you make eye contact with the person right in front of you. And you keep that contact until you complete your first sentence. You then choose a person to your left. Again you make and maintain eye contact throughout a sentence. You then move your eyes to your right, beyond your first listener, then back to the far left, then the far right. You then start all over again at dead center.

If you do this, you'll speak directly with each person a number of times. You'll have the attention of everyone in the group. Each person will think your message was intended especially for him or her.

Don't start at one end of a group and work your way across the group one person at a time. If you make that error, you'll have half an audience wondering why you don't care about them at all. To keep eye contact with an entire group, you must look often at each member of the audience.

Our most successful public speakers can maintain eye contact with audiences numbering in the hundreds. They look directly at someone in the audience with each sentence delivered. Their eyes lock with the eyes of that one person, then another, at all times. They make eye contact with someone near the front of the audience, then with someone in the middle left, then someone in the center rear, then someone in the middle right, and back to the front, never stopping in one target direction for more than a complete sentence. But they look at individuals, not at space!

Distance being what it is, every listener in the auditorium thinks he or she has the complete attention of the speaker for a good share of the time. What greater way to capture and retain the interest of the audience!

The importance of eye contact is demonstrated by a device developed for public speakers who are called on to speak before audiences numbering in the thousands. You have surely seen one or more of the national conventions of our political parties on television. Do you remember that the eyes of the speaker turned this way and then that during a speech? Every speaker appears to look directly at the various people in the audience, maintaining eye contact at all times.

How does this happen? Sheets of transparent plastic stand a little bit to the left and to the right of the speaker's eyes. On those sheets of plastic are projected the words of the speaker's prepared address. The audience can't see the words. One sentence is projected first to one side of the speaker, the next sentence to the other.

To keep up with the prepared text, the speaker must look first at one plastic sheet and then at the other. This movement of the speaker's eyes and head gives the audience the feeling that the speaker is looking directly at them.

When the audience has left the meeting, everyone is sure the next President of the United States has spoken directly to them! And all this because a device has forced convention speakers to maintain eye contact

3. LET YOUR EYES SPEAK FOR YOU.

When a situation calls for warmth, let your eyes show that warmth.

When a situation calls for sympathy, let your eyes show that sympathy.

Whatever feeling or emotion is called for, let your eyes help in sending the message.

You are a human being with all the warmth, sympathy, sincerity, frankness, interest, and feeling a human being has. Let your eyes do their part in punctuating your message whenever you speak.

If you are praising a group for its accomplishments, your eyes do their share in carrying the message. If you are criticizing a group for some reason, your eyes can show that too.

This use of eye contact makes listeners tie right in with you while you speak. They know and understand the message they are getting.

If your eyes are giving one message while your words are giving another, your audience will not know how to read you. Because people trust a speaker's eyes more than his words, the most common response is to distrust the message given in words. The speaker is not trusted and will have a tough time communicating successfully.

Try this experiment. Stand in front of a mirror and tell yourself what a fine person you are. Tell yourself you have been doing a fine job and that you will soon be given a raise. Notice your expression while you are speaking. Are your eyes friendly and warm throughout this wonderful message? If so, you will tend to believe the words you are saying.

Now give the message while looking unfriendly or downright angry. Do you see the difference in your eyes? Can you see how a real audience might respond to a message in which a speaker's eyes do not match his words?

Secret II. Speak Loudly Enough to Be Heard Clearly

A number of years ago, we were asked to help a large aircraft company win the most important production contract on which it had ever bid. The competition had been going on for two years. All the major aircraft producers had entered the race. Now only two were left. The purchaser—the United States Air Force—was willing to buy from either company: the designs were almost identical, the prices offered by the two companies were both acceptable, and both companies were judged capable of delivering excellent products.

To choose the winner, the Air Force decided to invite the chief engineer of each company to make a final presentation before the selection board. The ground rules? *No visual aids of any kind.* Just appear before the twenty-officer selection board and speak for fifteen minutes, telling the board anything the chief engineers wanted to say. Each man was to appear alone before the board.

Our role was to help one of these chief engineers prepare and deliver the best speech he had ever given.

By the time we began to participate, hundreds of ideas for the speech and several drafts had been put on paper. The chief engineer had one week to go before the big day.

When we met the chief engineer for the first time, we were impressed by his intelligence, his knowledge, and his engaging manner. He immediately conveyed an impression of great confidence and determination. As a candidate for this tough assignment, he left nothing to be desired—except that he was *hard to hear from more than a few feet away.*

We asked him about this characteristic, and he replied that he had never had any difficulty in being heard. Further discussion revealed that he had never given a speech except to small groups in his office!

Once the speech was put in final form, the chief engineer learned it easily and was able to deliver it well without using notes of any kind. But we wanted to be certain he would maintain eye contact with the board.

Since we were informed that the board would be seated at a long table in a narrow room, we established a rehearsal room much like it. We gathered a group of twenty people to be present at rehearsals. Whenever anyone could not hear a word the speaker said, that person would raise his or her hand. After several of these sessions, the engineer had learned to speak naturally in a voice that carried throughout the room.

We cannot say that the engineer's company won the contract award because he had learned to speak loudly enough to be heard clearly. But the published report of the selection board included a sentence that may indicate this: "The board was especially impressed by the directness of Mr. ____, who had a

firm grasp of his subject and by his manner conveyed the full
commitment of his company to success of the Air Force
project.''

The advice to keep your voice at a level that can be heard
is simple, but it is often ignored. A creative-writing teacher
we know, fed up with mumblers in his class, refers to the
Marlon Brando Syndrome. Asked to read their work aloud in
class, these mumblers seldom get beyond the second sentence
before being interrupted by the teacher and directed to speak
out.

While we sympathize with the feelings of shyness and
stage fright people have when called upon to speak before a
group, we have found that those speakers who try to speak
louder often overcome their embarrassment as a result. By
concentrating on raising their voices, they forget their reluc-
tance to speak.

So if you make the effort to speak loudly enough to be
heard clearly, your performance will automatically improve.

Secret III. Slow Down

If you are like millions of others, you think faster than you
can speak. Poor speakers often make the mistake of racing
through their words to try to catch up with their thoughts.
Excessive speed can numb an audience in a few minutes.

Test yourself now to find out how fast you speak. Find a
passage in a book that deals with a subject you may someday
be called on to discuss. Count off about five hundred words.
You can do this by counting the number of words in three
successive lines and dividing by three to get an average line.
Then count the lines you need to reach five hundred words.
Read aloud and time yourself. Read in the way you normally
speak before an audience. A good range is 130 to 165 words
a minute. How do you rate? If you are faster than this, try to
slow down. You will soon find that you can do so.

Do not think that you ought to hold a constant rate when
speaking before a group. A variety of speeds is more interesting.
When your facts or ideas are difficult, slow down. When your

facts or ideas are simple, speed up. Yet the overall average should be 130 to 165 words a minute

Secret IV. Sound Each Word Clearly

Many English words sound alike. By moving your tongue or lips a tiny fraction of an inch while saying a word, you can change the sounds you're making. By opening your mouth a bit more or a bit less while speaking, you can change the sounds you make.

If you do not make sounds carefully, then you risk serious misunderstanding. A tape recorder is a good investment for improving this aspect of your speech.

Using the same passage you measured for computing your rate of speaking, record your speech and then listen carefully to how you make every sound. Listen especially for the way you pronounce words beginning in *d, t,* and *th.* Can you hear the difference when saying *din, tin, thin,* and *then*?

Ask your friends whether they have trouble hearing your words clearly when you speak. Make a list of any sounds that are difficult for you. Use your tape recorder to practice all of them.

Secret V. Banish All Space Fillers

"Uh-h-h-h."
"Um-m-m-m."
"Like."
"Y'know."

In his book *Strictly Speaking,* Edwin Newman tells us, that "people collapse into y'know after giving up trying to say what they mean." *Y'know* is just one of the space fillers people resort to instead of saying something real, or *merely keeping quiet*.

Do you have friends who are guilty of this annoying practice? More important, are you guilty of it?

No one likes to listen to nonsense syllables or words. Try

recording a conversation with a close friend to hear your own space fillers. You can be sure that if you use them in conversation, you also use them when speaking before a group.

A mutual agreement with a close friend to call attention to one another's space fillers can help you discard this verbal crutch.

Practice Activities

You have been given five secrets:

Establish Eye Contact
Speak Up
Slow Down
Say Words Clearly
Banish Space Fillers

You probably can invent practice activities on your own to give yourself the increased strength you need as a speaker.

If you can't think of any, try these. Speak to yourself in front of a mirror from time to time to make eye contact natural for you.

Tape record yourself from time to time to esablish the habits of speaking loudly enough and slowly enough and clearly enough to be understood without difficulty. Sit or stand farther and farther from your tape recorder to see how well you project without hurting your speed and clarity.

Listen to yourself carefully as you speak to see whether you have banished your particular space fillers.

CHAPTER 2
Tapping the Speech Power You Now Have

Members of the clergy often are excellent speakers. This should not surprise anyone. Strength and conviction are vital to truly powerful speech, and people who preach their beliefs have plenty of both these qualities.

But preachers do not have a monopoly on power. In ancient Rome, Cicero had it. As a result, to Romans his was the voice of reason. Demosthenes had this power, and ancient Athens followed him to war. Franklin D. Roosevelt, four times elected President of the United States, had this power. When you have the opportunity, listen to his strength and conviction as he told a frightened nation: "We have nothing to fear but fear itself." In a single speech he wiped out the panic that had gripped his countrymen and united an entire people behind him.

You may not now be the match of any of these gifted orators, but you do have within you the strength and conviction they had. And the release of your power is the goal of this chapter.

Do you doubt the importance of strength and conviction in capturing your audience? Recall 1980, when strength and conviction in speeches given tirelessly through the previous fifteen or twenty years counted as the chief reason for success in winning the highest office in the land.

It was essentially as an orator and an actor that Ronald Reagan began to win a political following in the 1960s. He became notable for the effectiveness with which he argued in support of his sincere conservative views while speaking often on diverse occasions. He was not a lawyer, a prominent business or government manager, nor an authority on any subject whatever. Yet the power with which he spoke for his beliefs won his election as governor of California, and then as the nation's fortieth President.

Let's start now to release some of that power. Right now!

Ask yourself what really matters to you. We mean what *really* matters to you. There must be something that bothers you, some issue so pressing that you want to tell the world about it—and change the world if you can. Can you think of something? Is it politics? Is it housing? Is it unemployment? Are you having trouble deciding how you're going to spend the next thirty-five years of your life? Are your teachers or friends treating you with less respect than you think is your due? Are you concerned over nuclear power? The environment? The price of gasoline? Your career? What's bugging you? Pick a topic.

Got it? *Go right to a friend and sound off.*

Your purpose is to express your point of view and convince your friend that you are right.

Don't think twice about the words you use. Don't worry about whether you're speaking perfect English. Don't worry about your choice of words. Don't plan the speech at all.

What's going to do the job for you—what's going to persuade your friend—is the strength of feeling, the conviction of truth your words will carry. Because you will really mean what you say.

* * *

Have you tried it? If you have—if you really sounded off—the result was predictable. Your voice carried so much authority that your friend listened carefully until you finished. No listener dares break in on someone who speaks with strength and conviction.

Let us look hard at how this works.

Ignace Paderewski, the late Polish piano virtuoso, once said: "If I do not practice one day, I notice it. If I do not practice for two days, my friends notice it. If I do not practice for three days, my public notices it."

A well-trained voice is like a musical instrument. Care and practice are needed to bring the voice to its peak.

So what we are saying is that while vocal technique is no substitute for sincerity or sound reasoning, you will help your speech if you know something about how you produce sounds. With this knowledge you will be able to take greater advantage of your natural ability.

Breathing Properly

Breath is the basis of speech. Awake or asleep, we breathe continually. When we sleep, our breathing is automatic and quite deep. It resembles the breathing that supports the best speech and singing.

When we are awake, we breathe in two different ways. The first way is silent. Primarily through the nose we take in small amounts of air without thinking about it. Breath inhalation and exhalation are of approximately equal duration.

The second way is quite different. The breath we use to support words depends to some extent on our will. We know how much we want to say and we plan our breathing accordingly. We are likely to take in a good deal of air in a short period of time and then let it out more slowly. In order to get enough air, we must inhale through the mouth as well as through the nose.

As you breathe, you can feel the action of your rib cage and a sheet of muscle called the *diaphragm,* which fits below your lungs. When you inhale, your rib cage rises and your diaphragm falls. This enables your lungs to take in air as a result of atmospheric pressure. When you exhale, your rib cage falls and your diaphragm rises. This pushes air out of your lungs.

This is a natural way to breathe. It produces no tension. The body is not prevented from doing exactly what it knows how to do. Taking a deep breath before you speak—a mistake made frequently by frightened, untrained speakers—produces tension throughout the body. It makes nothing but trouble for the rib cage, diaphragm, and lungs. It makes breath control difficult and affects the resonance, tone, and pitch of your voice. (You will be reading more about these aspects of speech production shortly.)

So what can you do to improve your breathing for effective speech? To start with, if you merely hold yourself straight—but not rigid—and tuck in your stomach while you speak, you will be doing ninety percent of what's necessary.

Instead of thinking about taking full breaths as you finish each paragraph of a speech or each thought in a conversation, take advantage of the comfortable pauses that always occur in speech. They allow you to sip the air naturally. Tucking your stomach in and holding yourself straight will keep your diaphragm, rib cage, and lungs ready to do their jobs exactly when needed without any prompting from you.

Let's take a closer look at the role of posture—how we stand or sit—in speech production and see what effect it has on our voices.

Try this experiment now: Stand at attention. Bold as a U.S. Marine. Chest thrust forward. Lungs full of air. Straight as a ramrod. Shoulders square. Chin jutting out defiantly. Eyes straight ahead.

In this unnatural posture, say something strong and defiant. How about: "I'm angry. I'm not going to take it anymore. This is the new me. Dynamic. Full of life. Afraid of nothing. I'm ready to go out and shake the world by the throat until I get what I want."

When you finish, stoop a little. Relax. Let your stomach sag. Let your chest fall. Let your eyes drift back toward the floor. Let your shoulders droop.

Now say something appropriate to this posture. How about:

"Life is unfair. I can't get a break. I try. I always try. But somehow I cannot get ahead. Everyone is against me."

Now you have seen how the way you hold yourself while talking affects the way the words come out, the way you are heard by your listeners. But think further about these postures. They have something important in common. In both cases your voice sounded unnatural. Anyone who might have over-heard you would have felt uncomfortable. At Marine attention you sounded strained and shrill. In utter dejection you sounded pathetic. Both performances were painful for an audience.

What about your breathing? In both cases you were limiting the chest room you needed for full voice projection. The notes your voice can make during normal breathing were limited by the way you held yourself. In both cases you finished yourself off as an effective speaker before you began. You might say that you programmed yourself for ineffective speech. It doesn't matter whether you felt strong enough to walk through a wall in the Marine posture, weak enough to be knocked over by a feather in the second posture. You weren't making it possible for your full speech power to emerge in either posture.

An Effective Voice Is a Convincing Voice

The sound of your voice should be the least of your worries. In fact, it shouldn't be a worry at all. Most of us at one time or other have doubts about the way we sound. What many of us do not realize is that almost all of us possess the tools we need for a perfectly adequate voice, unless we want to become actors or opera stars.

As a law student we know discovered in her first year of law school, the enemies of good voice are the same old enemies many of us face daily: lack of self-confidence, tension, and plain old bad habits.

Sheila was forever being told by her law professors to speak up when she was called on in class.

"There I was, a woman trying to make it in a man's field. But I was still handicapped by my image of what a woman should be. Quiet. Demure. Anything but pushy. And after they told me to raise my voice, I'd suddenly switch into high gear. I hated the way I sounded. I felt as though I had gone from a whisper to an air raid siren."

One day Sheila was in a restaurant with some friends, having the usual give-and-take we all find comfortable, when she caught sight of one of her teachers a few tables away. He was watching her. Sheila halted in mid-sentence.

"I would gladly have vanished into thin air at that moment if I could have," Sheila told us later.

The teacher came over and asked for a private word with her.

"Sheila, if only you could bring into class the same skills you exhibit here!" he said. "Here you are competing beautifully with the sound of the jukebox, traffic noise from the street, and dozens of other voices. Yet your friends can hear you perfectly. They hang on your every word. Please, for the sake of your career in law, try to transfer your ability to where it will do you the most good."

Sheila says of the experience: "It was all a matter of finding the right level for the right audience. The trouble with speaking in class had always been that there was nothing to measure myself against. I could hear every word I said, but I didn't know how to gauge what was needed in those cold echo chambers we call lecture halls. To me, *louder* just meant *louder*. I didn't know what else to do. But when my teacher spoke to me in the restaurant it became clear suddenly. I wanted to carry with me into the classroom the *ease I felt with friends*. I didn't learn how to make it happen all at once, of course, but I finally knew exactly what I wanted to accomplish."

When you are in a social situation, you let the setting give you a mark to shoot for. Just as in tennis you hit the ball high enough to clear the net, in speech you pitch your voice and set the volume so you can be heard by all the listeners in the circle, no matter what the competition. Music, laughter, or other voices are compensated for automatically. Your voice is animated. Your stories, your jokes, your gossip, your arguments are given all the life they must have to be interesting.

You are excited in those situations. Your energy level is high because you are relieved to be out of the grind. You are relaxed. Your enthusiasm cannot be repressed.

Your speech shows all this.

What you must strive for in all your speech is the zest your speech has in the best of your private conversation. There's no substitute for conviction. Avoid the layers of self-doubt. Make it possible for your important ideas to find their way to the surface.

This applies to all situations you face in day-to-day living: You are the person for the job. Your plan is the right one. Your best friend is really asking for your help. The merchandise you were sent must be returned for full credit.

Don't be handicapped, either, by a shortage of breath at a critical moment. Or a crack in your voice. Or a plaintive whine that puts your listener off. These things shouldn't happen. And with a little effort they will not. It doesn't take a great deal of technique to turn you loose to become the best speaker you can be.

Good Technique— Your Untapped Strength

We possess the ability to speak well. It comes naturally, just as we breathe perfectly while asleep. But many of us have learned to doubt ourselves, to fear an audience, to be tense. And these characteristics harm the way we speak.

There's a saying that an adult should work with the seriousness of a child at play. Children don't think of their play as recreation. It's their job. They are exploring. They are in that sandbox because it's important to them. They are completely caught up in it.

For adults, work and play are different things. They worry about appearing foolish. They worry about not getting the job. They worry about everything—even while they jog. Thus, you hear them open a little speech with "I don't know how to say this . . ." or "I don't know much about this . . ." or "I haven't given much thought to this." It's almost as if they want to turn off their audiences.

Why can't we relax when we speak? If we could just relax and speak unself-consciously, if we could just be like children at play, we all would be better off.

Unleashing the full potential of your voice is just a question of a little practice. It is not a matter of becoming someone new at all. Michelangelo said that he didn't shape the stone into anything, he merely chipped away at it until he uncovered the form that was already there.

Think of your new speaking voice as something that's already there. Your shyness and your bad habits have kept it imprisoned up until now.

Sizing Up Your Voice

It is time to move ahead in your voice development by taking a bold step forward. Some people find this first step painful, but it is well worth the trouble: *Find out exactly how you sound to others*.

For this experiment you will need a tape recorder and a friend.

Be forewarned. When you listen to your own voice on tape, it will sound strange. Most people who hear their recorded voices for the first time are surprised, even shocked: "Is that me? Do I really sound like that?"

Recorded voices usually sound thinner and higher pitched to the speakers than natural voices. Remember that sound is vibration. Vibration carries through the bone and tissues of the head to the ears, as well as through the air. Cover your ears right now and hum a few notes. You do hear yourself, even though your ears are covered, don't you? So every time you speak, you not only hear yourself with your ears, but you also hear yourself with your blood, bones, and other tissues. All these parts of you transmit the vibrations that are sound.

Enough for this preliminary warning. You are ready to start your experiment with your tape recorder and a cooperative friend.

Select a topic you can speak about with that friend. It may be a personal problem. A complaint. The prospects of your local football team during the coming season. The advantages—the disadvantages—of having many children. It does not matter what topic you choose. You merely want to have a topic in mind that is worth a few minutes of your friend's time.

Turn on the tape recorder and get started. As you speak, watch your friend. You are talking to your friend, not to the tape recorder.

When you have spoken for a few minutes, turn off the recorder. The experiment is ready to move into its most important phase.

How did your friend respond while you were talking? Did you see amusement in that friend's eyes? Boredom? Skepticism? Did you see the kind of involvement with what you were saying to make your friend want to respond? Did you speak effectively? If you were complaining, did your friend sympathize? If you were explaining something, did your friend concentrate on the explanation and appear to understand? If you know this, you know whether you really were communicating.

Now rerun the tape.

Can you understand every word? Did you run out of breath at any point? Did your voice rise objectionably? Did it crack? Was there a pleasing variety of tone and volume?

When were you most forceful? Did you begin strong and then build to full effectiveness? Or did you get off to a good start and then gradually fade away?

When you sounded best, what were the qualities of voice that made you think you were at your best? Did you sound enthusiastic? Authoritative? Objective? Properly concerned? Good humored?

Can you recall the feelings you had all through the few minutes you spoke? Did you have to grope for the right words? Were there unnatural gaps in your sentences or between sentences? Or did the words just seem to flow?

When your voice sounded weakest, what qualities made it that way? Did you seem to choke? Did you lose control? Can you recall what was going through your mind when you began to lose control? Perhaps your friend made a face that indicated you were not making good sense. Or did you see boredom in your friend's expression? Did you mumble or did you seem to be screaming? Perhaps you could not get certain details quite straight as you were speaking and had to pour on too much energy to recapture your train of thought. This might have distorted your voice to the point of shrillness.

Did your voice seem monotonous? Nasal? Muffled? Weak? Was the total effect unpleasing in some other way? The explanation could be that you allow tension to reduce the natural resonance of your voice that makes your speech attractive when you are at your best.

Did you run out of breath completely one or more times while speaking? Were you caught up in a long, complex thought that demanded more of you at one stretch than you had breath for? Were you racing to get through to the end of the thought before pausing? Listen to yourself carefully on tape: you may actually hear yourself gasping for breath. A big gulp of air can usually be heard on tape.

Whatever problems you have discovered about your breathing can be overcome through analyzing your recorded speech and undertaking regular practice. Later in this chapter, you will find some exercises that will get you started toward better breathing in speech.

But let's take the time now to learn something more about pitch and resonance. These topics will supplement what you have learned about breathing to give you further insight into how you use your voice.

Pitch

Do you know what your vocal chords are? Think of them as the strings of a musical instrument called a voice. The vocal chords actually are part of the *larynx*, or voice box, the lump in your throat that bobs up and down as you speak. The Adam's apple is a man's larynx.

People have two vocal chords. They resemble flat bands a fraction of an inch long, and slightly longer in men than in women. When we are not speaking, the vocal chords are quite far apart and offer no resistance to the air that is taken into and expelled from the lungs.

When we speak, the chords are drawn together and offer a great deal of resistance to air. As a result of this resistance to air, the vocal chords vibrate to produce the various sounds that we call speech.

So this is how you produce sound. But think further about the vocal chords. We have said that men have slightly longer vocal chords than women have. The fact is that longer chords produce sounds of lower *pitch* than shorter chords produce. Pitch is the degree of highness or lowness of a voice or a musical instrument. Since men have longer vocal chords, you would expect them to have voices of lower pitch than women have.

You can understand this easily if you think of the strings of a violin. To raise the pitch of a violin string, a violinist moves his finger up the string, toward the body of the instrument. This has the effect of making the string shorter. To lower the pitch of a string, the violinist moves his finger back toward the neck of the instrument.

Now let's get away from violins and back to vocal chords, your vocal chords.

Your voice has a usable range of eight or more notes. You can make those notes higher or lower at will. Try singing a few bars of any song, first high and then low, to see how easily you can do this.

It is possible to train your voice to be deeper or higher than it normally is. Sir Laurence Olivier, the great English actor, lowered his by more than one octave—eight notes—in preparation for his role in Shakespeare's *Othello*. But this took him many months.

We are not suggesting that you retrain your voice to be eight notes lower than it naturally is. Yet there are certain advantages to a low speaking voice. A low voice is less apt to become shrill when a speaker is under stress. Even though the voice will usually rise in pitch at such a time, it will not become so high that the speaker sounds overwrought. Note, too, that the vocal chords are stressed more at higher than at lower pitches, and stress can lead to hoarseness and fatigue.

Too low a pitch carries only one danger: your voice may

not carry. A sure sign of too low a pitch is your experience with people listening to you. Do you often find that people ask you to repeat something you've just said? Or do people seem to lean in toward you when you begin to speak? Or—worst of all—after you have spoken do people's responses to what you have said indicate that they have misunderstood you or not understood you at all? Chances are they have not heard everything you said, and too low a pitch may be the problem. We shall deal with it shortly.

Too high a pitch is a more difficult problem to solve.

At worst, extremely high-pitched voices can become serious drawbacks both for women who may be considered childish, as well as for men who may be considered effeminate. Such responses of people to high-pitched voices may be unfair, but we cannot argue with people's feelings. Social and professional relations may be seriously distorted by such superficial personal characteristics.

Do you know the pitch of your own voice? It is quite possible that you have no impression of how you sound to others.

Pitch is easy enough to discover. To establish your truest and most comfortable pitch, all you need to do is read a paragraph aloud several times. Read faster than you normally do. Speak in a normal conversational tone. Don't try to make a speech. Don't try to make sense of the paragraph as you read. Just read rapidly. Leave out the pauses. Forget emphasis. Just pronounce each word distinctly.

After you have done this a few times to put yourself at ease and establish complete familiarity with the paragraph, *read it once more*. While you are reading this last time, turn on your tape recorder. When you finish, listen to yourself. You are hearing your natural pitch—your truest and most comfortable pitch—as other people hear it.

Does it please you? Are you neither too high nor too low? Or do you have a pitch problem?

If you do, you can begin to work on it right now. The important thing to remember is that you will be able to repitch your voice, either higher or lower, only by being aware of your pitch and being willing to practice speaking at the newer, more desirable pitch. At first, you will do best to talk at the changed pitch for a few minutes at a time with your tape recorder turned on. Read something aloud as many times as you can each day, but stop now and then to listen to what you hear during playback. Make any necessary adjustments as you practice. After you have begun to make progress, you can practice speaking at the new pitch with members of your family and your close friends. If things work out—and they surely will if you practice conscientiously—you can begin using your new pitch everywhere.

Caution: Don't try to move your voice all the way down or up all at once. A little bit of progress in a week or two is fine. Then a little more progress. Then a little more. You will find that the new pitch will soon become your true pitch. And new respect as well as better responses among your listeners will reward your effort.

Resonance

Physiologists tell us that vocal chords account for only five percent of the volume of speech. The vibrations produced by the vocal chords must be amplified by a set of *resonators*.

Think about the violin again. The body of a violin is a hollow wooden box. The hollow wooden box is a resonator. When you pluck the strings or when you draw a bow across the strings, vibrations enter the empty wooden box. The sound made by the vibrating strings echoes from the entire surface of the inside of the instrument. What is more, the echoes themselves cause additional echoes.

As a result, the sound of the violin has a depth and quality that go far beyond the sound made by the vibration of the strings alone.

Think of how a violin would sound if it were full of water. The instrument, no matter how well made, would sound flat. The strings would do their job, but the resonator would not be working at all.

What does this have to do with your voice? Your body has empty spaces that do for your voice what the body of the violin does for its voice. Your body has a chest cavity, throat,

sinuses, and mouth—in a word, resonators. Without full use
of these spaces, your voice loses the richness and power it
should have.

Do you know how you sound when you slouch in your
chair while you speak? Your voice is flat.

Do you know how you sound when you have a cold? Again
flat. Unpleasant. You have trouble speaking loudly enough, so
you try to compensate by shouting. This strains your vocal
chords and causes hoarseness.

You have all the equipment you need to achieve good
resonance. It is waiting to be used. Good posture opens up
your chest. Clear sinuses and your full throat—if not ob-
structed by a medical problem—are there and functioning.

So what goes wrong? Speakers develop bad habits. Many
of these habits are related to tension and lack of confidence.

People with bad posture often are fearful of sitting up
straight in the presence of others. They do not want to be
noticed. People who feel they must whine to get attention end
up closing off their sinuses.

As you know, whining gets the wrong kind of attention.
Whiners are annoying and tiresome, so we get through our
business with them as quickly as possible.

People who shrink from attention don't open their mouths
sufficiently to use their throats as resonators.

A deficiency in any of these parts unbalances the whole
system. If you don't use your nose in speaking, you can
throw off your breathing in general. If you keep your chest
rigid, you are not using its natural rise and fall to help
breathing. You end up shouting to be heard, because a rigid
chest cannot act as a good resonator for your voice.

Remember how you hummed earlier in this chapter to hear
yourself transmit vibrations to your ear? Try humming now to
feel the vibrations throughout your system. In your sinuses,
chest, and throat. Feel the different vibrations and listen to
what they add to your tone. When you close off any part of
your resonating equipment, you lose all-important resonance.

If you have habitually neglected any part of your resonating
apparatus, try to hum in that area. Try to direct the vibrations
into any of the cavities that have not been receiving their full
share.

Remember that your problems of voice production are

directly related to your general level of physical tension, so any special techniques you have for relaxing will also help your voice.

Things to Do to Help Your Speech

1. Tuck your stomach in and use your diaphragm to support your words.
2. Sit and stand straight but not rigid. Shoulders back but not uncomfortably so. Head up but not like a Marine at attention.
3. While sitting, keep your feet squarely on the floor. This means with legs uncrossed.
4. Use a comfortable, calm, low pitch as the basis for your speaking voice.

Things to Avoid

1. Slouching.
2. Deep breaths.
3. Straining your vocal chords by shouting.
4. Tension in any part of your resonating space: chest, sinuses, throat.
5. Tension in lips, tongue, or jaw. A stiff mouth hurts your capacity for clear pronunciation.

Call Your Own Tune—How Greater Control Can Work for You

A good speaker has more than a good vocabulary. A good speaker has a repertoire of voice notes. A good speaker has the ability to use inflections—small shifts in pitch and volume that provide subtle shades of meaning. A good speaker has the ability to lead the listener with the sound of the spoken sentence, as well as with the logic of an argument or the precision of word usage.

These extra vocal qualities are greatly helped by your new, improved speech habits. They are the *extras* of the successful speaker. With these extras, a speaker can convey the importance and excitement of the words and thoughts he is using.

Without these extras, a speaker can make dull words out of words as exciting as "Life, liberty, and the pursuit of happiness." Without appropriate pitch, without full resonance, without easy breathing providing support for your words, your listeners will neither be moved by, nor believing of, what you say.

Practice Activities

Be sure you have followed the activities already suggested in this chapter. In addition, make tapes of your speech from time to time over many weeks. Do not erase these tapes. They will become the record of the progress you make in tapping your speech power.

CHAPTER 3
Building Good English

Just as we all may speak English with individual accents, we also may have habitual phrases we've learned from those around us. But these natural turns of speech can pose a hazard: they may brand us as ignorant and low-class among those we see in our lives if what we say sounds inappropriate or incorrect.

The fact is that people can tell a great deal about you from the words you use, from the way you pronounce those words, and from your grammar.

In the Broadway musical *My Fair Lady,* Professor Higgins taught Eliza Doolittle the refined accent and diction of the British upper class as a replacement for the Cockney of her upbringing. She was then able to pass as a lady.

The purpose of this chapter is to help you work toward improving your diction so that your speech patterns will be a help, not a hindrance.

The Rough Edges

As you become a better speaker, you will want to make progress in every way. You will want to remove every barrier, no matter how small, between your thoughts and clear understanding by your listeners.

Every rough edge distracts from the message you want to get across. And some of the roughest edges of all occur in pronunciation, usage, and grammar.

The language that comes naturally to you and the phrases

you use habitually with your friends may not be the best for reaching the widest possible audience. Educated people may think of you as ignorant. Snobs may consider you lower class. Youthful slang will not be understood by people twice your age. If you want to earn respect from your elders, you must speak their language or else they will think you immature.

Bad pronunciation, usage, and grammar can affect listeners the way a scratch in a phonograph record does. No matter how good the music, the listener thinks only about the scratch every time it comes around—thirty-three and one-third times a minute.

A well-known example of poor pronunciation was President Eisenhower's difficulty with the word *nuclear.* Instead of saying *nuke*-lee-ur, as he should have, Ike said *nuke*-yu-lur. The effect on listeners was jarring. Every time he mispronounced the word, he lost his audience for a few moments. President Ford had a similar word problem. He pronounced *judgment* as *juj*-uh-ment.

Such mistakes create the impression that the speaker doesn't know what he's saying. Do you know whether you have any of these rough edges?

We want you to think of good grammar, usage, and pronunciation as part of your grooming habits. They are the washing, combing, and dressing of good speech. Appropriate speech denies people the opportunity to turn up their noses at you. Appropriate speech does not distract people's attention from what you say by the way you say it. It frees your audience to listen carefully and approvingly to the messages you send.

This chapter is presented in three major sections. The first section alerts you to words that are commonly mispronounced and to phrases that contain errors in diction.

The second major section of this chapter provides a Quick Reference Guide to Grammar and a Quick Reference Guide to Usage. The Guide to Grammar will reacquaint you with many of the rules that give our spoken language its structure. The Guide to Usage will acquaint you with correct ways of using words that are commonly misused.

Mistakes in grammar and usage can lead to misunderstandings in speech, particularly when fine shades of meaning are involved. Correcting your mistakes will enable you to deal with complex ideas with greater precision and confidence.

The third major section of this chapter deals with word choice. We tell you how to clean the deadwood from your vocabulary. We tell you how to aim your words at the widest possible audience, how to expand your vocabulary, and how to make your words as lively as possible. We give you a list of overused words and phrases, and the words and phrases to use in place of them.

Learning to speak better is like learning to play tennis better. It is difficult to improve your tennis by playing against your equals. You should play against people who are better than you are.

For this reason, take every opportunity to speak with people who speak better than you do. Listen to them carefully to learn their speech patterns. If you know some of these people well, ask them to correct you when you make mistakes. You will also find it helpful to listen carefully when you watch national news programs on television. And study this chapter. Even people who speak better than you do can make mistakes.

Improving Your Diction

How you pronounce words and how you use them, as we have said, affect the way an audience sees you. In this brief section, our purpose is to alert you to everyday mistakes in diction so that you become conscious of how you sound to others. We then suggest ways for helping yourself improve your diction.

In the left-hand column below are correctly spelled words. In the middle column are common mispronunciations of these words. The right-hand column provides the correct pronunciations.

	WRONG	RIGHT
accidentally	ak-si-*dent*-ly	ak-si-*den*-tal-ly
across	a-*krost*	a-*kross*
anyway	*en*-ee-wayz	*en*-ee-way
anywhere	*en*-ee-warez	*en*-ee-hware
burst	bust	burst
clique	click	cleek
drowned	*drown*-did	drownd
escape	ek-*scape*	es-*cape*
heartrending	*hart*-ren-der-ing	*hart*-ren-ding
height	hithe	hite
hold	a-hold	hold
hundred	*hun*-nert	*hun*-drid
incidentally	in-si-*dent*-ly	in-si-*den*-tal-ly
interesting	*in*-nur-es-ting	*in*-tur-es-ting
judgment	*judg*-uh-ment	*judg*-ment
nowhere	*no*-warez	no-hware
often	*off*-ten	*off*-en
pronunciation	pro-nown-see-*ay*-shun	pro-nun-see-*ay*-shun
recur	re-o-*cur*	re-*cur*
regardless	ir-ri-*gard*-liss	ri-*gard*-liss
scared	uh-*scared*	scared
toward	tuh-*ward*	tawrd
unaware	un-uh-*warez*	un-uh-*ware*
undoubtedly	un-*dow*-tuh-blee	un-*dow*-tid-lee

The dictionary is your best tool for checking pronunciations of new or unfamiliar words. A good dictionary indicates acceptable pronunciation through use of symbols. Once you master the symbols, you will be able to check the pronunciation of any word. In most dictionaries two or more correct pronunciations are supplied for many words. The first pronunciation given is usually the preferred pronunciation.

You know which words give you trouble. Some of them may appear in the list supplied above, but the list is far too short to include all the words that trouble speakers. Construct your own list, using your dictionary as a guide to correct pronunciation.

Say It Right

Correct grammar is important in speech, particularly in discussing complex topics. Thus, mistakes in grammar not only may mark you as poorly educated but can lead to serious misunderstanding.

The following list is intended to alert you to common errors in diction. How many of these errors do you make?

DON'T SAY	SAY INSTEAD
a phenomena	a phenomenon
a whole nother thing	another matter
Can I leave now?	May I leave now? (to ask permission)
I don't got; he don't got	I do not have; he does not have
enthused	enthusiastic (as adjective); showed enthusiasm (as verb)
finalize	complete
for free	free; for nothing
hardly nothing	hardly anything; almost nothing
hisself	himself
I ain't; it ain't	I am not; it is not
I been	I have been
I can't hardly	I cannot; I can hardly
I done	I did; I have done
irregardless	regardless; irrespective of
it don't	it does not
it's apropos	it is appropriate
my friend, he; my sister, she	my friend; my sister
off of	off (as in *take it off the shelf*)
oughta	ought to; should
out loud	aloud
over with	over; done with; finished with
quote (as noun)	quotation
reason is because	reason is
snuck	sneaked

supposing I am	suppose I am
theirselves	themselves
this here	this
thusly	thus
we had went	we had gone

Careful listening to good speakers will help you rid your speech of errors such as the ones listed above. When you hear a speaker use an expression that is unfamiliar to you, write it down so that you can look for it in a usage dictionary. There are many usage dictionaries available.

Improving Your Grammar and Usage

Many people think that grammar does not matter. How many times have you heard someone say, "So what if I'm not grammatical? You know what I mean."

Another complaint is often heard: "If I have to think about grammar all the time, I won't be able to say what I feel and mean."

As you advance in the business world, or in a profession, you will be expected to shoulder greater responsibility. People will look to you for leadership, and you will want to be understood the *first* time. You will want people to know exactly what you think. Grammar is a system for conveying information in an orderly way so that you can be understood instead of being misunderstood.

A Quick Reference Guide to Grammar

If you were building a house, you might use wood for framing, brick for the walls, glass for the windows, and nails and glue and mortar to hold things together. You would use insulation to keep heat and cold out. Every material would have its use, serving best in the function for which it was designed.

We know you can make substitutions. A house with a glass roof would attract attention, but what would happen inside your house on the first bright, hot day?

The parts of speech are the building materials of good speech. Each has its own purpose. The parts of speech are related to one another, and the best way to build sentences is to use each part in its own place.

Get to know the parts of speech and you will be a better builder of good sentences.

PART OF SPEECH	DEFINITION	EXAMPLES
noun	name of a person, place, or thing	John, Iowa, car, problem
article	used before nouns to limit their application	a, an, the
pronoun	word used in place of a noun	he, them, it
verb	word or words used to express an action, state, or condition	eat, go, grieve, is, exist
adjective	word used to describe or limit the meaning of a noun or a word used as a noun	short, loud, fat, blue
adverb	word used to modify a verb, adjective, or other adverb	quickly, happily, strangely
preposition	word used to show the relationship between a word in a sentence and a noun or a word used as a noun	into, upon, among, before, until

| conjunction | word or words used to connect other words or groups of words | and, but, because, so, nor, yet |

In addition to learning the parts of speech, you should learn several more terms. These terms are used in analyzing the functions of words within sentences.

TERM	DEFINITION	EXAMPLES
antecedent	word or expression to which a pronoun refers	When Emma left, she said good-bye. (*Emma* is the antecedent of *she*.)
direct object	noun or pronoun receiving the action of a transitive verb	Dick lifted the *cat*.
indirect object	noun or pronoun receiving a direct object	He threw *me* the ball.
intransitive verb	verb that does not require an object to convey meaning	John *runs* smoothly.
number	quality of nouns, pronouns, or verbs that shows that they are singular or plural	girl, girls; he, they; run, runs
person	quality of verbs and pronouns to indicate speaker, person spoken to, person spoken of	I do. Go home.
tense	changes in verbs to indicate *when* action takes place	I am; I was; I will be.
transitive verb	verb that requires an object in order to convey meaning.	We *found* gold. They *received* their money.

Now that you know the names of the parts of speech and some of the terms used in analyzing sentences, we are going to give you some tips on how to improve your spoken sentences. We will concentrate on the most common mistakes that people make. If you find that you make some of these mistakes, practice using the correct forms. If you do not understand all the terms used in the following discussion, be sure to look them up in your dictionary.

MISTAKE	CORRECT FORM	WHY?
	ADJECTIVES	
more smoother, most smoothest	smoother, smoothest	Adjectives have degrees of comparison. These are shown (1) by adding -*er* or -*est* to the adjectives or (2) by placing the words *more* and *most* in front of them. It is wrong to do both.
	ADVERBS	
He ran slow.	He ran slowly.	Many adverbs are adjectives with -*ly* added to them. *Slow* is an adjective, *slowly* an adverb.
I was real angry.	I was really angry.	People often omit the -*ly* in changing adjectives to adverbs. Adverbs that do not end in -*ly* include *now*, *well*, *very*, *quite*, *then*, *there*, *when*, *no*, and *almost*.

He studied good.	He studied well.	*Good* is an adjective. *Well* is an adverb. Remember that an adverb is needed to modify *studied,* a verb.

PREDICATE ADJECTIVE

I feel badly.	I feel bad.	A predicate adjective is an adjective that completes the meaning of a verb. It does not modify the verb.
It smells well.	It smells good.	

AGREEMENT

We was tired.	We were tired.	If the subject of the sentence is singular, the verb must be singular.
She have been waiting.	She has been waiting.	
Honesty and integrity is basic to good citizenship.	Honesty and integrity are basic to good citizenship.	If the subject of the sentence is plural, the verb must be plural.
Bill is one of the boys who has talent.	Bill is one of the boys who have talent.	The antecedent of the pronoun *who* is *boys,* a plural noun, so *who* is plural and its verb must be plural: *who have talent.*
Neither he nor I are to blame.	Neither he nor I am to blame.	When a two-part subject is divided by *or* or *nor,* the verb agrees with the subject closer to it.
Neither the dog nor the cats is healthy.	Neither the dog nor the cats are healthy.	
Either Ralph or	Either Ralph or	

the two girls is causing the trouble.	the two girls are causing the trouble.	
Everybody were having fun.	Everybody was having fun.	Use singular verbs for the pronouns *each, another, anyone, somebody,* and *everybody.*

CASE

He is the one whom can help you.	He is the one who can help you.	*Who* is in the subjective (nominative) case. *Whom* is in the objective (accusative) case. Since the pronoun is the subject of the verb *can help,* it must be put in the subjective case.
Marge is a woman who everyone likes.	Marge is a woman whom everyone likes.	The pronoun *whom* is the object of the verb *likes.* Other subjective pronouns are *he, she, it,* and *they.* Other objective pronouns are *him, her, it,* and *them.*
We can run as fast as them.	We can run as fast as they.	This is an elliptical construction. The words *can run* are implied by the sentence: *We can run as fast as they (can run).*
I liked you better than he.	I liked you better than him.	In this elliptical construction, the implied meaning is *better than (I liked) him.*

COLLECTIVE NOUNS

The majority of the group are for the proposal.	The majority of the group is for the proposal.	The speaker is treating *majority* as a single unit, not as many people.
The orchestra played as best they could.	The orchestra played as best it could.	An orchestra performs as a unit.
The audience clapped its hands.	The audience clapped their hands.	Everyone in the audience has hands, so *audience* is treated as plural.

PRONOUNS

Bill had not seen his brother Ralph for years because he had been overseas in the Marines.	Bill had not seen his brother Ralph for years because Ralph *(or Bill)* had been overseas in the Marines.	When you are telling a story that has several characters, pronouns can confuse your listeners. In speech you will be better off using nouns when there is any chance of confusion.

A Quick Reference Guide to Usage

There are many words in our language that are so much alike that speakers often mistake one for another. And every time our standards loosen in this way, the language becomes less precise. It's just like the edge of a chisel. The duller it gets, the less useful it is. We need to keep our tools sharp.

The following pages supply words with shades of meaning that are worth preserving in your speech. Study them to shore up your vocabulary. If you use them correctly, they can pay dividends. People may be accustomed to hearing poor speech, but when they hear good speech they take note.

AFFECT, EFFECT

These words are often confused. Even though *effect* does have meaning as a verb, think of *effect* as a noun meaning result. Think of *affect* as a verb meaning influence.

The *effect* of the storm was catastrophic.

The illness did not *affect* my performance.

COMPARE, CONTRAST

Compare—followed by *to*—is used to point out similarities between things not ordinarily compared.

Shall I *compare* thee *to* a summer's day? (Shakespeare had in mind the similarities between his beloved and a summer's day.)

Compare is used to examine both similarities and differences of things that are readily compared.

In the evaluation, my foreman *compared* my performance *with* that of my predecessor. (There were similarities and differences.)

Contrast—followed by *with*—is used for pointing out differences.

He *contrasted* the second year's attendance *with* the first year's and showed that business was better.

EACH

Formal: *Each* of the performers carried out *his* task perfectly.

Informal: *Each* of the performers carried out *their* tasks perfectly.

Formal: *Each* of these problems *is* an aspect of a larger problem.

EITHER

Used as a pronoun, *either* is singular.

Either is all right.

Either of the students *is* qualified for graduate school.

FARTHER, FURTHER

In formal speech, *farther* refers to distance and *further* refers to abstract concepts.

The village is twenty miles *farther* away than the next gasoline station.

If you carry this argument any *further*, I shall call the police.

INFER, IMPLY

These two words are frequently confused. A simple rule is that *imply* refers to the sender and *infer* to the receiver.

He *implied* that he hadn't finished yet.

I *inferred* that he had more to say.

IT IS I, IT IS ME

This is a problem of formality. In a formal speaking assignment, you may want to use *it is I*. *It is me* will do the rest of the time.

KIND OF, SORT OF

This kind of cookbook sells well everywhere.

These kinds of cookbooks sell well everywhere.

This sort of foolishness must stop.

Those sorts of fellows make enemies wherever they go.

KIND OF A, SORT OF A

Avoid them in formal speech.

LIE, LAY

Lay is a transitive verb, which means it takes an object. *Lie* is an intransitive verb, which means it doesn't take an object.

If you are tired, why don't you *lay* down your backpack?

If you are tired, why don't you *lie* down?

Learn the principal parts of the verbs:

    lay, laid, lain

    lie, lay, lain

LEARN, TEACH

Seth *learned* his lessons so well that he pleased his teacher.

Mrs. Kowalski *taught* English.

LESS, FEW

Less refers to amounts measured, such as gasoline, energy, air, and water, *Few* refers to things counted, such as cars, cigarettes, gallons, and fingers.

   We had *less* sugar than we needed.
   We had *few* things to consider.

LEAVE, LET

   Incorrect: *Leave* me go!
   Correct: *Let* me go!
   Incorrect: She told the bully to *leave* them alone.
   Correct: She told the bully to *let* them alone.

LIKE, AS

   Like is a preposition. *As* is a conjunction.
   The suit fits *like* a glove.
   He promised to look in on us *as* we were leaving.

NOWHERE NEAR

   Incorrect: We got *nowhere near* the top.
   Correct: We did not reach the top.

PLENTY

   Don't say "This is *plenty* good enough." Leave out the *plenty*.

SLOW, SLOWLY

   Slow is an adjective and *slowly* is an adverb.
   Tommy was a *slow* runner.
   Tommy ran *slowly*.

Improving Your Choice of Words

   Joe Flaherty, a policeman, had just completed a tour of duty. He changed into his street clothes and went to a local bar, where he commented to the bartender that he had had a rough night. The bartender, who had nothing better to do, asked Joe to tell him about it.
   Joe said, "At approximately oh-two hundred hours, a

nine-one-one came in at headquarters. A four-oh-six was taking place at a liquor store in the eight hundred block of Fourth Avenue. We responded to the call and spotted the perpetrators. One was a brown-haired male Caucasian five feet ten to six feet tall, entering the passenger seat of a dark station wagon. The other perpetrator was obscured from the rear by the automobile's head rest. We pulled in front of the store and radioed to our back-up car to give chase."

At this point the bartender said, "Joe. Wait a minute. This isn't the D.A. you're talking to. Just tell me what happened."

The mistake Joe Flaherty made in telling the story his way was that he allowed the specialized language of the police force to spill over into his personal life. The result was that he turned a rather interesting story into something no one but another policeman could understand.

This mistake in choosing words is not the only one speakers make.

Sarah James went to a party one night. The next day she telephoned a friend to talk about it. The friend asked how the party had gone.

"I don't know," said Sarah. "Everybody there was pretty strange."

"What were they like?"

"Well, they were weird, y'know. I mean I didn't know any of them. They were real hard to talk to."

"But what were they like?"

"They were just weird."

Sarah's friend still had no idea of what the party had been like. Sarah had been as uncommunicative as Officer Joe Flaherty. Neither Sarah nor Joe was able to tell a story in a way that most of us would understand.

Instead of saying things clearly in words that convey meaning, they hid their thoughts in a specialized language that had no generally understandable meaning.

Word Ruts

How do ruts form in roads? Too many people drive over the road too many times. The same is true with words. We hear the same ones over and over again. We use them ourselves. We stop thinking our ideas through completely. We are stuck. Our conversation becomes stale. When we want to say something important, we find that we cannot. We are deeply embedded in familiar word ruts.

Do you want people to listen to you and understand you when you speak? Of course you do. And one of the best ways to do this is to weed out all the lifeless words, especially the clichés, words that have lost their meaning through endless repetition. Replace them with words that specifically express just how you feel and just what you think. If you think you need help in staying out of word ruts, read the next section with particular care.

Words to Look Out For

FAD WORDS—such as *bottom line, time frame, viable*, and *in terms of*. Words and phrases that have leaked out of the sciences, politics, business, and social sciences may be useful in their original fields, but they add nothing when used in ordinary conversation.

PET WORDS—such as *boring, fabulous, cute, far out, right on*, and *weird*. These words may tell close friends how you feel but not what you think. Hanging the same labels on everything deadens communication.

EXTRA WORDS—such as *naturally, actually, frankly, to tell the truth, so to speak*, and most of all *you know*. These words and expressions, used mindlessly as pure habit, add nothing to your speech. They are merely variations on *uh-h-h* and *um-m-m*, and they deserve no place in your speech. Far better to be silent until you have something to say.

SLANG WORDS—Colorful slang, used in moderation, can add meaning and zest to your speech, provided its meaning is clear. But slang cannot replace colloquial and formal language when you find yourself in a situation where slang is unacceptable. If you are not certain of whether a word is considered formal, colloquial, or slang, consult your dictionary. When you are in doubt about the status of a word, substitute another that makes you and your audience comfortable.

EXAGGERATION—Everything that is good is not *great*, *fabulous*, or *fantastic*. You don't have to *love* everything. You can *like* some things. *Great, fabulous, fantastic, love*—these words were once strong. They were used carefully to convey strong meanings. Now, however, words such as these are used so often that we don't have any simple words left for expressing strong feelings. Instead of relying on these words, try to say exactly what you mean: *I believe he is trustworthy* may be much closer to the truth than *I love him*.

DEGRADING AND DEFAMING WORDS—Don't use words that defame or degrade other people. Chinese people are Chinese, not Chinks; Japanese are Japanese, not Japs; Polish people are Poles, not Polacks. The list can go on, and you may have to work hard to eliminate degrading words from your speech.

WORDS ENDING IN -WISE—Don't say *healthwise*, I feel fine. Say I feel *healthy*. Don't say *moneywise,* I am short, or *timewise*, we are in trouble. Adding -*wise* to the end of every other word in the language is an irritating one. People who do this habitually are stretching the English language out of shape.

PROFANITY—Twenty years ago, *hell* was never heard in polite society. Now, we hear profanity nearly everywhere. But the common use of *hell* and many more objectionable words doesn't make them acceptable in a formal setting. You can still make enemies by swearing, and you can hurt your career by slipping into this habit. Little is gained by swearing. Much can be lost.

The Right Words and How to Choose Them

When you speak, your audience cannot run to a dictionary to try to figure out what you mean. If you want to be understood, it is important that people understand you without having to mull over individual words.

Don't make the mistake of using rare words or big words to impress people. Those who root around in the thesaurus and the dictionary to find unusual ways of expressing themselves are marked as showoffs. What's more, they run the risk of misusing those words, bringing ridicule on themselves.

Words rarely can be substituted for one another without subtle shifts in meaning, since words often get their power from the ways in which they are used.

Do you know that many words have literal meanings, or *denotations*, and suggested meanings, or *connotations*? *Iron*, for example, is defined as a metallic element. This is the denotation of iron. If you describe someone as *iron-fisted*, however, you do not mean that the person has metal hands. You mean that the person is strong and dominating. This is a connotation of the word iron. You must be certain that you understand a word before you use it.

The connotations of some words are of far greater concern for speakers than the connotation of iron. In Jimmy Carter's first campaign for President of the United States, he used the phrase "preserve the ethnic purity of neighborhoods" and made many people uneasy if not angry. Regardless of what he meant by these words, *ethnic purity* carried ugly connotations among many who heard or read the phrase. They chose to interpret it as indicating that the candidate stood for segregation.

The message for you is clear: say just what you want to say in words everyone will understand in the same way. If you do not, you will be misunderstood. Murphy's First Law of Communication puts it this way: IF PEOPLE CAN MISUNDERSTAND YOU, THEY WILL MISUNDERSTAND YOU.

Don't go out of your way to find new words. You run the

risk of sounding artificial and pompous. Your new words may stand out like brand-new blue jeans: stiff, bright, shiny, but still uncomfortable. Words you are familiar with, words you can use with ease, have a comfort about them. Stick with them.

This is not to say that you shouldn't expand your vocabulary. But try to draw on words as you find them in your reading or in the speech of others. This is because the best way to discover words is in the context in which they are used. Authors or other speakers have already done the research on those words. They probably have taken into account the various denotations and connotations of the words. But check out the new words yourself if you're not certain about their pronunciation or the context in which they should be used. Nothing reveals ignorance and pretentiousness more than an impressive word incorrectly pronounced or used in the wrong circumstances.

Be a plain speaker. We are living in a time when specialized vocabulary is leaking from special fields into common speech. It is getting harder and harder to understand what some people are saying when they use long words that have no precise meaning when taken out of their original context.

An Air Force general told an audience that officers were "experiencing an upward obesity trend." What did he mean?

He meant that Air Force officers were fatter than they used to be. The general had a simple message. Instead of just stating it in a matter-of-fact manner, he cloaked it in jargon and probably confused his audience. Worse yet, he became an object of ridicule.

Use words that suggest images and pictures in people's minds. *Iron-fisted* is beter than *strong* or *dominating* because it is vivid. You want your words to stick in the memories of your listeners.

Clichés are the enemy of lively speech. They are deadwood: the shiny suits of your word wardrobe, the torn sandals, the frayed collars, the scuffed shoes, the bobby socks, the fur pieces, the Nehru jackets, the miniskirts—yesterday's chewing gum.

Some clichés take too many words to say something simple. Some clichés cloak good thoughts in words that sound more important than they really are. Some are exaggerations.

Whatever the fault, go through your vocabulary closet to find the clichés and throw them out. Replace them with clearer, more lively language.

The following list will help you. Notice that some clichés should be replaced by other words or expressions. Others should merely be removed.

DON'T SAY	DO YOU MEAN?
advance planning	planning
advance warning	warning
all things being equal	(nothing)
and stuff; and all; and everything	(nothing, unless you have something else to say)
as you know	as you may know
	let me remind you
	(nothing)
at this point in time	now
at that point in time	then
beautiful	good, kind, cooperative
be that as it may	but
bleep out	censor
by the same token	also
charisma	appeal
confrontation	meeting
consciousness-raising	educational
consensus of opinion	consensus, agreement
curiously enough	curiously
disadvantaged	poor
due to the fact	because
encounter	meet
escalate	rise, raise
estimated at about	estimated
expertise	knowledge
fabulous	good, excellent, acceptable
fantastic	(same as above)
far out	(same as above)
flash	idea

for free	free
frame of reference	background
game plan	plan, strategy
guesstimate	rough guess
head tripping	thinking
impact upon	affect
in my opinion	I think
in point of fact	in fact
insightful	perceptive
learning experience	experience
love	like, approve, admire
meaningful dialogue	discussion
meaningful experience	experience
my personal opinon	my opinon
needless to say	(nothing)
never before in the past	never before, in the past
out of this world	impressive
outta sight	impressive
personal friend	friend
presently	now
prior to	before
start off	begin
underprivileged	poor
valid	true, genuine
validate	confirm
with reference to	as to, about

Practice Activities

The following paragraph is written poorly. Read it aloud. See if you can find what is wrong. Repair it and read it aloud once more. Compare your corrected version with the version printed at the bottom of this page.

Martha, Agnes, Zelda, and Irene all are going to run in the race. Hopefully, all of them will finish. Each of them are good athletes. They all feel she can win. Agnes and Zelda probably has a more better chance than the others. Both of them has real strong legs. Zelda has a longer stride than Agnes, but her endurance may be better of all.

Martha, Agnes, Zelda, and Irene are going to run in the race. I hope all of them will finish. All are good athletes and feel they can win. Agnes and Zelda probably have a better chance than the others, because they have strong legs. Zelda has a longer stride than Agnes, but Agnes's endurance may be better.

Here is another list of words to watch out for. All are commonly used by people who want to impress others. If you use any of these words, find more common substitutes for them.

alienated	operative
articulate (as a verb)	oppressed
awesome	overreact
climate (except when discussing weather	paranoid
	politicized
concept	posture (for *attitude*)
controversial	prioritize
credibility	rhetoric
depersonalization	rip-off
dynamics	scenario
elegant	structure (as a verb)
enrichment	substantive
holistic	superlative
involved	ventilate *(feelings)*
manic	veritable
obscene	

Establish your own file of words you use loosely or too often. You will identify them yourself if you establish the habit of listening to yourself. Your friends can be enlisted to help in rooting out your clichés.

CHAPTER 4
The Vital Silent Elements

Your voice never tells the whole story. Your choice of words never gives the entire message. A major part of your speech effectiveness rests elsewhere: in the way you look, your grooming, your clothing, the way you stand, the way you sit, and the way you move your hands.

These vital silent elements are the key to the inner you. They reveal your self-confidence, your personality, your mastery of your subject—all the things you cannot put into words.

If you are skeptical about the importance of the vital silent elements, the following brief account may convince you.

Psychologist Edward Young conducted a fascinating study using a Mobile, Alabama, clothing store as his laboratory. Seven salesmen and their customers were his test subjects.

The psychologist compared sales figures for days when the salesmen wore suits and ties with sales figures for days when they worked in shirtsleeves.

The results were dramatic. Sales on suit-and-tie days surpassed shirtsleeve days by far. Sales were forty-three percent higher on full-suit days than when ties were worn without jackets. Sales were sixty percent higher on full-suit days than when collars were left open without ties.

It is the same with other aspects of your appearance. Think about how you react to people who dress badly. Do such people attract you? Do they inspire confidence? Or, perhaps because they lack confidence in themselves, do they look uncomfortable with themselves so that you don't feel comfortable looking at them? Or do they look too comfortable with themselves—so comfortable that they appear not to care at all about you?

These are just some of the factors that you pick up with your eyes—some of the vital silent elements that will be discussed in this chapter. What they all add up to is this: if your eyes are offended, then words count for little.

Good Grooming

Who has not heard the saying "Cleanliness is next to godliness"? But you'd be surprised how many people either don't know it or don't think it matters.

We live in a casual age. Our lives are conducted less formally than the lives of our ancestors. But casualness need not deteriorate into sloppiness.

We know a successful small business operating in a suburb of New York City in which everyone is glad to be away from the pressure and formality of the downtown world. Ties and jackets are shunned at the office of this business, but that doesn't mean there is no dress code.

Two young people recently appeared for interviews in response to an advertisement for part-time positions. One was a man, the other a woman. They both knew the reputation this business has for informality, but their understandings of informality differed sharply from the standards set by the office. The man showed two days' growth of beard. With his particular beard pattern, he did not appear to be sporting the beginnings of a healthy, dignified, luxuriant beard. His beard looked more like patches of dirt. And he wore a sleeveless T-shirt.

The woman wore faded cut-off jeans.

Neither one was hired. The company president summed it up simply: "It has been our experience that people who carry themselves like that are very sloppy in their work as well as their dress. Both of them had academic qualifications that indicated they could probably perform the work, but the job requires patience and attention to detail. We have learned that people who feel themselves to be above good grooming are also above the patience and attention our work requires."

So there you are.

In all personal grooming, adjust to your own individual

characteristics. There are some people who can have a single hair out of place and look as though they've just survived a hurricane. Others can pass a hand through their hair once in the morning and still look perfect all day long.

Some women can wear pale lipstick and look marvelous; others try this shade and look like candidates for a protracted health cure. Some women can wear their hair long and look attractive; others try this and look like terriers. The same considerations hold true for men. Long haircuts and bushy beard styles may add to the attractiveness of some men; others trying to achieve the same effects become targets for stares, jokes, and hostility. Look hard at yourself before you decide to adopt your own new look.

There is a danger in being overgroomed. Women must choose makeup suitable for the occasion. While blue and silver eyeshadow sometimes may look stunning in candlelight, daylight may not be equally kind. For business purposes, the best makeup accents the face. It cannot give you a new one. So choose makeup as carefully as you can to avoid the appearance of overgrooming.

Overgrooming draws attention to itself. Overgrooming says you are working too hard to achieve an effect. Overgrooming projects insecurity.

Clothes Make the Person

Soon after Jimmy Carter became President, he delivered a fireside chat from the White House.

The President of the United States was trying to change the image of the office of President from one of almost imperial power to something more familiar and accessible.

He sat in an easy chair. A log fire burned in the background. He had the text of his speech in his lap instead of using a TelePrompTer.

What people remembered and talked about afterward, however, was not the homey quality of the fireplace. Nor was it the content of the speech. It was, rather, the clothing he wore.

The President of the United States—speaking before all the

citizens of the nation—did not wear a suit. Instead he wore a cardigan sweater with a tie!

Why did he dress that way? Was his only good suit at the dry cleaner's? Of course not. Mr. Carter wanted to look like one of us. As we watched him, we were dressed casually, and the President wanted us to believe that he was just folks.

The press responded so well to the speech that for months afterward, many of the President's aides wore jeans and cowboy shirts to work.

And what was the reaction of the American people? How did we feel about a President and his staff being just like us?

Some liked it. They thought it pointed to a new era and a more open Presidency. But most didn't like it. They didn't want their President to be ordinary. And they thought that blue jeans meant that the country's business was being run by cowboys, cowgirls, and hippies.

While President Carter may have let his informal clothing represent him badly, another U.S. President may have gone to the other extreme. Richard Nixon gave the appearance of being too formal, even in extremely informal situations. Can you remember even a single photograph of him when he was not wearing a business suit? One famous news photo shows him walking alone on the beach near his former estate. What is he wearing? Yes, a business suit.

So, before we ever say a word, the clothing we wear speaks for us. And if it distracts our audience or, even worse, prejudices our audience, it is the wrong clothing for the occasion.

You know how important first impressions can be. If you are like us, the minute someone walks into a room, you size that person up. Most people do the same thing. So judge yourself with the same rigor with which you judge others.

What was it that made those salesmen in Mobile, Alabama, so effective? First, they looked well turned out. You usually feel you can trust a clothing salesman who has good taste himself. Secondly, they appeared to care about themselves. Finally, their clothing gave them an air of authority, in the same way a military officer in uniform has authority. (When military officers wear casual clothes at home, they look as ordinary as any homeowners cutting their lawns or taking out the garbage.)

Dress for the occasion. Don't overdress. And remember that conservative clothes never go out of style, so don't feel you have to keep up with the latest trends. Nothing is more dead than yesterday's trendy clothing.

Dress to suit your physique. A short man who wears bell-bottom trousers looks shorter than he is. A fat woman who wears stretch pants looks even fatter.

Some people think that dress codes stifle individuality, but we think the opposite. Sensible dress codes help the real you to come across. By ruling out clothing that distracts, sensible dress codes enable ideas to become more important than appearances.

But there is more to clothing than selecting it carefully. Take care of your clothes. As a man, don't go around with holes in your shoe soles or frayed collars. As a woman, don't go around with runs in your stockings or wear outrageous shoes that make you a potential hospital case every time you take a step. Even the details that people can't see can make a difference. How? What they don't know can't hurt. Right? Wrong.

A young man told us this story about a job interview he had.

"I had worn out the soles of my good shoes," he said. "I don't wear my good shoes when I'm not working, so it was easy to just put off fixing them. But this interview came up before I had a chance to go to the shoemaker. I sat there thinking I really would like to cross my legs. But I didn't dare pick a foot up from the floor for fear that the interviewer would see this hole. It just made me nervous when I already had plenty to think about."

So—to make sure grooming works for, not against, us—we must choose the right clothing, take care of personal details, and maintain our wardrobes carefully.

Now that we are dressed right, let's see how we behave fully clothed and how our behavior is seen by others.

How Your Body Talks and What It Says

Alert observers can detect tiny clues about your real feelings from the way you sit, from the way you cross your legs, and from the way you make all kinds of moves. This movement is called body language.

People don't have to be experts to pick up little hints. Certain patterns of movement are almost universal. We respond to them perhaps because we recognize bits of ourselves in the body language of others.

There are no magic tricks to body language. You cannot gesture expertly for success. The important thing is not to handicap yourself by the way you carry yourself. If your posture is bad, it affects the quality of your voice, but it also says to your audience "I am scared" or "I am not sure of myself" or "I wish I were in command of this meeting but I'm not." If your face is deadpan, you are signaling that you are not someone who gives away important information. This may be a strength at the poker table, but it can be disastrous in speaking. Your audience may never trust you or respond enthusiastically to what you say. If you frown or scowl or look scornful, it matters not what compliment you are paying, what flattery you are offering, your audience will not accept what your words express. Your face is sending a different message.

How do your physical characteristics affect your speech? We all have known fidgeters, but Jerry Taylor became one of the all-time great fidgeters.

Jerry was a popular man, both at work and in his social life. He was an industrial designer who always had interesting ideas to contribute in meetings of his department and could always be counted on to make excellent suggestions to his colleagues. At lunch and after work, he was an animated storyteller. People laughed at all his jokes. He was constantly being quoted. "Hey, did you hear Jerry's latest?" was a familiar question.

A few years ago, he went away for three weeks' vacation. When he returned he was sporting the healthy beginnings of a mustache. People were glad to see him. But things began to change.

Jerry found that people weren't as attentive as they had been. They asked him to repeat himself. They had trouble grasping his ideas. His stories didn't get instant laughs any more. It started to get to him. He became unnerved. He stopped talking as much. He didn't know what was going on.

One day he called up his oldest friend, Danny Cisco. Danny sensed the note of trouble in Jerry's voice and agreed to meet for dinner.

The first thing Danny said when they met was, "I like the caterpillar." He indicated Jerry's mustache. Jerry self-consciously brushed a finger across his upper lip.

They started with drinks and Jerry began unfolding his tale. He seemed to have lost his social grace. He wasn't thinking any differently, but the words somehow weren't coming out right. It scared him.

Jerry said, "You know what a glib guy I've always been. I'm not used to being tongue-tied."

As Jerry spoke, he noticed that his friend's eyes kept moving. They would flicker downward every so often.

At last Danny said, "I've got it. It's the mustache. You can't keep your hands off it. No wonder people aren't listening to you. You're making them nervous."

It turned out that Jerry had developed the habit of checking the progress of his mustache when he first started growing it. Despite the fact that his mustache was now fully grown, he still touched it constantly. He just couldn't keep his hand off his new adornment.

He shaved it off that night and quickly recaptured his ability to hold people's attention.

Fidgeters may twist their rings constantly. They may clench and unclench their fists. They may pick at their cuticles, bite their nails, rap their knuckles on the table, pull their ears, do many different things that annoy and distract others.

Some are scratchers. Some are lip biters. Some are chain smokers. But whatever they do, they are always distracting. These little quirks, like "y'know" in your speech, can take the fine edge off what you say.

The way you hold your head, the way you cross your legs, the way you sit forward or back in your chair, and the angle of your chin can all affect your performance as a speaker.

It is a well-established principle in selling, for example, that when dealing with someone highly placed in a company you should never lean back in your chair.

People with rank and status expect to be treated specially. If you sit back, you are telling them you don't have proper respect for their rank. On the other hand, someone with less status will feel better if you do sit back and relax a bit. A younger person should treat an elder with this same kind of respect, regardless of status. This means sitting forward, just as they would with their superiors.

Young women in business complain that the rules of etiquette apply unequally to them and to men. Men can relax and cross their legs while women are expected to sit with their legs together or with their ankles crossed. Fair or not, etiquette must be observed.

A word about how you cross your legs. Psychologists have found that when we sit in a row or circle with others, we cross our legs in the direction of a person we like, away from a person we dislike. Test this observation on yourself next time you cross your legs.

Crossing legs away from someone you are sitting next to surely has the effect of making conversation awkward. So see whether you are losing contact with someone next to you because one or both of you are crossing legs away from, rather than toward, the other.

A Disappearing Act

When Elroy Tatum was hired as a management trainee by a big electronics firm, the company sent him to a conference center a thousand miles from home. His company put every new trainee through this particular two-week indoctrination. He rose early every morning and went to the coffee shop for breakfast, where he would open his newspaper and begin to read. After a few minutes of being lost in the paper, he would look around for a waitress. Somehow, the waitresses always managed to miss Elroy. He would raise his hand to catch their eyes, but they would walk past him with the coffee pot to refill someone else's cup.

When he went to his classes, Elroy sat in the first row, but the lecturers never seemed to be talking to him. When he prepared an assignment overnight and walked to the front of the class to present his oral report, the other trainees always seemed more interested in their notes than in listening to him.

After a few days of this, Elroy decided that he might be the invisible man. Not the best attribute for someone just starting out in a new job.

Elroy made an appointment with his instructor after class and told her what was bothering him. "Take a good, hard look at yourself—I mean in a mirror—really look at yourself when you get back to your room tonight. Watch how you sit and stand and walk. Then I'll talk with you tomorrow."

That night he went back to his hotel room and did not change his clothing. He looked just as he had looked when he had gone out to breakfast. He picked up his newspaper and sat down on the bed, pretending that it was a stool at a lunch counter. Then he examined himself in the full-length mirror on the bathroom door.

He saw that he was hunched over. He looked meek, almost afraid. He seemed to blend in with the wallpaper.

He then got up and walked a few steps, as if he were going in front of his class to give a talk. His feet seemed to shuffle along the surface of the carpet. There seemed to be no purpose to his walk.

Elroy had all but made himself invisible. His body showed that he felt out of place. He acted out of place. He decided that if he were ever to get anywhere in his career, he would have to act as though he *belonged*.

From then on he walked proud. He straightened his shoulders. He kept his eyes alert, eager to catch every eye in any crowd. The response he received the first day was a revelation. It was as though people could feel his boldness and openness. People were drawn to him. No more trouble catching a waitress's attention. When he strode to the front of his class now with crisp, strong steps, people looked at him instead of at their notes.

If you have a disappearing problem of your own, you should find ways to get attention. Don't be content to blend in with the woodwork. Move with authority, with command.

Use your eyes. Have them send this message: "I am a person worth listening to. I deserve your attention."

Left to their own devices, people will pay attention to their own affairs. You must make them feel that it is in their interest to attend to you. That round-shouldered look is an apology. Don't apologize. If you ask for their attention by the way you look, they will give it without qualification.

The Way You Stand

When you stand, your weight should rest not on your heels but on the balls of your feet, which should be placed a few inches apart. This will give you the appearance of leaning toward your audience. Chin up. Stomach in. Chest out. Not *military attention,* but not *at ease* either.

It shouldn't surprise you that the posture of a speaker is closely linked to the mood of the audience. If you are stiff, your listeners will feel uncomfortable. If you are too relaxed or, worse, if you slouch, your audience will relax to the point where you will be ignored. An audience that is too relaxed is an inattentive audience.

There is more to it than that. Correct posture gives you the freedom of movement you need to make eye contact with every member of an audience. It enables you to face your questioners when you are fielding questions. It gives you free use of your hands for stong, natural gestures. You are poised.

Poised. A crucial word. Not *tight.* Not *nervous.*

Keep your neck relaxed so that your head can move effortlessly. Remember that a taut muscle must ease before movement can take place.

From the neutral stance, you have freedom to move in any direction. You can use your body to help you convey your message. If you want to step forward for a moment for emphasis, you can. If you want to bend forward from the waist to let your audience in on a little secret, you can.

Facial Expression

An aircraft company hired a new president from outside the ranks of the corporation. He seemed pleasant enough. He always had a handshake and a smile. When the older executives spoke, he nodded, as if agreeing with them. And he smiled. Oh, did he smile!

After six weeks, some of the old guard met at dinner to compare notes. They were getting uneasy.

"It's that smile," said the treasurer. "You can never tell what he's thinking."

"That's right," said the director of marketing. "I told him that inventories are up and orders are down because of a downturn in the business cycle. He just smiled."

One day the new president fired six of them.

A smile is an asset in business and social settings. But a face that always smiles is another thing. Why would anyone smile when bad news is offered?

A smile, like any other habitual facial expression, can mask true feelings, can make other people wary. A flexible, responsive face can be a huge asset. It can gain allies. It can instill confidence.

Do you know how casting is done for the movies? It begins with the face. Not just for classic good looks, but for the feelings projected by the actor. Good *acting* is partly *reacting*.

If you make eye contact and keep it, your eyes will pick up information as well as send it. Your face will then translate directly into a reaction to what is going on.

Many people, especially in business, cultivate a deadpan look, one that remains the same regardless of what they see or hear. They feel that masking feelings puts others on the defensive. Is this desirable? Not in a well-managed organization.

In Hollywood, the deadpan actors always end up playing the heavies and getting blasted by the good guys. When such actors are cast as sympathetic characters who are supposed to register happiness and sadness, they get bad reviews from the critics. Poet and critic Dorothy Parker once said of an actress, "She runs the gamut of emotions from A to B." People may even respect those whose faces never change expression, but they never feel drawn to them.

Allow your face to register both warmth and intelligence. Lack of expression may not give away information, but if your face shows people that you don't trust them, they are not going to trust you either. They won't hire you. They won't buy what you're selling. They won't want to be your friends.

So it is far better to let your face follow your feelings.

If you are being earnest about something, your forehead may wrinkle. If you are feeling positive, your mouth may curve up at the corners, on its way to a grin. If your eyes are narrow and your brows get lower, you may appear deep in thought. When you raise your brows, you may look skeptical or amused. People—now able to read your body language—will communicate more freely with you.

Practice before a mirror. Talk to yourself on a wide variety of topics. Good news as well as bad news. Hope as well as disappointment. Look for the signs of genuine feeling that must be there. If you can spot it, you can use it with others.

It's there in your warmest smile. Try to let your eyes glow with interest and sympathy and joy and all the other positive responses people like to see. Your ace in the hole is the look that will line people up on your side. When bad news calls for a look of concern, see whether you can achieve concern without conveying despair or alarm.

Gestures

Presidents are often remembered for the gestures they make when they speak. President John F. Kennedy used to point. Richard Nixon, well before he became President, had an elaborate repertoire of arm wavings. This later diminished to more controlled levels during his Presidential press conferences. President Reagan always offers a friendly wave.

Franklin D. Roosevelt did not gesticulate. He needed his hand to grip the lectern because his paralyzed legs could not hold him up. He compensated by developing a system of head movements that had the same effect as hand and arm movements.

When Woodrow Wilson was President, he studied an elaborate system of movements that were used by orators. In those days speech was a popular form of entertainment. Speeches were given before enormous crowds. Grand movements were necessary for making the speaker visible from great distances.

When President Carter gave his second major energy address, he clenched his fists for emphasis. This was so unlike Carter that afterward people talked as much about his fists as they did about his politics. That's because on television facial expression is much more important than the speaker's hands, and trained speakers do not gesture in television speeches.

Gestures do not always add to your meaning, so be careful when you use them. If you gesticulate too much, your audience, whether it is a class or a sales group or your family, will not take you as seriously as it will if you make your case without the overemphasis that too many gestures impart. Constant hand wavers are looked upon as ravers. If you have your hands in the air all the time, people will regard you as too emotional.

Convincing use of the hands depends on the content and emotional pitch of the speech. If you start out at your peak, you have nowhere to go.

Begin in that neutral position we mentioned earlier—weight on the balls of your feet. Keep your hands at your sides or on the lectern.

If you want to appear casual, it's acceptable to have one hand in a pocket, but both hands in pockets will round your shoulders and make you look less confident.

As you work up to an emotional pitch in your speech, you might begin to let one of your hands rise a little. You might punch the air for emphasis. The higher your hands rise, the greater the emphasis.

But don't go over the top. Hold back. If you were conducting a symphony, you wouldn't throw both hands in the air to signal a piccolo solo passage.

Gestures are not limited to public speaking. A person being interviewed, a person explaining something to one or two people, a mother speaking with her children—all of us in everyday conversation—can increase the emphasis in what we are saying by pointing, by ticking off arguments on our fingers, by raising our hands to express wonder, despair, concern, or many other feelings.

The trick is to use gestures—like all body language—naturally and easily. Gestures that are forced appear mechanical. Gestures that come easily will capture attention and convince.

Practice Activities

1. If you are a fidgeter, ask your friends to interrupt you every time you fidget, whether it's playing with your mustache, fiddling with an earring, drumming your fingers on the table, or any other distracting habit.

2. If you are a sloucher, try speaking aloud in your room while your back is touching a wall. See how long you can maintain this posture. With only a few minutes of daily practice over a period of two weeks, you should be able to correct the slouching habit.

3. If you are a hand-swinging talker, try to speak for an entire day without moving your hands at all. When you can get through most of a day in this way, you are on your way toward reducing your gesturing permanently.

4. If you never gesture at all, it's back to the full-length mirror. Introduce a gesture or two while talking aloud. Find out which gestures look good for you. Then try the good ones out when you speak with friends or before a group.

CHAPTER 5
Practicing the Basics of Giving Good Talks

The basics for giving good talks in any situation have remained the same since Aristotle wrote his *Rhetoric* about twenty-four hundred years ago:

1. Have a central idea.
2. Know your audience.
3. Divide your talk into a beginning, middle, and end.

What happens to speakers who try to get by without observing the basics? They say things like this: "I'm here to talk about. . . ." "The first thing you should know is that. . . ." "But before you can understand that, you'd better be aware of. . . ." "On the other hand, it could be stated another way."

In short, they ramble, sometimes actually touching on the subject of the talk but more often veering away from it. When a speaker is interrupted again and again by an increasingly hostile audience—dead silence is almost as bad—you can be sure the speech is a failure. The audience knows it has heard—but not listened to—a speech that had *no central idea*, was delivered by a speaker who *did not know the audience*, and that *had not been given a beginning, middle, and end*.

Such speeches never accomplish what they are supposed to accomplish. It doesn't matter what the purpose of a speech is: sell a new shade of lipstick, talk a friend into seeing a movie instead of going dancing, explain a new company procedure, or describe American foreign policy since World War II. An unorganized speech can be effective only if the audience is exceptionally motivated—and most of us cannot depend on that.

As a speaker, then, you may know everything there is to know about your subject, but unless you satisfy the three basics, you will never get your ideas across clearly. Bear that in mind the next time you have to convey a message to an audience of any size.

Meeting the three basics does not mean that you have to work long hours to prepare a simple speech. It does not take long to identify your central idea. If you don't know your audience, ask someone who does. Beginning—middle—end: these take a little more time, as you will see.

But remember, the three basics must be there whether you speak with or without formal preparation—whether you speak for a few minutes or for the better part of an hour.

The three basics are your best tool for organizing your talk. They help you pin down what the speech is really about. They eliminate ideas and information that are not worth presenting. They keep you from losing your audience by presenting too much.

Once you begin to use the three basics, you may wonder how you ever got along without them. You will find yourself automatically organizing almost everything you say with the basics in mind.

It is very likely that you already use the three basics in your speech some of the time without being aware that you are doing so. And once you begin to see where the basics come into your everyday speech, you will be able to apply them effectively to most speaking opportunities.

The Central Idea

Before you speak, have in mind one idea you are trying to convey and choose words that will make that idea as clear and as simple to understand as possible. Don't try to squeeze in everything you know about a subject, or you will confuse yourself, as well as your audience.

Edit while you talk. Stick to what you feel is your most

important point. Make your language clear. Don't force your listeners to guess at what you are talking about. Give it to them straight.

We have never heard of a speech whose central idea could not be given in one or two sentences.

Do you agree? Think for a moment of what you remember hearing other people say.

Have you ever been to a town meeting? After hours of discussion about taxes and schools, the most pressing item on the agenda is raised. A company wants to build a factory next to the local high school. Permission of the zoning board is needed before construction can begin.

A representative of the company rises to speak in favor of the project. She tells the people at the very beginning of the talk that if the company moves in, the town will benefit from more jobs and increased tax revenue. Other industry will be attracted. Again, more jobs, more revenue. She speaks for half an hour, giving figures and facts and projections to support her central idea.

When she sits down, a man gets up to speak against the project. His central idea is that the high school will deteriorate and families will move out, thus depressing real estate values. He has a daughter in the high school. He says the new factory will be a fire hazard, it will drift into the school's ventilating system, and the noise of machinery will interfere with learning. This speech also lasts for half an hour.

Someone asks you the next day how you feel about the new factory. Whether for or against, you have an opinion and you can explain your stand. You may not recall all the details of the two speakers' talks. After all, they went on for a total of an hour. But you do remember the central ideas because they were stated so plainly at the beginning of each talk: FOR, the factory will bring jobs and tax revenues; AGAINST, the high school will be ruined and residential real estate will be depressed.

Two competent speakers did their jobs well. They met the first basic requirement: *they had central ideas*.

Your Audience

Who are those people out there listening to you? Are they your friends? Strangers? Family? Are they old or young or somewhere in between?

Do you work with them? Are they your equals or do they have more experience and seniority? Or do they have less?

Are they your classmates? Your students? Your teachers? Are they as knowledgeable as you on the subject you will speak on?

Are they potential customers? Do you want to sell them a product? Are you trying to sell a service? Do they have something you want? How high are the stakes?

In short, WHO ARE THOSE PEOPLE? The more clearly you identify them, the better your chances of speaking successfully.

Every time you have to speak, make it your business to know your audience beforehand. Learn what makes them tick and you can tailor your message to their needs. If you can gain their confidence as soon as you begin talking, you have a good chance of keeping them interested until you have finished. But if—like the hapless candidate for President of the United States who opened his talk before the citizens of St. Louis by saying how glad he was to be in Kansas City—you never gain the confidence of your audience, you are in trouble.

You want to achieve two things with every audience you face: *understanding* and *acceptance.* You want your ideas to be heard and understood by everyone you speak to. You want your ideas accepted. Otherwise, you would not bother to present your talk. To gain understanding and acceptance, you must know your audience and shape your presentation to suit that audience.

How earnestly, how beautifully, how forcefully—and how unsuccessfully—a young Harvard Business School M.B.A. once spoke to an interviewing committee when he applied for a job in management! He did only one thing wrong in his prepared talk. The committee included three members of the family that years before had founded the business but had since yielded management of the company to a new team.

The young man spoke admiringly of the company's current management team, disparagingly of the former management. People present at the unfortunate meeting say the ice that formed during that interview many years ago has not melted yet.

A classic case of a speaker who had not done his homework. He did not know his audience. He was on his way home within minutes.

How do you learn enough about your audience to be able to do your best?

Here is a list of questions you should consider. You don't have to memorize them. You don't have to ask them every time you want to speak. Just think about them carefully now. They are commonsense questions. If you read them over a few times, you will find that you will begin to ask them automatically as you prepare yourself to make any kind of speech.

- How many people will be there? (You can be less formal in front of a small group.)
- Are they friends or strangers? (Who are the strangers? What do they expect to hear?)
- What do they have that you want? (A job? Money with which to buy something you are selling?)
- Are they a general audience or are they specialists? (A general audience will want to hear words and ideas that are broadly and readily understood.)
- How old are they? (If your speech has any historic references, you may have to explain them to the younger people in the audience.)
- Are they men, women, or both? (The examples you use to illustrate your ideas may be affected.)
- What educational and cultural level are they? (The depth of your presentation may be affected.)
- What social, political, economic, and racial backgrounds do they represent? (You cannot impress an audience favorably if you offend them.)
- What do they know about your subject? (You don't want to bore people by repeating what they are likely to know already. You don't want to confuse them by assuming they know more than they do.)

- How do you feel about the subject itself? (If you are going to ask people to think about changing a deeply ingrained habit, expect a hostile audience. Incidentally, when speaking before a hostile audience, you can do as much good with your good nature as you can with the logic of your ideas. Stick to your guns, but be fair and open-minded.)
- What do they know about you? (Do they know your good reputation? Are you meeting the friend of a friend? Are you representing a reputable firm or organization? Are you well qualified by training and experience to present your ideas? All these factors will influence the way people see you when you talk to them for the first time. Make sure you fill them in on who you are. Try to live up to or surpass their best expectations.)

If you know the answers to all these questions while getting ready to speak before a group, then you have met the second basic requirement: *Know your audience*.

Beginning, Middle, and End

The three sections of a good speech are more than just the starting point, the finishing point, and everything in between.

They are distinct units. Each has a purpose of its own. Start thinking of the parts of a speech in that way.

The beginning must (a) capture the attention of the listeners and (b) introduce your central idea. It must be appealing enough for your audience to want to listen to the rest.

The middle presents your ideas in greater depth. It provides information to support your central idea. It must be appealing enough so that your audience will want to hear you through.

An effective ending sums up the central idea and the supporting evidence. It provides a powerful close that will stick in the minds of your listeners.

The late Bernard Baruch, known for decades as advisor to U.S. Presidents, was deeply committed to the dream of lasting peace among nations. His favorite place for meeting with government officials and members of the press was a particular bench in Lafayette Park, across Pennsylvania Avenue from the White House.

When he was given the opportunity after World War II to address the opening session of the newly founded United Nations, he opened his memorable talk with these words: "We are here to distinguish between the quick and the dead." Having established at once in this way the high stakes of the enterprise that was being undertaken, he went on to elaborate the need for ensuring success of the U.N. and concluded by restating his theme in a forceful manner. His speech was widely quoted in the press and had a lasting impact on the considerations of the U.N.

Remember that you must plan talks that have beginnings, middles, and ends. When you have made these elements the grand plan of every talk, then you have met the third basic requirement.

The Basics in Everyday Life

The three basics apply even in the most ordinary situations. No message is so simple that it does not require logical presentation.

In fact, because the three basics are so logical and universal— as important today as they were for Aristotle in ancient Greece—you may already be in the habit of using them without realizing that you are.

But if your speech is not as effective as it should be in *all* situations, it will help to see how the basics fit into the way you talk. Not just with employers, customers, or town officials but with your friends over a cup of coffee or a luncheon table. If the basics worked for Aristotle, they can work for you.

Read the following speech. It was given on an evening in autumn. Four friends were watching television together. Two of them wanted to see the football game. The other two wanted to watch something else. After a few minutes of argument, Roger began to speak:

I can't stand football on television. Let's watch *The Rockford Files* instead. TV football has no excitement. It's not like being at the game. And the announcers say idiotic things. The guy who plays Rockford is one of the best actors around. He's funny and clever, and the other characters are always interesting. Besides, everyone likes the show. You can always check the football score during the commercials. Last but not least, I really don't want to watch football. If you insist on it, I'm going home.

Roger's speech was spontaneous, but it had all the points of a well-prepared longer address. See if you can analyze how it fulfills the basics. What can you say about the central idea; the audience; the speaker's efforts to tailor his words to his audience; and the beginning, middle, and end? (We will take a hard look at this speech later, but it would be good for you to analyze it first.)

Here's another speech given in a commonplace setting on an ordinary issue. It is early morning. A married couple are in the kitchen. Both have to go to work. The husband is looking into the refrigerator. He asks; "How would you like some pancakes for breakfast?" His wife replies:

Not pancakes. I still feel full from dinner last night. Pancakes just make me feel bloated all morning. Not only that, but they're so much trouble to make. You have to mix the batter, cook them, and then wash all that sticky batter and syrup off everything. We don't have much time before we leave for work. I'd rather just have orange juice, yogurt, and coffee and look at your handsome face. So let's skip the pancakes.

Now let's analyze these brief talks to see how well they satisfy the three basic requirements.

Mini-speech 1: TV Football?
- Central idea—The speaker can't stand football on TV.
- Audience—Friends. The speaker knows they like Rockford, so he can appeal to them on that basis.
- Beginning—The central idea is stated firmly. The speaker offers a positive suggestion.
- Middle—The speaker backs up the points stated in the beginning with sound reasons. The speaker couples sound reasoning with concern for the feelings of his audience.

• End—The central idea is stated again with a powerful close: If you insist on watching football, I'm going home.

Mini-speech 2: Pancakes for Breakfast?
• Central idea—She doesn't want pancakes for breakfast.
• Audience—Husband. She knows he has to go to work and that he will respond to flattery.
• Beginning—Forthright. Central idea stated firmly: Not pancakes.
• Middle—Sound reasons, physical and practical, for not making pancakes.
• End—Upbeat, flattering (your handsome face), practical suggestion, followed by a restatement of the central idea: So let's skip the pancakes.

Get the idea? The little speeches of everyday life that prove effective have the same logical construction as major addresses. They may not be as finely crafted, but they don't need to be.

Practice Activity

Sit down with a friend to talk. Record your conversation on tape. Just go ahead and chat. When you are relaxed—and the conversation permits it—introduce something along the lines of the mini-speeches you just read.

Speak on any subject. For instance, talk about a movie you saw recently—not the plot but whether you liked the movie and why. Or talk about a book you've just finished. Just choose a subject on which you can express a point of view.

This is very much like what students do when they write a paper for a course in school: state a thesis, give information to support the thesis, then restate the thesis at the end.

When you have a chance to play back your speech, analyze it just as we did with our two previous examples.

Does your central idea come out clearly in the first or second sentence? Does your word choice reflect your understanding of, and feelings toward, your audience? Does the middle of your speech support the central idea and present evidence clearly? Does the end of your speech restate the central idea in such a way that your audience will remember what you said? If you had a chance to give that speech again, how would you do it better?

Now that you have listened to the way you speak, put together another speech on a topic you consider important. Build the basics into the structure.

Suggested subjects: Problems at work. Problems at school. A domestic dispute. Advice to a friend who is in trouble. A plan for finding a job.

This time you have the opportunity to plan your speech in detail. Just what are you trying to say? What facts can you gather to convince your audience that what you say is correct? What is the best way to end the talk? Is the talk right for your audience?

It is not enough to think about these lessons only when you are reading this book or when you are practicing. Incorporate the three basics of giving talks into situations you face in your daily life. You will find that this logical system for speaking strengthens your communication with others.

Beyond Everyday Speech

The basics of giving good talks are used at every level of speechmaking.

Theodore C. Sorensen, speechwriter for President John F. Kennedy, wrote in *Kennedy,* his memoirs of life at the White House, that he and Mr. Kennedy "always discussed the topic, the approach, and the conclusions in advance." Speeches were designed "for an orderly presentation of their substance." Sorensen said further, "Our chief criterion was always audience comprehension and comfort."

They're all there—the central idea; the audience; the beginning, middle, and end.

While we may never get to the White House, except as visitors, there will be occasions when we will want to speak more carefully than we do in discussing what to watch on television or what to have for breakfast. Later in this book you will find advice on how to prepare for such special activities as writing an important speech.

Right now, however, it is important to think about expanding your speech preparation toward more advanced levels.

Always Begin in the Middle

Begin in the middle? Isn't that a little strange? Isn't it customary to begin at the beginning? Not in planning a speech.

Remember, you want to get the substance of your message across. And the substance is discussed in greatest depth in the middle. The middle is where you make the case for what you want to say. It is where you put the facts.

The beginning is a statement of the central idea, in terms that will appeal to the audience and interest them enough to listen further.

The middle is the part of the speech where you put the evidence. No matter how good your beginning is, your listeners will not take you seriously unless the middle, the body of the speech, supports the beginning. It doesn't matter whether your speech is intended to convince, inform, or praise.

A lawyer will never make an opening argument in a trial without knowing the evidence first. Everything the lawyer argues must be based on evidence.

A scientist will never accept a theory until experiments have backed it up.

You won't buy a car until you have done a lot of research.

Without evidence, the most eloquent statements can be picked apart.

We have heard lots of people start bravely at the beginning and suddenly find themselves out on a limb. After the first sweeping statement, they have nothing further to say. All they can do is repeat that statement over and over again in different words. No one was ever convinced by that type of speech.

So the work of planning a speech begins in the middle. What is required is a bit of thought—plus whatever quick research is needed to help your thinking—just enough to enable you to draw up a list of points you can make in support of your idea. This exercise shows you quickly whether you have anything worth saying. It guarantees that "We need another secretary in our branch" will receive careful attention. It guarantees that "School taxes must be raised this year" will not be hooted down.

Another Secretary Needed

1. Two secretaries now each averaging ten hours a week overtime—at time and a half.
2. Office not covered adequately when one secretary goes off on trip or vacation.
3. Sales department phones not adequately covered.
4. Typing backlog—it takes three days to get a letter out.

Now you know you have what you need to back up your statement: "We need another secretary." Try outlining the middle for the school tax speech yourself. (Take either side.)

When you know that you really have a middle for your speech, you can go on to the beginning.

How to Begin

Don't feel that you have to be funny or wise in your opening remarks. We all know speakers who can draw us in right away with their charm and wit, but don't measure yourself against them now. Speakers who can capture their audiences from the start have had a great deal of practice.

All you have to be concerned with now is making your message as clear and as simple as possible.

If your ideas are worth listening to, people will listen *if you state the ideas so that they are easily understood*.

Jokes are effective only if you are a good joke teller. Professional speechwriters never put jokes into speeches they write for others unless the speaker absolutely insists, or unless there is a natural sense of humor already there to exploit.

People who can't tell jokes well will inevitably turn their listeners off with bad jokes. (And they ruin good jokes!)

If you try to tell a story in order to make a point, it has to be very well told or people will wonder what the devil you are talking about.

Don't take a chance on losing your audience by being fancy or clever until you have more experience. Later in the book we will discuss such techniques. For now, concentrate on clarity and simplicity.

One last hint. The phrasing of your central idea should contain key words that can be repeated many times during your speech to reinforce the idea in the minds of your listeners.

- *Good teachers* are leaving our school system.
- Our children need *good teachers*.
- Will my younger children have the opportunity of being taught by *good teachers*?

All these sentences follow naturally the central, opening statement: School taxes must be raised this year to keep our *good teachers*.

The central idea is the hub of the wheel. Repetition of the key phrase, *good teachers*, supplies spokes for the wheel.

The End

The end of the talk restates the central idea, summarizes the evidence presented in the middle, and demands action.

Don't make the mistake of trying to introduce new evidence at the end of a speech. Don't repeat too many points. These mistakes will confuse your listeners and distract them from the logic of your arguments.

If a speech is intended to inform, the listeners should be invited to ask questions.

If a speech is intended to rouse people to action, the

listeners should be invited to sign petitions, to give money, or to take whatever action is appropriate.

If a speech is intended to impress a prospective employer, you ought to be ready to receive a job offer.

Whatever effect you want your speech to have, a powerful close will help. The most famous powerful close in United States history came in Patrick Henry's statement before the Virginia House of Burgesses: "I know not what course others may take, but as for me, give me liberty or give me death."

Gear your close to what *you* feel. Your conviction is the most important element in your speech anyway. Just remember: restate your central idea, summarize the facts, and don't try to present any new evidence.

CHAPTER 6
Good Speech on the Telephone

At six P.M. the telephone rang for the fourth time at Harry Edwards's desk. His office, crowded with company officers, was the scene of an important meeting. A complex bid for a substantial contract was under discussion. The finishing touches had to be completed by eight P.M.

Annoyed that a call had come in even though he had told his secretary to hold all calls, Harry spoke angrily when he answered: "Yeah?"

There was a pause at the other end of the line. Finally, a voice said, "Harry, is that you?" It was the chairman of the board.

"Yes, sir!" Harry was deeply embarrassed.

"I just wanted to know if I could be of any help."

"We're going to be finished on time, sir, and I am confident we have a winning price. Of course, if you want to come by. . . ."

One Harry, two voices. One resentful at an intrusion, one deeply respectful.

An important lesson learned: The way you answer a telephone call can profoundly affect your relations with other people.

Of course Harry should not have answered the call angrily. How was the caller to know that Harry's secretary had left her desk for a few minutes? How was the caller to know he was interrupting the very meeting in which he was interested? We cannot blame the caller, the chairman of the board.

Can we blame Harry? We would hope that no one ever

answers a telephone call in the angry way Harry did. But tension rises at times, and the chance of such behavior increases.

All you can do to keep yourself from making such errors is to adopt a uniform, warm telephone response that becomes second nature to you. Thus, without having to think again about how you answer the telephone, you will be spared future embarrassment.

In the world of today we spend so much time on the telephone that no program intended to improve your speech can neglect your use of that instrument.

Your Telephone Personality

You may be one of many people who spend more time talking on the phone than face to face. The average American puts in an hour a day on the phone. An hour. That's all talking and listening. Unlike face-to-face conversation, the telephone doesn't make use of silence. You cannot read someone's face on the phone. When you are quiet, nothing's happening except that message units are ticking by. So if you've never done it before, now's the time to consider what kind of person you are—what impression you make—during that hour.

When you speak on the phone, three factors make up your personality—voice, attitude, and courtesy.

How many times has someone put down the telephone while you were speaking? How many times have you done that to someone else? How many times have your telephone calls begun in a friendly way and then gone sour? How many times have you found yourself unable to make your feelings or opinions clear to someone on the telephone? You can count each one of these situations as telephone failures.

Let's examine *voice, attitude,* and *courtesy* one at a time to see whether you can explain past failures on the telephone.

VOICE. You have to speak with as much resonance and warmth on the phone as you do in person. Not with the same volume, but certainly with the same fullness of voice.

Remember, your voice is all you have going for you. It must convey your attitude and the courtesy you extend. How do you do this?

Hold the receiver about an inch and a half away from your mouth. Speak into it. Do not whisper. No matter whether you are calling someone on the other side of the earth, do not shout.

Don't depend on the telephone to do the work of your diaphragm. The telephone can only transmit vibrations, so you must send the vibrations.

ATTITUDE. The right attitude on your part will improve your phone conversation immensely. Although you cannot see the person you are speaking with, that person can tell a great deal about you from the sound of your voice, almost as much as if the two of you were sitting across a table from one another.

Smiling callers sound like smiling callers. Angry callers sound angry, even though they may not have raised their voices. Bored callers sound bored. Nervous callers sound nervous.

Have you ever had a call from an inexperienced telephone salesperson? The sales talk may be well rehearsed. The words may be marvelously engaging. But something is missing. You almost think that the caller expects to have the phone slammed down at any moment. You wonder whether the caller is frightened and uncertain, unconvinced of the quality of what is being offered for sale. All of that may come through on the phone.

To improve your telephone attitude, see in your mind's eye the person you are calling. Smile. Make eye contact. Gesture. Let your hands really move, as much as you would in person. Your warmth, your sincerity, your interest and enthusiasm will come through.

An executive editor we know likes to walk up and down, moving his free hand in wide swings while talking on a telephone.

"It helps me keep my energy level high," he says. "My hand rises and falls and waves about according to what I'm saying. It makes the conversation more fun. And when I have fun, the people I'm calling have fun also."

Treat every call as important. This, of course, means personal calls as well as business calls. The importance you attach to a call translates into effective use of the telephone.

COURTESY. First of all, think about the person you are calling before you reach for the phone. What is that person likely to be doing when you call? Are you calling to make a complaint? You don't want to call just before the close of the business day. Are you calling someone within your office? Consider that person's routine. Are you calling someone at home on community matters? If you are calling at home in the evenings, avoid the dinner hour. Be considerate of bedtimes.

When you reach someone on the telephone, be aware of the attitude that person conveys. What may go unsaid, yet be clearly apparent, is that you have called at the wrong time or on the wrong topic, or that you are an unwelcome caller at any time and on any topic.

In those cases it's up to you to assess the attitude.

On the other hand, if you'd rather not talk when the phone rings at your office or home, you can say so: "I'll call back" or "Can you call back?" Your associates and friends will appreciate this more than having only half your attention.

What about attitude when speaking to an answering machine? You may hate to speak into a recorder, but it's your responsibility to leave your name, number, and message. While it is understandable that you may resent missing the chance to speak with a person, at least the machine provides the opportunity to leave a message. Respect the judgment of people who use these devices. So when you hear the beep . . . speak warmly.

Preparing to Make a Call

Know why you are calling before you place a call. When making personal calls as well as business calls, you will find that people appreciate callers who are considerate of their time.

Organize your ideas! For business calls, arrange your ideas in the appropriate order. If you want information, prepare your questions as if you were interviewing the other person. It's up to you to steer the conversation. Don't depend on the other person for direction.

If you are trying to sell something over the phone, prepare as carefully as if you were making a sales visit. Be direct. You might describe the problem the potential customer might be having and then give the solution—your product. Or you might announce the service you are selling and ask whether the person you are calling has need of it.

Telephone salespeople make two big mistakes: They may act too friendly before getting down to business. They may try to disguise a sales pitch as something else. A favorite trick is to pretend that they are conducting an opinion survey or are offering a free service. These are examples of bad telephone manners. Don't make such mistakes.

Unless you are working for a company that has a secret formula for beguiling customers with a line of extraneous patter, be straightforward and efficient when calling. Be polite. Be enthusiastic. But don't pretend to be something you are not.

Efficiency will enable you to determine quickly whether you have a potential sale. If there's no interest, no further conversation is in order. If there is the possibility of a sale, your forthright manner will create good will and inspire confidence.

Be prepared! Have at hand whatever equipment or reference sources you will need: pencils, paper, order blanks, catalogues, prices, facts, figures. Don't ever make someone wait while you go off to find a pencil.

Check the number! Wrong numbers waste your time and that of an innocent stranger. If you do get a wrong number, repeat the number you wanted. Chances are you dialed wrong, or the number you called is out of date. Above all, avoid dialing the same wrong number twice.

When the Phone Begins to Ring

Hold the receiver about an inch and a half from your mouth. Unless you have a shoulder grip, don't cradle the phone between your shoulder and chin. It will cramp your style. If you need to have both hands free, you aren't fully prepared.

Identify yourself: "Good morning. My name is Ron Hansen. I represent Corinth Engineering." If you have reached a switchboard operator or if the other party does not make any effort to identify himself, ask for the person you are trying to reach or for the department.

"I'd like to speak with Alan Pierson in purchasing." Or "I'd like to speak with the buyer of engineering services."

When you have reached the right person, state your business. Get right to the point: "I would like to set up an appointment with you to describe a new drafting service we are introducing in this area." If you will need more than a few minutes to complete your business, say so at the beginning. Offer to call back at a more convenient time. Ask when it would be most convenient to call again.

When you have finished your business, end the conversation politely: "Thanks for your help. I'll send the information immediately." Or "Sorry we couldn't help you. I'll send our services brochure in case you ever need any drafting help. Good-bye."

The Little Hassles of Telephone Conversation

Even the largest companies may not be staffed to handle all incoming calls at once. You may have to let a phone ring for a long time (there are ten rings per minute) before you get an answer. For a business call, you should hang on for as long as it takes. For a personal call, ten rings are more than enough.

Don't be put off by apparently less-than-polite receptionists. They may pick up and then ignore you while they take another call. They may put you on hold and then leave you there. They have a lot to do. If you ever have the opportunity to watch a switchboard during a busy time of day, you will be amazed by the high level of activity. Be patient. Most people try to do their jobs efficiently.

Yet no matter how polite you are and how careful you are in your own telephone style, there will always be some people who treat you badly. Chalk these rare occurrences up to experience.

Life on the Receiving End— Answering a Call

When the telephone rings, put that cigarette in the ashtray. Set aside your coffee. Stop laughing, no matter how funny you just found that joke.

Pick up the receiver as soon as you can—just because you have to hold on for ten rings when you make a call doesn't mean that everyone else should. Some callers quit after three rings. If you don't pick up, they will have to try again—if they do. You may be missing an important call.

If you work the switchboard, answer by giving your firm's name. If you are a secretary, answer by giving the name of the person you work for. Then give your own name: "Ms. Anderson's office. Mrs. Davis speaking." Department secretaries and assistants should name the department first, then say their own names.

If you work alone and answer your own phone, or if your secretary informs you that a call has come, state your name: "John Wood speaking."

When the right person is not available, say, "Miss Jacobi cannot be reached. May I take a message?" Or, "Miss Jacobi will return at two o'clock. May I have her call you?"

Jot down the name and phone number, the time of the call, and the message. Repeat the message to the caller to make sure you have it right. Spell the caller's name back if the name is strange to you. Be sure that the right person gets the message. Make sure that your handwriting is legible.

Listening—Artful Silence

When you listen to a speaker face to face, you watch and you respond. The speaker is watching and responding to you.

Many phone listeners feel the temptation to do other things while listening. In some cases it doesn't matter. We've all seen movies in which someone takes a call from a doting mother who chatters away. The actor does not even bother to listen. He puts the phone down and, every once in a while, picks it up to say, "Yes, ma."

It doesn't often work that way in the real world. You need to pay attention. Listening is not a passive process. You have to participate.

To pick up the full meaning of what someone says on the phone, you have to pay attention to the way the voice rises and falls. Where the pauses come. The attitude reflected in the voice. Is your caller smiling or frowning? Does he sound confident? Does he sound pleased? Is he getting ready to give you bad news? Are any of these extra messages signals to you that you must do something quickly?

Listen for all the information in a voice that you would seek otherwise in the body language and facial expression of a person with whom you are talking face-to-face.

But there is, of course, the actual message to be absorbed, and this also requires attention. Keep a note pad next to the phone. Listen for key words and phrases you can write down. This will make recall that much easier.

Try to avoid interrupting. From time to time say "I see" or "Yes" or "Of course" as appropriate to let the talker know you're there. But make sure that you *do see,* or that you *mean yes* or *of course*. If you don't really pay attention, your response will be inappropriate and the speaker will know.

A careful listener earns the right to interrupt.

If a caller has omitted some significant piece of information or has made something less clear than it should be, stop and ask.

If a friend is rambling on and on, tell him you've got to run.

If a salesperson is peddling something you don't want or don't need, tell him. Tell him nicely, but tell him.

Transferring a Call

If it is clear, after hearing a caller speak, that you are not the person who can handle that call, say politely but with authority, "Mr. Shea in the tax department can give you that information. I'll signal the operator to transfer your call."

Do your best to direct calls to the right person. You owe it to your firm to get such business handled with dispatch. Every time the wrong person answers the phone, time and money have been wasted. If you end up with the same caller on the line a second time, you will be annoyed, and the caller will be frustrated.

Signing Off

A polite "Thanks for calling, Mr. Jones" is always in order. If there is no further business to follow, say, "Thanks for your help" or "Sorry we can't be of service."

If more remains to be done, say whatever is called for: "I look forward to hearing from you." Or "I'll talk to you on Thursday."

Calling Someone in a Large Company

It is easiest to call someone in a large company if you can dial directly or if you know the person's extension: "Hello, I'd like extension 416 please." The operator does not have to look up the person or department.

In some cases, it will not be that easy. You may want to

speak to someone who performs a particular function in a company, for example, publicity. But you do not have a name to call, and the company does not have a publicity department. The thing to do is think of some other name that might serve the same function. Advertising. Marketing. Public relations. When someone answers the phone, give your name, the company you represent, and your reason for calling. People try to help someone who is open and frank in making such a call.

You may want to complain about a bill.

Here's a sample conversation. Read it. Haven't you had similar situations in your own life? Play both parts as you read. See if you normally do as well with your own complaints.

The phone rings. A voice answers: "Northeast Gas and Electric."

"I'd like to inquire about a bill."

"Just one moment. I'll connect you."

"Billing department. Miss Arnold speaking."

"Good morning, Miss Arnold. My name is John Barnes. Account number 6187794."

"Yes, Mr. Barnes. I'll get your file." Miss Arnold brings the information from computer memory to her CRT display screen.

"Thank you for waiting. I have your file in front of me. Now what is the nature of your complaint?"

"I believe I was charged for gas I didn't use in March and April. I was on vacation. I know I shut off the gas at the back of the stove, so unless there is a leak in my line, I could not have used any gas."

"That is possible. We do not always have the meters read. My guess is that because you were away, our man could not get in to read the meter. When this happens we bill on a monthly average. The next time we read the meter, we will make the adjustment."

"Thank you."

Both callers used their telephones well. They were prepared. They had all necessary information. They knew what they wanted to say.

Practice Activities

1. Taking a message for someone else.
2. Leaving a message with someone.
3. Making (or answering) a complaint.

In all these activities, make a conscious effort to improve your voice and telephone manner as suggested in this chapter.

CHAPTER 7

Speak for Success in Job Interviews

Getting a job is a series of steps, not a single task. Getting a job can be extremely difficult. By the time you reach an actual interview, you will have answered advertisements, written and typed résumés, visited agencies, made many phone calls, and read some of the many books on the subject. You will have followed lots of advice, some bad and some good.

Through it all, doubts hang over your head—doubts about yourself, doubts about all that you are doing and whether it will ever accomplish anything. Fear of rejection stays with you. It can be harrowing.

With an interview ahead of you, you have reached the final and, possibly, the most difficult phase—a face-to-face meeting with the representative of a company that may offer you work.

It is a crucial time for you, but it may help you to know that it is also crucial for the interviewer. If you are selected and are right for the job, hiring you will mean profits and success for the company as well as for you. If you are selected and are wrong for the job, the company will lose money and you will lose time and self-esteem.

Sudden Death

It is commonly known that many interviewers make up their minds about candidates within the first two or three minutes of meeting them. This doesn't leave much time for a bad start. The interviewer's state of mind at the beginning of the session is all-important.

So, with your future hinging on gut reactions, it is important that you know how to avoid disqualifying yourself by looking wrong or by carrying yourself badly. Your dress, your grooming, and your attitude (as pointed out in earlier chapters) are always as important as what you say—but particularly in a job interview.

This chapter is laid out to help you with the preliminary hurdles first: how to look, how to act, and what to bring with you to the meeting. Then we move on to what to say and how to say it.

The Vital Silent Elements—Revisited

The silent elements are so important that they are reviewed here.

Scene: A company office.

You are shown to a seat. The interviewer shuts the office door so the two of you can talk without distraction. It is two o'clock in the afternoon. The interviewer feels good because she has returned from lunch and has had time to think through the job requirements once again. You feel good because you've just treated yourself to your favorite dish, spaghetti marinara. The interviewer asks you a question. You are enthusiastic and launch into a detailed, thoughtful answer. Suddenly a sour look appears on the interviewer's face. You falter. What has gone wrong?

As the television commercial used to say, maybe it's your breath. One of the cardinal rules of preparing for an interview is to avoid garlic for at least twenty-four hours before the appointment.

When it's just the two of you in an office and the air is still, the interviewer can observe you with more than just her eyes. As Jimmy Durante used to say, "The nose knows."

And what about the eyes? What are your eyes and the interviewer's eyes saying?

In the first place, the most natural pattern in an interview is for people to look directly at one another only part of the time. Staring constantly at a person can make that person uncomfortable.

Make eye contact when you start to speak and at points along the way for emphasis. Then look again when you are through. You can be sure that your eyes will be met when they look at the other person, because it is precisely while you are speaking that the interviewer's eyes will look most thoughtfully at you.

While those eyes are looking at you, they will notice whether your shoes are scuffed, your clothing wrinkled, your hair carelessly combed.

The interviewer's eyes are studying you from the moment you walk into the office until the moment when something clicks, and you are judged acceptable or unacceptable. Thus, before an interview, get your clothes cleaned and pressed. Shine your shoes.

And remember, it isn't just eyes that are busy.

Shower, use a deodorant, brush your teeth, and gargle with mouthwash. If you use aftershave lotion or perfume, be sparing. In an office, even a pleasant aroma can become overpowering.

Cigars? Alcohol? Not before an interview. If you smoke cigarettes, freshen your breath with a mint after you put the last one out. And know that clothing can pick up all kinds of smells, especially smoke.

Wear clothes suitable for the job you are applying for. If the job is in sales, dress like a salesperson. If you are applying for a secretarial job, dress like a well-groomed secretary.

Here's some evidence for anyone who doesn't believe what we say about grooming and dress:

Study Shows Neatness Pays Off in Job Hunt

Neat, well-dressed college graduates have a better chance to land a job than those who appear in jeans or refuse to wear a bra, according to a Stanford University study.

The wearing of jeans, shorts, sandals, or dispensing

with bras creates an impression ranging from "mildly" to "strongly negative," the survey shows.

Applicants who use jargon, have dirty fingernails, or fiddle with objects on the desk also earn negative ratings, according to the study by two Stanford students who received doctoral degrees in educational counseling and guidance.

The researchers, Jane Anton and Michael Russell, questioned more than 100 recruiting officers from 17 different industry groups, ranging from accounting and aerospace to government and utilities.

They found that a male creates a mildly positive impression if he wears a sport coat, shirt, tie, and slacks. But he creates a stronger impression if he wears a suit.

And the shorter, more neatly trimmed the hair and beard on males, the better the impression on recruiters.

Applicants considered "assertive, intelligent, independent, and inquisitive" registered only a mildly positive influence in job interviews.

(From the *Cincinnati Enquirer*)

A Winning Attitude

Now let's get on to the role of speech in your job interview.

Without a winning attitude, you will find that your credentials, your clothes, your clean fingernails, and the rest are all just parts of a machine with nothing to hold them together.

You are trying to sell yourself. To sell yourself, you need to have confidence in the product—you. You have to make your customer—the interviewer—feel that your product is right for him.

Here's a story about someone with something to sell, but whose deep-seated doubts came back to haunt him.

Harry Ryan wanted to work in sales and he had a lead for a good starting position with a tool and die manufacturer. He was scheduled to be graduated from college in May, three months away, and get married in June. He had good grades, excellent recommendations, and a new dark-blue suit.

But Harry also had doubts.

"I wanted to go into sales," he told us, "because if I

worked hard enough I knew I could make a lot of money and rise to a sales executive position. But in the back of my mind, I had a lot of doubts. I thought that the product sold by that company wasn't very exciting and that the company wasn't innovative. In addition, the territory that was open was an area in which I had lived all my life. To top it off, I suddenly felt very young to be getting married. When I went into the interview, I guess I felt that the rest of my life was on the line and that if I took the job I would be stuck."

All of us have uncertainties when we are preparing to commit ourselves to a career, but Harry's worries showed up in the interview. He didn't get the job. To land a job as a salesman, he needed to show confidence. Harry failed to sell himself.

You may never have thought of yourself as a salesperson, but in any job interview you must become one. So maybe you'd better pay some attention to one expert in the field. In his long-time best-seller, *Successful Salesmanship* (Prentice-Hall, 1947), Paul W. Ivey defines four elements as keys to a good sales personality.

- Enthusiasm
- Sincerity
- Tact
- Courtesy

Ivey calls enthusiasm "a spirit which animates the whole body and makes an attractive and convincing salesman out of an assortment of dead flesh and bones."

To show your enthusiasm, you must allow it to charge your speech with excitement. You can't convince anyone that you are interested unless your voice sounds interested. You don't have to bubble over, but don't sound detached or uninterested either, especially if you have the opportunity to talk about your accomplishments and interests.

A recruiter we know who works for a nontechnical division of a large aircraft company told us, "I like my job. I like my company. I expect people I hire to do the same. If someone wants to work for me, the worst thing that person can do is act like he can take it or leave it.

"That doesn't mean that new people shouldn't ask questions.

But people who act blasé in an interview may not care about their work either.''

But enthusiasm should not be artificial. You have to be sincerely enthusiastic. Sincerity is the attitude that must underlie your enthusiasm. If it doesn't, an experienced interviewer can tell.

"I know when they are trying to fool me," says this recruiter. "Some are better at it than others. But the ones who think they are the cleverest are the easiest to see through. If the job has nothing to do with their real interests, they are desperate or they are liars. Would you want those qualities in your workers?''

Tact is another test of character. In any company you will have to deal with people whose attitudes and personalities are quite different from yours. You will have to deal with them tactfully so as not to give offense or stir up trouble. We are not all cut from the same cloth, so you cannot expect all the people you work with—or any job interviewer—to agree with you on everything.

One college senior, who had demonstrated against nuclear power and worked for an antinuclear organization, listed this fact on her résumé. The interviewer had just read about a demonstration at a nuclear plant in the newspaper and said, "These people are the first to complain when their stereos and electric guitars don't work.''

The applicant recalled, "I just assumed that the interviewer was testing me, so I let his comment pass. I put down that information because it was important to me, but I knew it would have nothing to do with my job.''

She got the job.

Sometimes, because you are asked to comment, you can't let remarks go by. So be prepared with phrases like "I know what you mean, but . . ." or "That makes sense, however. . . .''

If you are interviewed by a person who expresses an opinion in the course of asking a question, you must be tactful in your reply.

A man who landed a job in the personnel department of an electronic equipment manufacturing company told us this story: "The interviewer had given every indication of being ready to offer me a job as personnel counselor, when he said, 'You know, you'll have to work a lot with Hispanics. I'm afraid they give us a lot of trouble. Do you think you can deal with people who are chronically late and take every possible day of sick leave?' I answered that I was sure that I could deal with individual employees in a counseling environment and would be sure to be supportive and encouraging as I examined the facts in every case I was assigned. I added that I was confident that the right attitude on the counselor's part could do much toward helping solve the company's problems.''

What might have been construed as an offensive remark was defused in a forthright way without creating controversy. Just imagine what would have happened if the job applicant had decided to take offense at the interviewer's remark. As it turned out, the interviewer proved to be anything but prejudiced in his attitude toward minority workers. What he said reflected the fact that most newly hired people in that company did take advantage of company rules, and the company had just begun to hire minority workers, which made them very visible to the personnel department.

Finally, there is courtesy in an interview. Courtesy should be present in everything you do. It's like that rule of the road, "Watch out for the other guy."

You must be on time for the interview. You must show good manners during the interview. You must follow the interviewer's lead.

Sit when you are offered a chair. Shake hands only if the interviewer offers first, not before (and make sure your hand is dry and your grip firm).

Remember names and pronounce them correctly. If you have trouble with names, make a point of repeating the name as soon as you can after you first hear it.

"I'm Arnold Tarnovski," says the interviewer.

"Glad to meet you, Mr. Tarnovski. . . ." "That's an interesting question, Mr. Tarnovski. . . ." Find a couple of chances to use his name so that you won't slip later on.

Carry a pen and a notebook in your jacket pocket or purse so that if you are asked to write something down you will be prepared.

Have all relevant documents in a briefcase or folder: extra copies of your résumé, work samples, and letters of reference, or names, phone numbers, and addresses of references.

Courtesy means being sincere, honest, and enthusiastic—

the real you—without offending anyone or hurting anyone's feelings.

Being Assertive Without Being Aggressive

You have to make some kind of impression. The interviewer has to feel there is something there.

Assertive people stand up for themselves and do everything they can to succeed. When they fail, they pick themselves up immediately and, learning from setbacks, do better in their next interviews.

Nonassertive people are too shy. They cannot make their personalities felt by others. In interviews they come across as dull. They kick themselves afterward, when they have thought of the right things they should have said. Too late! They will make the same mistakes again unless they become assertive unless they learn to speak out.

Aggressive people make their personalities felt all too strongly. They put their personalities first, ahead of the jobs for which they are applying. When they are turned down for a job, it is never their fault—they think. The recruiter we mentioned earlier has interviewed all kinds Here are her feelings:

"You like the shy ones the way you like stray kittens. They're cute but you can't afford to keep them. They are hard to work with because, while they do everything you tell them, they don't have much initiative.

"Aggressive ones act like they're doing you a favor. They are so cocksure. Usually, however, their bright ideas are ones that the company has rejected before. And don't forget that the interviewee has to keep his eyes open during the interview. No job is right for just anyone. But the arrogant ones are too busy showing off to take in any new information. I like to hire people who want to know what they're getting into, who are assertive enough to get the best *from* me while they are doing their best *for* me."

What separates the assertive, successful type from aggressive or nonassertive failures? Above all, real confidence and self-knowledge.

The shy ones beat themselves. They've convinced themselves either that they can't succeed or that they can't ever do more than hold down a low-level job.

Aggressive people are scared too. They compensate for lack of real confidence and self-knowledge by offending anyone who can do them a good turn.

The Confidence Game

You must think positively: *I will get this job*. This does not guarantee success, but negative thinking guarantees failure.

Try to keep a level head. You want to have the strength to "keep your head as those around you are losing theirs."

If you have that attitude, you will succeed sooner or later. It's the same in every aspect of life. Confident people attract people who will go out of their way to help them.

People become leaders if they have the confidence to select a course of action when there are several attractive alternatives; people become leaders if they have the confidence to reject all unattractive alternatives and resume the search for a better way.

Believe in yourself. Accentuate the good things. Don't dwell on the negatives. Instead, do something to change the negatives.

Easier said than done? Of course. But not impossible. Part of the problem that people have in job interviews is that they have avoided thinking about their own strengths and weaknesses. Suddenly they are asked a probing question by an interviewer. The following activities are designed to help you come to grips with such things—to help you recognize your strong and weak points—before your next job interview.

1. KEEP A JOURNAL. In just a few minutes every day, list the things you have done that day. What was good and what was less than good? This will help you understand how you have become the person you are. It will also give you pride in your achievements and help you become a better person.

2. DRAW UP A RÉSUMÉ FOR YOURSELF. Give a copy to a friend. Then have the friend sit at a desk and act the role of nasty interviewer. It is the friend's job to comment on the information in the résumé.

"You were in the glee club (or on the football team or in the drama club or a sociology major)? So what? What does that have to do with working for a living?" The comments should be very harsh. It's up to you to put yourself in the best light in the face of such an attack. No interviewer will ever be as cruel as your best friend can be in trying to help you.

3. PICK OUT THE SKELETON IN YOUR CLOSET. Most people have some weak spots in their background that show up in their résumés. A low grade-point average. A year in which they bummed around. A job from which they were fired. Your friend should know you well enough to spot the weakness. Ask him to pump you with questions about it, really embarrass you. Then explain it, putting it in the best light possible, but without lying, while you try to deal with the adrenaline flow that accompanies your embarrassment.

4. CHOOSE SOME ACCOMPLISHMENT YOU ARE REALLY PROUD OF. Something you do so well that your head threatens to explode every time you think of it. Tell your friend about it. Use such extravagant terms that it sounds like boasting. Tell it again. And again, until you both are sick of it. The point is to burn all the boasting out of yourself. You want to speak with self-respect but without sounding smug. Now see if you can tell the story quietly, honestly, and with self-respect. That's how to impress an interviewer.

Other Kinds of Preparation

If you are looking for work, it helps to know exactly what you want to do. You can then do research on different companies to find out if any of them have departments offering what you want. This kind of research can be done at most public libraries. Check out business directories and industrial publications.

Job searches are helped by knowing something about a company and the products it makes. Your library will be helpful in this regard. You don't want to become an expert, but the interviewer will appreciate it if you have taken the time to learn something about what the company does.

At the last minute before the interview, you cannot prepare yourself further. But you can warm up. It helps to hear your voice before an interview since, in your nervousness, you may find yourself speaking a couple of notes above normal. Or you may listen to your voice and wonder if you sound natural. If you can, have a few words with someone before entering the interviewer's office. Just give yourself a chance to hear your voice.

Questions and Answers

There are a few things to keep in mind before you go for your interview.

Take every question seriously. Inexperienced interviewers may be as nervous as you are and ask questions just to keep things moving along. But any question, no matter how superfluous it seems, can be a precision tool in the mouth of an experienced interviewer.

If the meaning of a question is unclear, like "What do you want from life?" you are allowed to ask for some clarification. Chances are the interviewer is throwing this at you as a test. If you answer quickly, "Six children and a house in the suburbs" or "To be chairman of the board," it may be good for your case or bad. But you can do most for your cause by appearing thoughtful and careful.

Jarring Questions Most Often Asked in Interviews, and Truthful, Effective Answers for Them

1. HAVE YOU EVER HAD A DISPUTE WITH YOUR SUPERIORS THAT INTERFERED WITH YOUR WORK?

In answering this question, be tactful. You don't want to portray yourself as a malcontent. You don't want to slander anyone. The stronger the terms you use to decry your former colleagues, the more suspicious your interviewer will be. Chances are that if he checks up on you, you will be described in similar terms at the other end. Tell the truth politely and unspecifically. If appropriate, describe the disagreement as a policy conflict. Be sure you say nothing that may be seen as badmouthing. A person who speaks against others speaks against himself.

2. WHAT KIND OF PERSON ARE YOU?

Accentuate the good, but don't put a halo over your head. Be forceful and clear. Use your reading of the interviewer and the job to give pertinent information that will help your cause. What you want to emphasize is your reputation as a hard worker, as a person who cares about his company's interest, as a willing worker who knows how to follow instructions and give instructions.

3. DO YOU INTEND TO STAY IN THIS JOB IF WE DECIDE TO HIRE YOU?

Say that you have thought firmly about your plans. You want to make your career in the company, and that is why you are applying. As long as your position is fulfilling, you have no intention of changing employment.

4. WHY DO YOU WANT THIS JOB?

This is where your research will pay off. Be honest. Don't be afraid to list income as one factor. But surely there are other good reasons. The company is known as a good place to work. There is opportunity for growth. You have always lived in the area and want to remain. You intend to continue your schooling after working hours in subjects that will be useful in the company.

5. WHAT ARE YOUR IDEAS ON SALARY?

Unless you have a yardstick on which to base your answer and a firm income goal, it doesn't hurt to ask what the job pays. You may also find a helpful response in one or more of the following:

- You were paid X dollars in your previous job and hope to better yourself now.
- You understand that the job pays a salary between X and Y and would be glad to start in that range.
- You look upon the job as a promising opportunity, so starting salary is not important.
- You don't know what to expect, since this is your first job.

6. WHY WERE YOUR SCHOOL GRADES SO LOW?

Perhaps you spent all your spare time at college working to support yourself. Maybe you become too absorbed in running your college newspaper. Maybe you were too immature to think about grades. The point is to compensate for gaps or low spots in your record by showing interests, abilities, or newlyfound maturity that make up for them.

But stay away from lying, no matter how difficult and embarrassing a question may be. If you know and recognize your problems in advance of a job campaign, you can develop answers for embarrassing questions that are thoughtful enough to turn minuses into plusses.

What Mistakes Did These Job-seekers Make?

The interviewer seemed pleased. Carol felt quite comfortable. Then the interviewer asked, "What would you say is your most important asset as an employee?"

Carol answered, "I've thought about that before and I guess the answer is that I make very good coffee."

She didn't get the job. Why not? Because she made a joking answer to a serious question. She could have said she types eighty words a minute. She could have said she gets along well with all kinds of people. She could have said she handles pressure very well. Instead she made a joke. The interviewer noted, "Not serious enough."

John went for an interview at a bank for a job as teller. He wore a suit the color of a putting green. The manager said, "Don't call us. We'll call you." What went wrong?

Banks like their image gray and solid. They don't want their money handled by people who look like blackjack dealers.

Barry wanted to make some extra money, so he decided to take up caddying at the local golf course. The caddy master decided that Barry should have some practice shagging balls for one of the members. Shagging balls didn't pay as well as caddying, so Barry said he preferred to caddy. He sat there all day while all the other boys shagged balls or carried bags. He sat all day and next day and the next. What did he do wrong? He refused to do the work he was asked to do.

At the close of the interview, the manager of the store said he was pleased with how things had gone and would be getting in touch with Fred within the next few days. "Can't you tell me now whether I have the job? I'm going on a camping trip for the next few days."

"Oh? You told me you were ready to start work as soon as we called you."

"You can't expect me to sit and wait for your call."

"Well, all I can say is that we'll get in touch with you if we need you."

The manager never did call Fred. What had Fred done wrong? You might say he showed the interviewer a trait he had not previously revealed. Again, if Fred had mentioned the camping trip earlier, the interview might have ended more pleasantly—and more successfully for Fred.

The personnel manager started things off by describing the job as management trainee that Sheila was applying for and then asked whether she had any questions before they went on.

"Yes. I would like to know your policy on maternity leave."

The manager supplied the answer and then told Sheila she was one of several people under consideration and he would notify her promptly of the company's decision.

You can guess that Sheila was not hired. A trainee normally does not become productive on the job for some time. Besides that, a company invests a good deal of money in training a newly hired person. What did Sheila do wrong? She gave the personnel manager the impression that Sheila's training would be interrupted soon after it would have begun. Why did Sheila ask the question? She told us she was engaged to be married at the time and thought the question might one day be important to her. As things turned out, the engagement soon was ended.

What are you to learn from all these true stories? First, people who do not develop their ability to speak well at interviews through thinking, planning, and rehearsing can make terrible mistakes. Secondly, any approaches you develop for answering questions in job interviews must be examined from the interviewer's point of view as well as your own.

CHAPTER 8
Good Speech in Selling and Persuading Others

Successful salespersons are essential in business. So true is this that successful salespeople can usually find work anywhere.

Age is no barrier. You've seen high school students working behind the counters of retail stores after school and during vacations. Thousands of college students earn impressive sums selling books door-to-door during their summer breaks. Senior citizens in great numbers supplement their pensions and fight retirement blues by getting out and selling.

Then there is the dynamic class of professional salespeople— all persuasive speakers—who log hundreds of thousands of miles on the nation's highways in selling everything under the sun. Their median income as a profession is higher than that of lawyers, according to a survey in *The American Salesman*.

What does it take to become a good salesperson? Aren't you born with it? Don't some people just have the knack? Doesn't it take a certain amount of cynicism to go out and pretend you are doing people a favor by selling them something?

No. You are not born with it. It takes hard work. Some people seem to have the knack, but they still have to put in time learning their markets, learning how to deal with people, and keeping up with product changes and changing needs.

Finally, most salespeople are not cynical. They depend on doing business with their customers year in and year out. If salespeople were cynical about their customers or their products, they wouldn't survive. In fact, salespeople and their customers value sincerity more highly than almost anything else. So success in sales requires persuasive speech as well as some traits you may not have thought much about until now.

Most people have the ability to master effective salesmanship. What's more, most people practice effective selling all the time, even though they probably are not aware that they are selling.

Everyone practices effective selling? How can that be?

Because the basics of selling are the same as the basics for all persuasive speaking.

But can selling be learned? Yes. And can it accomplish miracles? Well, almost.

The Essentials of Persuasiveness

Knowledge, sincerity, empathy, and enthusiasm are essential elements of persuasiveness.

KNOWLEDGE. You want to be able to show people that you know what you are talking about, because no one will buy from the ignorant. But the kind of knowledge it takes to persuade is more than simply what, where, and how knowledge. It is deeper than that. It shows real understanding of the reasons why people will or will not buy the service or product.

Jack Robbins, a salesman with an excellent annual income, sells lockers for installation in schools. He once prepared a bid for an Ohio school system for an installation of two thousand lockers for a junior high school that was about to be built. He presented his bid in a meeting with the superintendent, who looked only at the total price and said, "I'm sorry, Mr. Robbins. Your bid is several thousand dollars higher than that of your nearest competitor. We cannot consider it."

"That's too bad," Jack replied as he rose to leave. "Of course, my lockers are not dangerous."

The superintendent couldn't let that remark go unexplained. "What do you mean, 'dangerous'?"

Jack reeled off a list of the companies that made lockers. From the look on the superintendent's face, he could see that they were his competitors on this project. Then he explained that the other lockers had rough edges on the insides of their doors, that sometimes children would close a locker door by grasping the door itself instead of the handle.

"The other bids you have may be lower than mine, but when you start adding up the medical bills and the lost class time and the lawsuits, you'll wish you had spent the money for our safer lockers."

Jack's claim was correct. He made the sale.

Get the idea? It doesn't matter what you are selling—a product, an idea, or a plan. Know what you are selling and know what it takes to make a sale.

SINCERITY. It isn't enough to know what you are selling. You have to believe in it as well. Don't even try to sell a third-rate product. Don't try to collect signatures on a petition for a cause you don't fully support.

When you are not sincere about something you're trying to sell, you cannot help giving yourself away. Eye contact is difficult. You are susceptible to giveaway slips of the tongue. You appear uncertain. You appear falsely enthusiastic. Even if people don't actually think you're lying, they will not buy if they sense that you don't have complete faith in what you are trying to sell.

EMPATHY. Sympathy is feeling *for* other people. Empathy is feeling *with* them. When you feel empathy with someone, you get inside that person and see the world through that person's eyes.

Why is empathy important for persuasion? Because people buy for various reasons, not all of them strictly rational.

Think about the last presidential election, for example. Did you support a candidate because of what he said on the issues or because you trusted him as a person? Because of his record or because of the way he spoke? Which issues did you support him on? All of them? Or did you disregard the issues completely?

Did your candidate address people in your hometown in the same way he addressed retired people in Florida or wheat farmers in Kansas? Of course not. The candidate tried to see the world in the same way that the voters before him saw it.

Like a campaign speech, a sales talk is quite complex. Each sales talk has to be adjusted to address the needs of a particular audience in the same way in which a candidate adjusts to different voting blocs. But this is just part of empathy.

Empathy also means showing respect for your customers' attitudes and feelings. This means that they must believe you recognize their importance. While you speak and while you listen, you watch for signs that indicate they have more important things on their minds than the business you have in mind. "May I come back tomorrow?" "Would you rather talk another time?" "Have I said something to offend you?"

A salesperson who shows empathy is a listener as well as a talker, a watcher as well as a performer.

Let's see how this works.

Carol Barton is not a professional persuader. Last year, feeling that she wanted to get involved in community activities as a welcome change from her work as a wife and mother, she volunteered to sell raffle tickets to raise money for the volunteer fire department. She went from door to door with her daughter. At one house, her daughter said, "Don't bother to go in there. That man yelled at me when I was selling Girl Scout cookies and told me never to come back again."

"Well," said Carol, "these aren't cookies." She went up to the house and rang the bell.

When the man came to the door, Carol said, "Save your house!" The man was startled and didn't slam the door.

Carol explained that the volunteers had saved thirty-two lives and twelve homes in the last six months. She sold—he bought—ten tickets.

By appealing to the man's instinct for self-preservation instead of community spirit, town pride, or anything else sentimental, she made the sale. She had put herself inside the man and found his weak spot—himself.

Don't think there's something wrong with people who look out for their own interests. We all do it. When you ignore this fact about people, you limit yourself to trying to convince people to do things for your reasons instead of theirs. With what result? Doors slam. People say "No." "My husband gives at the office." "Just mail me the information."

When you show empathy, you find it easier to understand people. Once you understand their motivations, you find it easier to sell.

ENTHUSIASM. One salesman called his job "transferring enthusiasm." Enthusiasm supercharges your words. It makes you exciting and your service or product exciting. The customer feels that something extraordinary is happening.

Steven Switzer, who sells shoe accessories such as laces and footpads to shoe stores and shoe repair shops, places enthusiasm right at the top of his list of important qualities for salesmanship.

"It isn't hard for me to get enthusiastic over my merchandise, because what I sell is a good buy for the money. But I also enjoy the challenge of selling and I like to get out and meet new people, just as I like seeing my regular customers every so often.

"I think the result is that my customers like seeing me. I lift them out of their routine, and they remember what I say because of the way I say it. When customers walk into stores while I'm there, I often hear the storekeepers recommend my products, and they usually use the same words I've used with them."

In all persuasive speaking, enthusiasm is important. Unless you are enthusiastic, you won't enjoy what you do. And if you don't enjoy what you do, you won't succeed and you won't be doing it very long.

Here is a list of things buyers dislike about salespeople. The list is really about two elements we have been discussing: sincerity and empathy.
1. Overpromises and oversells.
2. Misrepresents and exaggerates.
3. Abuses telephone privileges.
4. Talks prices in front of customers.
5. Sells customers without buyer's consent.
6. Carries stories about other people in the business.
7. Tries to bribe prospects.
8. Interrupts when buyer is busy.

Notice how many of these dislikes are related directly to the qualities of sincerity and empathy. Numbers one and two, both signs of insincerity, are at the top of the list. Obviously there's nothing these buyers hate more than a con man.

And the rest are all critical of salespeople who, lacking empathy, show disrespect for the buyer's feelings. Having empathy is more than understanding how to reach a customer's receptive nerve with your sales talk. It also means being sensitive to people's feelings at the right time.

Here is a list of what buyers like about salespeople.
1. Respects buyer's time.
2. Talks about "us" instead of his company—showing how he feels a part of it.
3. Tells how product serves buyer's needs.
4. Knows his products.
5. Helps train buyer's employees in use of products.
6. Makes appointments for sales calls.
7. Lives up to promises.
8. Doesn't inventory buyer's needs without consent.
9. Is courteous and neat in appearance.
10. Pronounces buyer's name and company name correctly.

Do you see the emphasis on knowledge, sincerity, empathy, and enthusiasm? While this list and the one before it refer to salespeople in a particular industry, you can see that they apply to any sales situation. Indeed, they apply to any situation in which one person is trying to persuade another. Refer to these lists before you set out to persuade anyone to do anything.

Grabbing Attention

We said earlier that every speech has to have a beginning, a middle, and an end. Well, nowhere is this sort of structure more important than in a persuasive speech. The beginning captures attention, the full development occurs in the middle, and the end ties everything together.

How do you capture attention?

People do all sorts of things to set themselves apart from other people. One job applicant attached a dollar bill to his résumé when he answered a want ad, so people remembered him in the interview as "the guy with the dollar."

A young Dutch actor went to Paris to look for work. As he entered each casting office, he would leap over the secretary's desk. No one there ever forgot him. Whenever they needed an actor of his type, they called the "fellow who jumped over desks."

When you are attempting to persuade people, you don't have to do tricks. But you should try to get people interested right from the start. Once you have done this, you can launch into your explanation of the facts. You may have started off with a claim that what you are offering will benefit your customer substantially; you may have appealed to your customer's pride, greed, or vanity; you may have merely grabbed attention by some stunt. Now you are ready to back up your opener with a strong statement of the facts. There are various ways to do this.

Inverted Pyramid Persuasion

Newspaper writing uses a technique called *inverted pyramid style*. The most important information is placed first in a news story, and the rest of the story is structured to offer facts in order of declining importance. This enables the editors to trim from the end if there isn't enough space for the whole story.

In effective persuasion, follow a similar pattern. After your attention-grabbing approach, put forward your most compelling information and shoot your big guns first. You have your listener's attention for a limited amount of time, so don't waste it by starting small and then building to a ringing climax.

What is your most compelling information? To borrow a phrase from the world of advertising, it is your *unique selling point*. This is an aspect of your service or product so outstanding, so different, so important that it distinguishes your service or product from all others. It is a reason, all by itself, for the customer to buy what you offer.

Here are some examples of unique selling points: The automobile with *the best mileage rating by far*. The telephone answering service that sells at *a far lower price than any other*. A pair of binoculars that is *half the size of any binoculars of equivalent power and field*. A grass-cutting service that employs *quiet mowers*. A pizza that *does not drip while being eaten*.

But what about the service or product you sell? Can you take the time to look hard enough at it to find its unique selling point? Your company may have trained you in selling, but no one knows the customers in your area as well as you do. Look hard at what you sell. You may find a unique selling point that is perfect for your customers.

When you have identified your unique selling point, develop the persuasive speech that explains it. This is a surefire way to success in selling.

Emotion and Reason in Persuasion

Several years ago, British health authorities embarked on a campaign to convince young people not to smoke. They distributed literature to schools describing the effects of cigarettes on smokers' hearts and lungs. They had warnings printed on the cigarette packets.

Smoking continued to increase.

When this reasoned approach failed, they set out to show that smoking could be harmful in other ways. A commercial was made showing a beautiful woman entering a lunchroom. Two handsome men start to talk about her. One says, "She has lovely hair."

His friend replies, "Her hair smells."

The first admires her clothes. His friend replies, "Her clothes smell."

As the camera pulls in for a close-up of her mouth, the first man says, "Look at those luscious lips."

His friend replies, "Her breath smells. She smokes cigarettes. Being near her is like sitting next to an old ashtray."

We're still waiting to find out whether the new approach worked, but this story illustrates that when people will not act for totally rational reasons, you may have to blend appeals to reason with appeals to emotion to accomplish what you want.

Fortunately, most of us do not have to sell things as difficult to sell as the breaking of a lifetime habit. Notwithstanding, the fastest and best way to sell many products is to appeal to personal feelings. That's how smoke detectors, deodorants, diet pills, denture adhesives, and a host of other products are sold.

People harbor fear, insecurity, vanity, pride, and all sorts of other feelings that influence their thinking. As you watch people and listen to them, you will learn to adjust your persuasive speech accordingly.

Good Speech in Retail Selling

Retail selling is much more than standing behind a counter and waiting for people to bring you money. You mustn't assume that because people come into the dress department of a department store or into some specialty shop, such as a camera shop, greeting-card store, or bookstore, that they know exactly what they want. The salesperson must play an active role.

Be an Expert

When you take a job selling in a store, you must soon become the resident expert in the goods you are selling. That's what customers expect of you.

They expect you to know which are the best items and why they are the best. And they will be suspicious of you if all you do is steer them to the most expensive item in the store without some clear explanation of why it is rated above the rest.

What sorts of things should you know about your merchandise? If you are selling appliances, you should learn all their unique features and be able to show the differences.

For products that demand some skill to use properly, you must learn to match the customer's experience to the product's degree of sophistication.

For example, if a person without experience in taking photographs wanted to buy a complex camera from you, you would be honor bound to explain the difficulties that might be encountered. You would do well to suggest an automated camera that would give them good photographs without requiring a lot of fine tuning. On the other hand, you would lose a customer if you tried to sell a simple camera—because you were out of more complex cameras—to an experienced photographer.

Another bit of advice in selling: There's nothing worse than appearing ignorant of your service or product.

A department-store buyer of men's furnishings brought in a shipment of cotton shirts and installed them between silk shirts and woolen shirts that cost only a few dollars more.

Across the aisle were synthetic-fiber shirts that cost only half as much and looked just as good.

Customers would ask the salesmen what made the cotton shirts so good that they cost almost as much as wool and silk. The salesmen could not answer.

When the buyer returned, the salesmen asked him what they should say to the customers. He unpinned a cotton shirt and showed them its workmanship. The fabric was a very tight weave, which made it stronger than ordinary cotton and almost as sturdy as wool. The stitching was very tight, which meant that seams would never come undone. In every detail, the shirt was stronger and finer than other shirts. It would last more than twice as long as the synthetic shirts that cost half the price.

Armed with this information, the salesmen were able to sell the cotton shirts.

The Delicate Matter of Taste

What do you say to a customer who wants to buy something from you that would be in poor taste for that customer?

There is no greater problem in store selling than the matter of taste. You are obliged to accommodate customers' wishes by selling them what they ask for. You must not insult them by saying, "It's all wrong."

But you also have to know that if customers don't like what you've sold them when they get home, they will return it. If someone at home tells them they look ridiculous, they will blame you, not themselves.

One of the best ways to establish confidence in your taste is to make a recommendation right away, before the customer has expressed an opinion.

If a slim man comes into a store and asks to see overcoats, you might say to him, "I think you would look good in a double-breasted coat. May I show you that?" Or, "We just received a gray wool that would look perfect on you."

Always be careful to recommend according to the customer's characteristics.

A customer wants to feel as though he is the only person in the world. A salesperson belongs to the customer the way a doctor belongs to the patient. While you're together, no one else counts.

Don't say, "These are very popular." Say, "This would look good on you." "I think this is exactly right for you." "These colors are good for you." The idea to convey is that you've thought of the customer's needs and best interests.

Good Day, Madam May I Help You?

In stores with lots of salespeople and few customers, salespeople sometimes lurk by the entrance, each one jockeying for position to be first to help when someone enters. This practice emphasizes the store's lack of customers. It also gives a customer the feeling of being the victim of birds of prey. Salespeople swoop down on them as soon as they enter, declaiming: "May I help you?"

If customers are encouraged to look around in a store for a while until they find what they want, they will feel more receptive to an offer of help. But watch them from a distance. If you follow them about, they will get the feeling that they are being spied on.

Your Best Face

Your personality and speech have as much to do with your effectiveness in selling as the merchandise you sell. More, in fact. People will want to buy if they like you, if they feel you are warm and honest. So you must show them these qualities by how you look and how you speak.

Some people can switch their warmth on and off. While this might seem like an advantage, it can be a liability. Have you ever entered a store and seen salespeople chatting with one another? Sometimes you can tell from the looks on their faces that their minds are not on their work. Well, you may think, there's nothing wrong with that, but how do you feel when a salesperson finally turns to you and it is clear that the last thing he wants to do is break up the little party? The message is clear. The customer is a pain in the neck.

Your sales personality should be genuine.

Don't be loud, pushy, or too friendly.

You are in a service job. Customers should feel that they are in charge of themselves and can exercise judgment.

Offer as much help as your customer wants, but help in a courteous manner.

Listen as your customer talks so you can respond intelligently.

Telephone and Face-to-Face Sales Calls

In a sales call, it is the approach that lays the groundwork for a successful presentation. The first thirty seconds may make it possible or impossible to make a sale. Dramatic and attention-grabbing approaches have proven effective in telephone and other sales calls.

Customer curiosity is useful, for example, in selling a product such as insulation. You can call on a homeowner or a business person and say, "My name is Joe Jones and I represent XYZ Home Insulation." An approach that stopped there gives the customer a chance to think, "Who cares?"

But if you went right on to say, "Our studies have shown that every month you pay ten percent more than you should to heat your home. We know your house on Lylewood Drive from having driven by on our way to your neighbor Mrs. Jewett's place, where we just finished a job. We are quite sure we can save you that ten percent. Could we come by and give you a free estimate?"

Chances are you have aroused curiosity: Can they really save me ten percent? I saw that truck in front of the Jewetts' house. I wonder what she would say about XYZ. A free estimate? What can I lose?

"Certainly. I wonder whether you could come by tomorrow at six, when we're both home from work?"

The *appreciative approach*, which salespeople use when they call on a client, is not the same as flattery, which would be insincere and breed suspicion on the part of the customer.

But inevitably you can find something to admire. If possible, make it something that the customer has obviously taken some real effort to accomplish. "The layout of this store is excellent. Everything is so easy to find." "I want you to know that I appreciate your seeing me and giving me the opportunity to show you our fall line." "Your people are always so warm toward me when I come in with my sample cases. I really appreciate it."

The *end-result approach* is dramàtic: "How would you like to have an extra ten thousand dollars to spend over the next ten years?"

Who would refuse to listen a little longer? "Ten thousand dollars is what you'll save if you insulate your home fully."

You have been asked to make telephone solicitations for a fund to provide summer jobs for boys and girls in your community: "I'm calling to guarantee another trouble-free summer for all of us this year, Mr. Hawkins. May I enlist your help?"

You have just finished writing up a substantial order for a sale you concluded at one of the automobile-accessory stores you call on regularly: "Mr. Albert, there's one more item I want to tell you about. This is a surefire add-on with every one of the customers who walk into your store—and it's a long discount article that will pay your rent for every month between now and Christmas."

An approach should be just enough to get the person on the hook. You want to get past their impulse to say that they've bought all they want or they're too busy to talk.

Ask Questions

Questions are very useful in any sales speech. They help you uncover useful information. They help you make the presentation into a two-way discussion. They enable you to establish whether your sales message is getting across in the way it should.

For information, the most direct questions begin with who, where, what, why, and how. But there is a problem with these questions. You may appear to be prying. You may also be embarrassing your customer by asking for something he doesn't know.

To soften the hard edge of such questions, preface your questions with "May I ask . . . ?" "I wonder if you'd mind answering a question or two. . . ."

An indirect question can accomplish the same thing as a direct question while it enables the customer to feel in charge. Instead of saying, "How much are you spending for oil now?'' say, ''If we knew how much your present oil bill is, I'd be able to make a more accurate assessment of your insulation needs.'' ''By giving me a broad indication of your tax bracket—below forty percent, above forty percent—I could easily draw up a list of bonds and stocks that would bring you the best net return.''

Other kinds of questions can help you uncover all sorts of attitudes and information that will help you target your appeal.

What to Do When People Complain

The best way to defuse the anger of a customer is to sit and take it. Ride it out until the anger subsides. If you want to keep it going, look angry and ready to argue.

Many salespeople report that some customers will unleash all the anger they feel toward salespeople in general on the next one that comes along. If this happens to you, when the tirade starts, take it, wait patiently, and when it flags, offer to make amends.

To make a sale under these circumstances is not easy. Like you, all people want to be treated well. They want to be special. They want respect.

Show them respect and you'll be successful.

Talking About Money

Money is a touchy and difficult subject to talk about, even for experienced salespeople. So follow the rule, *dwell on the gains and soften the costs.*

A one-year newspaper subscription may cost seventy-five dollars, but in selling it, you can say, ''Only a dollar fifty per week.'' If an air conditioner sells for $350 and has a useful life of ten years you can truthfully say, ''About twenty cents a day.''

A real-estate salesman we know has developed the technique of showing one house in the price range the customer requested and then a much nicer house nearby. After showing all the wonderful features of the expensive house, the customer asks, "How much more is this house than the other one?"

His answer: "Two cartons of cigarettes and a bottle of good wine a week over the life of a twenty-year mortgage." That may be thousands of dollars, of course, but it doesn't seem so much when put in terms of a few luxuries. And it helps sell houses.

The Close

After you have been talking with a customer for some time, you should be able to tell whether the customer really wants or can afford your product. The time has come to conclude the sale, and this may take a bit of effective speech.

Before you can fully appreciate why an extra bit of prodding is often necessary, you should realize *why people choose not to buy*. They are afraid to make decisions. They are afraid of failure. They are afraid of making mistakes. They are afraid of consequences. They feel they ought to consult a friend, father, or mother. Many leaders in all fields owe their leadership positions to their ability to make decisions. And most people, fearful of making decisions, never become leaders.

So here are some ways of closing a deal:

THE CHOICE: "Do you want it packaged in sixes or twelves?"

"Would you prefer a Thursday or Friday delivery?"

"Do you prefer the monthly or quarterly payment schedule?"

"How soon do you want this delivered?"

THE GENTLE SHOVE: "Why not start right away?"

"You're losing money every minute that goes by."

> "Say the word and I'll have it on
> your desk in the morning."
> "This is the last one of its kind in
> the store."

FISH OR CUT BAIT: When a customer is demanding more
of your time than you feel he is worth, or when you think
that spending another sales session with a customer won't
be worth the money you might earn, you may find it
worthwhile to write up the order, give it to the customer,
and say, "Mr. Smith, you either want this or you don't.
Now why don't you sign this so I can ship it to you right
away?"

Remember that any of these closes entails a certain risk. In
time you will become familiar with the signs that show the
degree of interest of your customers, and you will know when
and how to close effectively.

As you can see from this chapter, selling is an art that
depends heavily on understanding people and speaking
persuasively with them.

Practice Activities

1. With the cooperation of a friend, develop and give a sales
   talk for something you own—for example, a transistorized
   radio or an automobile. Instruct your friend to try to
   counter any sales point you make. Remember to have a
   beginning, middle, and end in your sales talk.
2. Ask a friend to play the part of an angry customer who has
   come to you as you stand behind the counter in a department store ready to serve customers. Have your friend try
   hard to get under your skin. Deal with him in a courteous
   manner.
3. Give a five-minute sales talk for a product of your choice
   before a group of your friends. Have them rate you on a
   scale of one to ten for knowledge, sincerity, empathy, and
   enthusiasm.
4. Join a community project and volunteer for an activity that
   requires door-to-door or telephone solicitation.

CHAPTER 9

The Business Conference —Respect and Leadership Through Good Speech and Small-Group Dynamics

You're at a meeting with your boss and three coworkers to discuss office procedures. You'd like to ask for an increase in the automobile mileage allowance your company pays employees when they use their own cars on business.

Or you're a member of your company's research and development committee and you're watching some of your pet proposals being shot down.

Or you're at a committee meeting of the League of Women Voters and you feel that a recommendation you favor is not being supported properly.

You know you're going to speak up. All you're waiting for is the right opportunity.

Such situations occur almost daily when your career begins to flower. But do you concern yourself about how you'll speak when you present your opinion? You're with people whom you see almost every day, right? It's not like standing on a stage, addressing a crowd of thousands of strangers. Right?

Right. And that's precisely what makes good speaking skills essential in such situations.

Why? Unlike a roomful of strangers, the men and women at these everyday meetings are people you deal with frequently. The impression you make on them and your success in getting your ideas accepted can directly help you advance your career or advance the political and social causes on which you spend so much time. Moreover, because the setting is intimate, everything you do—from the words you say to the way you sit—can have an immediate impact on people who may be only a few feet away.

Some of the general advice we've already talked about applies also in these everyday meetings: maintaining eye contact, avoiding incorrect phrases, being sincere and knowledgeable. In addition, however, there are special skills that apply particularly to small-group discussions. In fact, an entire theory of sociology, known as small-group dynamics, has been developed to analyze and to make the best use of such situations.

Communication Is a Two-Way Street

We have all heard that communication is a two-way street. This is true in groups of any size. But in small groups verbal traffic really does flow both ways—sometimes even colliding head-on. During the course of a meeting, for example, you may be arguing a point, answering questions, listening to someone else, asking questions, commenting on a point someone has made, and bringing up new ideas of your own. And so will everyone else. And not necessarily in an orderly manner.

Such situations cry out for leadership, and sociological studies have found that (1) the best leaders are those who are sensitive to the interests of all group members and (2) groups that work best are those in which every person feels as if he or she is participating actively.

If you want to be seen as a leader, then, it's important to speak as often as necessary and to initiate ideas. The person who speaks most or first in a small group, according to psychologist Edwin P. Hollander in his book *Leadership Dynamics,* will usually become the leader of the group. But remember the two-way street: Speaking as often as necessary does not mean hogging the floor. You must do your share of listening and note taking. Above all, when you speak, be sure to show that you have been paying careful attention to what others have been saying.

There are other general ways you can make a good impression in a small group. Take note of what sociologist Philip E. Slater found in his studies of twenty small groups. Two types of people seemed to rate the highest marks: *idea people* and *best-liked people*. Idea people stimulate discussion—even at the risk of provoking disagreement and causing opposition. Best-liked people speak less, are more sympathetic in their comments, and ask more questions.

Those are the theories. Now, how do they work in practice?

How to Get the Floor at a Meeting

Be aware that opportunities to speak don't always come by themselves. You may have to create your own opportunities. And you must be ready to do so in a way that flows easily into the discussion yet still catches everyone's attention.

If you're lucky, there will be a lull in the conversation after one person finishes and before anyone else can think of something to say. Or the group may be structured so that every member speaks in turn. Or the chairperson may call on people in random order. Your job is to listen to others and be ready to speak.

There may be some kind of unexpected interruption—a phone call, a loud noise, someone spilling coffee. A joke may be told. A wisecrack by someone in the room. Something breaks the thread of conversation, and you can jump right in with your remarks. If you get any chances like these, take advantage of them.

More likely you're going to have to create your own opportunities. It's easiest if you want to comment on a topic already under discussion. You can begin talking as soon as the speaker before you has stopped. From what you say, it will be clear that you have been listening and you will be listened to in turn. If you want to bring up a new subject, you have to use judgment to make sure the group is ready to turn to something new.

But when speakers are merely repeating the same points and agreeing with each other over and over, when there has been a vote or decision, when people are spending most of their time looking through papers or around the room—it's time for you to step in.

One of the oldest tricks in the book, points out sociologist Robert F. Bales, is to begin by expressing agreement with what someone else has said. That gives you the floor—and guarantees you the approval of one or more people. You can go on and talk about whatever you want to bring up.

In a large manufacturing company that the authors are familiar with, two executives have a system of cooperation at staff meetings. While one of them speaks, he will glance at the other to see whether he also wants to talk. If the signal is *yes,* the executive who has the floor will turn to the other and ask, "Didn't you do some work in that area too?" or, "I think you've also shown an interest in this problem." By holding the floor in this way, the pair can often influence the others at a meeting.

You may be surprised at how easy it can be to connect a subject you want to raise with something another speaker has just said, even if the topics seem worlds apart. For instance, consider how you might propose an increase in mileage reimbursement at the meeting we mentioned at the start of this chapter. You might do so as follows if any one of these three widely different subjects had just been discussed:

• Lowering thermostats in winter to save energy.
  You say, "The energy shortage goes beyond saving expensive heating fuel. We all know how the price of gas is going up. . . ."
• A review of the company's sales records for the quarter.
  You say, "Of course, to make a lot of those sales, we had to drive a large number of miles. And the way gas prices are going up. . . ."
• Increasing office efficiency.
  You say, "We do try to do as much work as we can on the phone in order to save time and money. But often you must

talk with a client face-to-face. And you know the way gas prices are going up. . . ."

Get the idea?

It's not enough just to get your audience's attention. You also have to keep it. And since, in most small groups, as we said, a lot of communication is constantly going back and forth, the chances are that no one is going to want to let you hold the floor for too long.

The first point to remember in learning to sustain the interest of a group is *be brief*. A good rule of thumb is *make your point in three or four sentences*.

Does this sound impossible? Consider this: a study of five corporate executives found that fully half of all their activities, including conversations, lasted five minutes or less.

In other words, if you want to be a leader, you have to learn to be efficient not only in your actions but also with your words. Besides, the people you want to impress—your boss, your client, your club president—are leaders themselves. They expect the people they deal with to get to the point quickly.

You don't have to pour out all your ideas, justifications, arguments, and suporting facts as soon as you get the floor. Instead just bring out one basic point—your best one, of course—and a brief explanation of your main reason for making that point. Your idea will get the group's full attention without having to compete with all kinds of lesser information. Don't worry. If your idea has merit, you'll have additional time later on to add ideas and explanations once the group picks up the discussion and people ask questions.

And being brief doesn't mean speaking fast to get it all out in under a minute. Speak clearly. Speak a little more slowly than you do when you chat with a friend. Slowing down and speaking clearly will help emphasize your ideas.

When speaking with three or four people, cut your normal rate by 10 percent. When speaking with five to ten people, cut your normal rate by 20 percent. (And when you're speaking before a really large group—unlike those discussed in this chapter—cut your normal rate by at least 30 percent.)

Be Simple

The second point to remember in learning to sustain the interest of a group is *be simple*. Remember, a small group is not the place for a formal presentation. You're talking with people you know fairly well and see frequently. They share your business or interests. A small group is usually fairly relaxed, and you are expected to be at ease.

But you don't want to speak exactly as you do in casual conversation. For one thing you should avoid slang and speak correctly. In addition you'll probably want to organize your ideas in advance of the meeting, and that is something you don't generally do in everyday speaking. As part of your preparation, you'll find it useful to prepare an apt example or comparison. A good phrase can have a dramatic effect in catching your listeners' interest, and most of us are not gifted enough to think of one on the spot. The best ad-libs are usually rehearsed well before they are spoken.

If you're talking about that mileage reimbursement proposal, for instance, you might try one like this:

> I figured out that the amount of money we're reimbursed for driving one mile would just pay the cost of driving from the parking lot to the corner and back—if I didn't have to warm up the engine first.

You'll undoubtedly do better than that, but notice that the statement is simple. No one has any trouble at all figuring out the point.

Another reason to keep your language simple is that your participation doesn't end after the three or four sentences in which you state your idea. You're going to be answering questions, dealing with criticism, considering other ideas, and generally discussing the merits of your idea with the group.

Don't make the mistake of trying to prepare a speech in a formal style, which may not be comfortable for you. It is not easy to keep up that style in spontaneous discussion and a simple statement is best for bringing good ideas to the attention of a group.

Be Ready to Shift Gears

The final point to remember in learning to sustain the interest of a group is *be ready to shift gears*. This is another way of saying you have to be alert and flexible.

A few years ago the authors taught a class in discussion techniques at a large accounting firm in the Midwest. Jeff, one of the CPAs in the class, faced a tough situation when his company set up special meetings to encourage employees to discuss any aspect of company policy that was on their minds. Since he and his wife were expecting their first child, and he wanted to spend time with his new family, Jeff decided to ask about policy on maternity leave for fathers.

He was just in the middle of his second sentence when the section manager curtly interrupted: "That idea came up a few months ago, and the vice-president turned it down."

For a moment Jeff's mouth hung open. No one else said anything. As Jeff recalled, "The tension was the kind you can cut with a knife."

Jeff knew he had to react quickly—both to ease the tension and to regain the initiative. He had a lot more to say about maternity leave, but it seemed pointless to pursue the topic. Yet he wanted to keep the discussion going on the general subject of spending time with his family.

Finally, after a brief pause, he said, "Are there other company policies that might apply to new fathers? Maybe there's some way to work part-time for a few months, or work overtime now in exchange for time off later." He glanced around the room. "Does anyone know of any other employees who've been in this situation? You know, it isn't very often that I can expect to become a father for the first time."

Jeff's youthful, earnest compliance changed the atmosphere. Everyone was totally relaxed again. Someone in the group remembered a case in which a male employee had taken a brief leave of absence for the birth of his child. The section manager promised to look into the questions of part-time work and overtime. The discussion went on. A couple of people complimented Jeff for bringing up the issue—adding that they wished they had had the chance to take some time off when their children were born!

By being ready to shift gears, Jeff had managed to salvage what could have been a disaster. Once he knew his original idea was not going to make it he was willing to abandon it. Instead he thought fast on his feet and came up with a new idea. You will often have to do the same thing.

Think of it this way: If you were in the middle of a conversation with someone, and a third person suddenly interrupted to say you had a phone call, would you just keep on talking as though there had been no interruption? Of course not. What you might do is ask the third person to tell the caller you'd be there in a minute. Then you would finish your original conversation as quickly as possible. Or you would excuse yourself temporarily from your conversation to take the phone call. You will find that speaking in a group is a lot like that conversation: full of interruptions.

In his meeting Jeff faced the added problem of trying to defuse a tense situation. That can be especially hard. Sociologists tell us that the mood of a group usually feeds on itself. Antagonism provokes more antagonism. Agreement encourages more agreement. Jokes inspire more jokes.

The method Jeff used to lighten the mood—asking a question that was seen as personal and important—is a good way to break a negative mood that feeds on itself. The disadvantage of the question technique is that it usually means handing the initiative to someone else. But if things go right, a question can be a good way to ease tension and force people to look at things your way. Other people have a chance to speak their minds and, in a small group, that is probably what they want.

You can also try to lighten things with a joke. Jeff did this well. However, jokes can be tricky, and you run the risk that your humor will fall flat.

Silent Clues from the Group

Susan Turner was in line for a promotion at the magazine where she worked as a junior editor. In a way, as Susan knew, the first editorial conference she was invited to attend was to serve as a kind of test: How well she presented and defended her ideas for future articles could determine whether she got the promotion. All the top and middle-level editors of the magazine would be there.

We won't keep you in suspense. Her promotion was announced three days later.

As soon as Susan walked out of that editorial meeting, she knew she'd made a good impression.

How did she know?

"I could tell that the editor in chief was listening," she explained later. "In fact his eyes really began to glow when I came to one particular idea for an article. He even took a few notes on what I was saying, and my boss had told me that the chief almost never took notes. Then I sneaked a glance over at my boss, who really had been sponsoring my promotion— and he was grinning."

As Susan's story shows, what people say does not always tell the whole story. The nonverbal reactions of the people listening to you also are a key part of communicating in a small group. Without saying a word, people can let you know if they are interested or bored, in agreement or opposed, skeptical or respectful. To make sure your points are getting across and you are making a good impression, you have to be sensitive to all kinds of reactions—and respond to them yourself.

There are obvious signs. If the other people in a group are shifting in their seats, glancing at their watches, looking around the room, shuffling through papers, or rattling coffee cups, it's a good bet they're getting bored. Maybe you're speaking in a monotone. Maybe you've been going on for too long. Maybe you're way off base in your line of reasoning. It could be time to stop talking or move on to another topic.

On the other hand, if only one person seems itchy, it may

be that he wants to speak but that others are still interested in what you have to say. In that case keep an eye out to make sure that one person's fidgeting doesn't begin to spread.

Stronger movements could indicate that your listeners are more than bored. They may be becoming antagonistic. Some signs of this may be tapping of fingers or feet, audible exhaling of breath, frowns, and quick glances exchanged between people. As the level of tension rises, the annoyance is probably directed more at what you're saying than at the way you're saying it. It's time to use the techniques we discussed for easing tension.

And what if everyone's eyes seem to be riveted on you, and the room is quiet—except perhaps for the scratch of a pen scribbling rapid notes—and nobody is sipping coffee? You have them hooked. Get ready to pull in your fish.

Special Tips for Rough Times

Sometimes—especially when what you've said is particularly controversial or when there's a lot of rivalry to begin with among the members of your group—the going can get rough. Questions start flying thick and fast. Voices rise. Disagreements become hostile. When this happens you may find yourself forced into a corner and saying things you don't want to say.

Such times call for special handling. The techniques we've already shown you for defusing tension may not be enough. It may be too late to calm down the whole group. Instead you have to concentrate on maintaining your own good image. There's no point in worrying about everyone else.

Good advice for use in such situations comes from the field of assertiveness training. Assertiveness training was developed a few years ago as a way of helping people who have trouble putting themselves forward. Typically, these are people who tend to be manipulated by others. Much of the training has been targeted for women who face the double pressure of breaking down stereotypes and moving ahead in their careers. But it has also been used to help men as well.

A few key techniques are especially useful when the going gets rough.

NO CONTEST. Someone has come up with a criticism of one of your ideas that you can't really argue with. The criticism is right on the money. Why argue? Accept what the person says. Accept quickly and calmly. Don't bother with a huge apology. The best thing you can do is to agree with the other person's criticism, accepting it as a general fact without admitting that it applies directly to you. "I agree with you. Increasing the reimbursement for mileage will cost our company more money. That's exactly right." Then change the direction of the critical argument: "But right now everyone who uses a private auto on company business is subsidizing the company."

I UNDERSTAND. This technique is especially useful for responding to an argument based on feeling or opinion rather than fact. You can't counter feelings with facts because feelings are not facts. Understand that you will not want to agree with the feeling being expressed. But trying to argue would be useless. Your best response is to accept the other person's feelings as a personal expression: "I understand how you can feel that way." Then go on to your next factual point: "Gasoline alone costs me eight cents a mile. And that's just the beginning of my car expense."

CALM REPETITION. Try this when someone insists on asking you the same question over and over. Try this when someone tries to badger you into saying something you don't want to say. Keep your voice level. Just continue to repeat your point. If you change the wording slightly each time, you will avoid hostility. "Any extra cost would be tax deductible." "The company could deduct any extra cost from its taxes." "The company is in a high tax bracket and would benefit from the deduction." This will help you stick to your guns. You won't have to point out that the other person has already asked you that question several times. Your repetition will make it obvious.

Finding the Right Place to Sit

You read earlier of the importance of sitting correctly in a chair. You should be relaxed. You should not slouch. You should keep your gestures restrained. In meetings of small groups, *where* you sit can be as important as *how* you sit.

Jeanne Page didn't realize how much difference seating arrangements could make until she went to a meeting of her PTA's steering committee a few years ago. She and her husband were co-chairpersons of the entire PTA. Eight folding chairs were grouped in a circle in the sixth-grade classroom. Without paying much attention, Jeanne took the first empty place she came to. Her husband took his seat to her right. It happened that Jeanne was seated next to the PTA member who was making the main report of the evening. What difference did this make? For the next two hours, Jeanne felt invisible.

The speaker did a pretty good job of making eye contact. He looked at everyone he could see—but never looked right at Jeanne. In fact, he couldn't see her. When it came time for asking questions Jeanne's hand ached from being up in the air. The speaker never called on her.

Finally the committee leader, who was seated across the circle from Jeanne, took over the rest of the meeting to go on to other business. After that Jeanne was called on frequently.

From that meeting, Jeanne learned an important basic rule of group behavior: we tend to talk more with people we can see as well as hear. Translate this fact into seating arrangements in any small group of which you become a part: You will be most likely to speak after the person across from you or farthest from you has spoken. You will be least likely to speak after the person next to you speaks. So, to make an impact on a small group, you are probably best off distancing yourself from the person who is most likely to do a good deal of speaking.

There is one important exception to this rule. It is often a good idea to sit next to the leader of a meeting—even though he or she may do the most talking. According to Philip L. Hunsaker, a professor of management and organizational development at the University of San Diego who has been observing gatherings of executives: "It's like the old cliché. Judge a person by the friends he keeps. It is better to sit next to influential people so that others will type you as being one of them."

In short, where you sit depends on what your goal is. If you want to make an impression by speaking out, sit across from the group leader. If you do not intend to do much speaking and if you're interested in having the group think you have important connections, sit next to the leader.

What if no one has been selected as group leader? You may well want to become the leader yourself. In this case the best place is at the head of the table, with the others sitting along the sides near you. Positioning works wonders. For example, sociological studies of jury members have shown that those jurors who were the first to sit at the end of the jury bench nearest the judge were most likely to be selected as foremen. So you might get to a meeting early and seat yourself at the head of the table.

There's one catch to this advice. You risk losing your chance for leadership if everyone else sits at the far end of the table instead of sitting near you.

There are two solutions. Try to be in place before the others arrive and engage them in conversation before they sit down. People are inclined to sit near a person they are talking with. Another solution is to time your move carefully. Wait long enough for a few people to settle at one section of the table—but not so long that someone else takes the end seat.

Practice Activities

Before you try any of these techniques at an especially important meeting, it's a good idea to get some practice in situations that carry less risk. You might begin in a discussion at home or at a club meeting.

1. AN ILLUSTRATIVE HOME SESSION. For instance, in a family that includes teenage children, the telephone often creates domestic troubles. Messages are missed. One or more members of the family monopolize the telephone. What should be a convenience turns out to be a source of annoyance.

You decide that a system should be adopted that would make it easy to see that telephone messages are not missed. How to proceed? A good way is to launch a family discussion with a real incident that can attract interest and attention.

"Jane, I am sorry you missed seeing your friend Pamela off at the airport last week because you never got her message."

The door is now open. Jane has not been challenged or threatened. She remembers her disappointment and is listening hard.

"What would you think of putting up a bulletin board by the phone? Anybody who takes a call for someone else can put the message on the board. We'd have a pad and pencil right there so no one would have to worry about remembering a complicated message."

2. PRACTICE WITH FRIENDS. When you plan such a session, it's good to anticipate questions or arguments that may be raised and to think of some answers to them as well. To help develop your skill in speaking before small groups, you will find it helpful to ask friends to act out situations with you—and have them think up their own criticisms and questions on the spot. Choose situations as close as possible to real-life conferences you have at work—you will be amazed to find how much playacting helps you learn how people think and act. Here's a situation you can try now.

3. YOUR MILEAGE QUESTION AT THE OFFICE CONFERENCE. You're ready to face that meeting with your boss to try to raise the company's mileage reimbursement.

The atmosphere is cordial. The group has just finished discussing another issue, and there's a brief lull in the conversation. What are you going to say?

Write out a brief script and read it aloud. When you think you've got it polished, compare your work with one we've prepared.

A Sample Brief Script on Mileage Reimbursement

I'd like to raise the question of reimbursement for mileage when we take our cars on company business. [Brief pause]

We all know how high the price of gas is, and it seems to be getting higher every month. The company set fifteen cents a mile two years ago and still pays fifteen today. At that rate, taking into account costs of insurance, depreciation, and wear and tear on the car, I figure that those of us who drive on company business pay our own money for twenty out of every hundred miles we drive making sales calls to customers. It seems to me it's time to increase our reimbursement rate. Don't you agree?

This script takes less than a minute to deliver. It covers all the points that need covering. Above all it is brief and simple and, because it ends with a question that invites agreement, the speaker has limited the need to switch gears. It is hard to imagine rejection at this point.

How does your script compare?

CHAPTER 10
Writing Good Prepared Talks

Most of what we've explained so far about speaking well applies to talks you make up right on the spot, or in your head as you go along. Spontaneous talks of this kind actually do account for most of the decisive occasions on which you speak.

Extremely important to you at times, however, can be talks to prepare and write in advance. You almost certainly do or will face opportunities for giving prepared talks in connection with your work, your community, your church or social organizations, or your education. And being able to write prepared talks well represents an important means of winning the respect of other people. Such ability can also be very helpful for getting ahead in a career—especially in upper reaches of a career, and in prestigious careers.

How Writing a Talk Should Differ from Writing a Report, Article, or Student Essay

First, the methods for writing a talk must always preserve the natural cadence of speech, and particularly your own speech. Secondly, the methods must enforce certain essentials for a speech which are not as important in material that is intended to be read. The methods we outline in this chapter

138

for writing a talk are ones that we think work best. You may find that they differ from the methods you've learned or developed for writing reports, or articles, or assigned essays in courses. However, this is because our focus is on writing material that will be *heard* rather than *read*.

EASY-TO-USE METHODS ARE GIVEN BELOW: You will find our methods particularly valuable if, up to this point in your life, writing has been hard for you. Our methods are largely painless ones, differing from the usual techniques recommended in English composition classes. Our methods build on what comes naturally to you.

I. Fix the Basic Points for Good Talks Clearly in Mind

Writing a prepared talk begins with a clear focus on the basic elements of good speech, as we described earlier in Chapter 5. Let's look briefly once more at these fundamental elements. Our methods for writing a talk use them directly.

1. CENTRAL IDEA. Have in mind one major thing you want to convey, and choose the words you will say to make it as clear as possible.

2. AUDIENCE APPEAL. Think carefully about the members of the audience to whom you're talking, in order to have your talk fit them. Most importantly, you should tailor your appeal to the intended audience to win acceptance of your central idea. A second factor is to make the talk clear and understandable to everyone in the audience.

3. BEGINNING, MIDDLE, END. Shape the three main parts of your talk for maximum impact, whether you are to talk no more than two minutes or as long as two hours. In a good beginning, you capture favorable attention and introduce your central idea and its major appeal. A good middle

presents your idea and its appeals as fully and convincingly as time permits. A good end sums up your idea and appeal with the most powerful close you can put together.

II. Begin by Jotting Down Three Kinds of Notes

You now move on to write your talk, using the three basic elements. Begin by jotting down three kinds of notes, so brief that correctness of spelling or grammar doesn't matter or delay you at this point. The three rules for this are:

- Jot down your central idea in about ten words.
- Jot down in a few words the one big appeal to use for your audience.
- Jot down the main connection you'll make between your central idea and the main appeal.

Here's how to carry out each of the rules, with illustrative examples.

Your Central Idea in About Ten Words

Any talk of yours, long or short, should have one central idea—*a main point,* the most important single conclusion you want your listeners to remember and act on.

Your first step in writing your talk is to jot down this central idea in very brief form. Ten words should be enough for almost any idea, but use as few words as possible. The fewer the words, the greater your impact.

Let's suppose you're active in civic affairs in your town. You've helped get a bipartisan proposition on the ballot in this fall's election. Proposition 3, if passed, will provide for commercial zoning of certain areas. You've backed it from the start as a means of easing property taxes on family-owned homes. It's the main topic on which you want to focus in the ten-minute talk you've been asked to give on the town's future at the Rotary Club lunch.

After reflecting a bit, you jot down the central idea: "Vote yes on Proposition 3."

Take another example. You've worked for several years at a large factory. You like the company and your job a great deal, and you've been asked to give a ten-minute talk to a group of new employees going through orientation. You've been active in the employee credit union at the plant, and you think it is a good example of the many benefits of working for your company. The personnel department says, sure, it's all right for you to talk mainly about the credit union.

Accordingly, you think and then jot down your central idea: "Our credit union can do a lot for you."

Take another situation. You're in student government and plan to speak at some length at the next joint meeting of the student council and faculty committee on student affairs. You've felt more and more that a real effort should be made to help students get part-time jobs, and learn skills to fit them for such jobs. In this situation, you jot down your central idea: "Let's start a jobs bureau to help our students."

A Few Words on the Big Appeal for This Audience

As the next step in writing your talk, think carefully about your audience and jot down the one big appeal you'll use to get your central idea accepted. Be sure your appeal fits that specific audience.

Let's turn again to our examples to illustrate such tailor-made appeals. For your talk before the Rotary Club, you jotted: "Vote yes on Proposition 3." Many Rotarians are homeowners and resentful of high taxes. It seems to be less compelling that they also favor business and commercial development, which Proposition 3 also fosters. As a result, you jot down after the central idea, "Main Appeal—lower taxes on your home."

Or, in connection with your talk to new employees about the credit union, you turn to the concise central idea: "Our credit union can do a lot for you." The new employees to whom you'll be talking tend to be younger people and not especially thrifty. But you suspect they often are interested in arranging credit for cars, for major appliances, or for homes.

And the credit union can often do better on down payments and interest than banks can do. So you jot down, "Main Appeal—we help you get more of what you want, in cars, in color TVs, in homes."

As a member of the student government, you realize that you'll be talking to a group of students and faculty members in an effort to start a jobs bureau. You'll need to emphasize not only abundant opportunities for part-time student jobs but the benefits of having those opportunities. The benefits should be summed up in terms that appeal to students and to faculty. A bit of thought leads you to jot down, "Main Appeal— financial aid for students and improved work habits."

The Prime Connection Between Your Central Idea and the Main Appeal

The writing of your talk moves briskly along for you as you turn to a third step. In it, you write down the major link you will forge between your central idea and the main appeal. Your notes sum up the prime logic and evidence you plan to use.

For example, suppose you want to connect "Vote yes on Proposition 3" with "lower taxes on your home." As part of your work for the plan, you have learned of other towns where this kind of step actually has cut homeowners' taxes. You decide to use the data for a community much like your own, so you write: "How a Proposition 3 worked in Medford— actual cases of homeowners who benefitted."

Or, in your urging to have new employees join the credit union, you make plans to use actual examples—some cases of individual buying by loans from the credit union, and other illustrations of the kinds of purchases made possible through the credit union. All illustrations, in contrast with bank financing, involve less money down and lower interest. You write down: "Real people and real buys prove how you can be helped by using your credit union."

Or again, in our third example, your proposal to start an active jobs bureau for students is based on what you have learned through reading information supplied by organizations such as the College Placement Council. Several other new bureaus like the one you are proposing have proven very successful. According to reports you've read, students served by the new bureaus have expressed enthusiasm and satisfaction with them. Accordingly, you write down as the prime connection between your central idea and the main appeal: "Jobs bureau ventures generate high satisfaction with the students they serve, both for the income received and the work experience."

You are ready to use your initial knowledge or research at this stage. As our examples suggest, at this stage of writing, you can draw on your special knowledge of the topic or on any initial research you have done. Often, you will have chosen a subject for your talk that you already know something about. And beyond what you already know, you may have done some exploratory research to settle basic points in your approach. You probably need no further research at this stage. How to do more detailed research will be explained shortly.

III. Write a Complete First Draft in Three Main Blocks, and in Note Form

Move ahead to produce a first draft of your talk. Write as quickly as you can, remembering to use words you'd speak naturally. Talk to yourself while you do it. Talking will help give your words a natural flow and ring. Don't worry over being fully correct or complete. Phrase the talk in brief notes to be fixed and fleshed out later. Guess and surmise as you wish for the moment. In the next stage, you'll turn to making the talk completely correct, authoritative, and polished in every respect. In this phase of work, the idea is to capture your spontaneous ideas and words so your talk will be lively.

Two factors can best guide your writing of the first draft. One is the talk's overall length. The other is the talk's overall form. Here's how to use both factors to help in writing your first draft.

Estimating Time-Limit and Length for Your Talk

It is worthwhile to make a rough estimate of how much to write to fit the time-limit planned for your talk. All too often, speakers write far more material than time permits. Then they either talk too long or waste preparation time in cutting their work.

You may be amazed to realize how long it takes to do a good job of delivering a page of written material in a talk. For instance, one fairly standard length for written text is that of the letter-size page (8½ by 11 inches), carrying a full page of reading matter that is typewritten and double-spaced (normal margins). The time needed to deliver a page of material in a talk, with careful enunciation, needed pauses for emphasis and frequent eye contact with your listeners, can easily run two to three minutes.

Apply figures like these to estimate in advance how many pages of draft material you should plan to produce your talk. Suppose you have been asked to talk for ten minutes—or that you decide on your own to get your message across in a lively, direct ten-minute talk. That means you'll need only about three to five pages of material!

But don't take our word for it. Use anything you have written in the past to see how long it takes to read aloud. Time your own delivery, pretending that you are giving a talk before a group of people. Be careful to keep your delivery at an easy pace, to look up frequently, and to emphasize as needed. You might even practice such timed delivery to a friend. The results will give you information that enables you to estimate the number of pages you will have to write for a talk of any length.

Once you have the fundamental factor of correct length in mind, you can turn to writing your talk. Remember, you want an effective overall form, with three main parts that really work: beginning, middle and end.

Beginning Block: Courtesy, Idea, Appeal

Three elements make up a good beginning block for your talk—an expression of courtesy to your listeners, introduction of the central idea of your talk, and first mention of the main appeal of that idea to your audience.

Open the written draft of your talk, then, with a gracefully polite statement of thanks to fit the occasion. For your talk on rezoning before the Rotary Club, for instance, you might say you're especially honored to be asked to speak to a group that has already accomplished a number of good works for the community—and cite two or three telling examples. Or, in starting to talk on the student jobs bureau, you could briefly express thanks for having the floor in order to outline an exciting new project. Anything natural and direct is fine at this point.

Introduce the central idea of your talk as the next step. For this, you can draw on the phrase you jotted earlier to state the idea briefly. Use your judgment on whether to lead into your central idea with a few sentences paving the way, or to give it almost immediately and then follow the idea with a couple of short paragraphs of necessary explanation.

In the beginning, give just enough on your central idea so that your listeners clearly understand what your idea is, without confusion or doubt as to what you mean.

Then, with similar clarity and brevity, give the main appeal favoring acceptance of the idea by your listeners. Say only enough about the appeal to make sure they understand.

Middle Block: Central Idea and Its Appeals Driven Home

Having begun your talk well in this way, turn next in the middle block of your talk to make the strongest case you can for your central idea in the time open to you. Continue writing easily spoken words as you write on into the middle block, making the case for your idea.

In our example of your talk on the employees' credit union, for instance, your beginning will have conveyed how "our credit union will do a lot for you" because "real people and real buys prove how it can really help you."

"Let me give you some of the proof," you might say in swinging into the middle block of your talk. "First, here is how using the credit union has saved money for fellow employees who are friends of mine." You tell how one employee borrowed his $4,000 down payment for a sports car from the credit union for $600 less in interest cost than he could have gotten through his bank. You explain how a married couple who work at the plant got a twenty-five-inch, instead of an eighteen-inch, color TV set because of the amount they saved on a credit-union loan compared with buying on installments.

You continue with further examples of friends and add a few illustrations of large purchases your listeners may want to make at some point—perhaps a vacation trip, a fine stereo, or a boat. After your examples, you sum up: "As you see, in each case the credit union can really save money." You add a touch of team spirit for heightened appeal, noting: "We employees help each other through our credit union. That's why we're in it together."

It is in ways like these that the middle block of your talk—on whatever topic, whether long or short—convincingly drives home the point of your central idea and its appeal.

End Block: Strongest Summary of Your Idea and Its Appeal

Just as your beginning block flows naturally into the middle of your talk, the middle moves smoothly into the end block. Your end sums up what you've been saying in the middle block, dramatically and as strongly as possible. It climaxes your presentation.

In almost all cases, you won't want to introduce any new facts or appeals in your ending. All the various facts and advantages you may want to present are most effectively gotten across in the middle block of your talk. The ending packs the most punch when it repeats, when it emphasizes, when it condenses and restates and hammers once more on your key messages.

Using the same kind of sentence repeatedly (in what is called *parallel construction*) might give the ending of a talk of yours special force. For example, your ending in the credit-union talk might run something like this: "For all these reasons, do consider joining our credit union—which is really *your* credit union now, too. Remember how one man saved six hundred dollars on his car down payment. Remember the couple who saved on their color TV. Remember that vacation trip. Remember that great outboard runabout. Remember all these, and I'm sure you'll join us."

One last detail for your ending will come to you almost automatically. Be sure to include it anyway. It's a word of thanks to your listeners. Something simple usually suffices: (PAUSE; LOOK AROUND THE ROOM AT YOUR LISTENERS) "Thank you very much for your kind attention."

Add to, Revise, Polish Your Talk

The heart of your talk is down on paper—without any agony on your part. It already has all the essentials in it. At this point you can be sure it's already better than four out of every five talks actually given in America this week. And it's roughly the right length.

Moreover, you're now in a position to fix it, complete it, change it, check it, and otherwise improve it in any way you want. Now that it is down on paper, you'll find it much easier to work on than if it were merely swimming around in your head. You can also do as little with it as you want, perhaps just a little polishing and rounding out here and there.

Whether you want to do a little or a lot, here are suggestions to help you put your talk in finished form.

Figuring Final Time and Length for Your Talk

Once you have completed your first draft, you will find it useful to deliver your talk several times as written. This is an excellent check on the actual time you need for giving it. Your original estimate of length was based on approximations, and may be off by some substantial margin.

Giving your talk aloud in first draft provides you with the

actual time for this specific talk and audience. It also supplies you with an average delivery time per page. You can use this information when determining the exact length of your talk as you put it in finished form. By adding or cutting material, you should be able to adjust the length of the talk to any precise limit wanted.

In addition, giving your talk aloud several times can help you notice spots where you may want to improve or add to it in your revising.

Research for Your Talk Made Easy

Some additions you may want to make in your talk could involve supplying further facts, examples, statements by authorities, and other material collected in research. Either at this point or earlier, research should be relatively easy for you if you carry it out along the lines of the following suggestions.

FOR YOUR RESEARCH, CONSULT NOT ONLY ARTICLES AND BOOKS BUT ORGANIZATIONS AND EXPERTS. Most research for talks is done best in a good library, with the help of good librarians. Library research should prove effective for you even if you know very little about using a library card-catalog or reference works like the *Readers' Guide to Periodical Literature*. Librarians will show you where to look for what you need. And librarians can also be very helpful even if you happen to know a great deal about using libraries.

You need not limit yourself to library sources. You can also do research by requesting information from organizations active in the field about which you're talking. As an example, you may recall that an association called the College Placement Council was mentioned earlier as the source of information on job bureaus for students. The addresses of most associations or companies likely to be useful as information sources may be obtained in libraries, and letters to them often bring helpful replies.

Similarly, individual men and women who are experts in their fields are often glad to furnish comments or opinions when such information is tactfully requested by letter or by phone. Government officials and their aides often will provide pertinent information on issues of public import. As public servants they tend to reply promptly to inquiries.

MAKE NOTES ON YOUR RESEARCH, WITH ONE ITEM PER SHEET OR CARD. When you've obtained likely material through research, record it in a form usable in your talk. Take one item or small batch of material you might cite at one place in your talk—a group of key statistics, an incisive quotation, decisive facts, a telling anecdote. Write each item or small batch on a single sheet or file card, and note the source in all essential detail. You may find it useful to put a catchword categorizing the item in the top left or right corner.

Keeping notes in this manner will be some trouble, but it makes the results of your research accessible for easy use. Having the items on separate sheets or cards enables you to select one or another for your talk as you may need them. It also enables you to sort your items into the groups and sequences that best fit your talk.

MAKE NOTES EARLY, AS IDEAS COME TO YOU. In the days before actually sitting down to write your talk, you may want to make notes for it as ideas come to you, or as you come upon information or anecdotes for it in reading or conversation. For convenience, you could consider keeping these in the same way suggested for your research notes—one item to a sheet or file card, with a top-corner catchword. Whatever early notes you make may be woven into your talk while you're writing your first draft. You may also, if you wish, combine them with later research notes that you prepare.

Four Important Tips for Writing or Rewriting Your Talk

In particular, four modest tips can go a long way toward helping make a talk of yours appealing, lively, and easy to draft. You can apply these either after you've done the first draft and are revising it, or while writing it for the first time.

1. USE SHORT WORDS. People find it easier to understand most short words rather than long ones, especially when the words are spoken. Short words often make statements

more forceful than long ones. Even Shakespeare used short words for greatest effect. He didn't say, "Indubitably, the difficulty is located at precisely this juncture." He said, "Aye, there's the rub."

So, for the most part, use short words of the kind natural to you in everyday conversation. Change long words in a draft to short ones if the short words serve as well. In fact they probably will serve even better.

2. USE SHORT SENTENCES.
Short sentences also make things you say easier to understand. Try, then, to make your sentences short and direct.

You need not worry too much about keeping your sentences short while you're writing the draft. As editors know, it's often a simple matter to break up long sentences into short ones after a passage with longer sentences has already been written.

For example, that last sentence is a long one—twenty-six words. Here's how easily editing can break it up. When divided, it's stronger too. Reworked, it goes:

"Here's one thing editors know. For them, it's very simple. You can easily break up long sentences into short ones. And you can do it after a passage is written."

3. USE PERSONAL WORDS: YOU, THEY, I, WE, AND PEOPLE'S NAMES.
Personal pronouns and the names of people tend to make a talk more informal, direct, and lively. By the same token, depersonalized talk tends to be dull. When you write, then, change impersonal phrases to personal ones. Don't let a sentence stand as, "It is thought that lying is always bad." Say instead, "I think that lying is always bad." Or again, don't say something like "How would a typical person react?" Say instead, "How would you react?"

4. SAVE HUMOR AND JOKES FOR THE REVISION STAGE.
You may find it easier to add a light touch and an appropriate joke or two to your talk after you've done the first draft. If an idea for whimsy or a chuckle comes to you as you're doing the draft, put it in. But generally, while drafting, concentrate on getting your basic message across without

being distracted by putting in humorous touches too. Relax. You can add these later.

Source books for speakers provide rich collections on which to draw for humor. Suggestions for using these books are given in a later chapter, and a number of the books are listed at the end of that chapter. Two that might be particularly handy are the *New Speakers' Handbook* by Sylvia H. Simmons and *The Public Speaker's Treasure Chest* by Herbert V. Prochnow and Herbert V. Prochnow, Jr. For either light or serious additions, you might also draw on one of the large collections of quotations, like the well-known *Bartlett's*.

Practice Activities

1. Starting Notes for a Talk in Your Company

Assume you work as a middle-management executive in a manufacturing corporation. You're associate director of the purchasing department, numbering seventy employees. Over recent months you have helped lead development of a new flextime system of working hours for the department, with other managers and departments. A special half-hour meeting of the whole department has been set for three weeks away. You are to give the talk announcing the flextime program, and generating employee support and enthusiasm for it. Weekday working hours now are 8:30 A.M. to 5:00 P.M. Under the flextime plan, working hours will still total eight hours per weekday, but any employee in the department will be permitted to put in those eight hours on any one day as follows: starting at any time from 7:00 A.M. to 10:30 A.M., and leaving at any time from 3:30 P.M. to 7:00 P.M.

For your talk at the department meeting, start the draft by jotting down the three beginning elements as follows:

- Central idea
- Prime appeal for your audience
- Main connection between central idea and prime appeal

2. Starting Notes for a Talk in Your Community

Assume you serve as chairperson of a community committee on the local high school. The committee has worked out a proposal for a solar energy program in the high school, with the help of teachers, students, and administrators. Under the program, students in shop courses would build small solar-collector units to make hot water for the school. Students in courses in general science, physics, and home economics would analyze these units in lab exercises on solar energy, and would learn related fundamentals of solar energy in small portions of their coursework. Savings in the cost of making hot water would return the costs of running the solar-energy program after several years.

You have been asked to give a ten-minute talk on the proposal before an open meeting of the school board. Start your draft of the talk by jotting down the three beginning elements, as follows:

- Central idea
- Prime appeal for your audience
- Main connection between central idea and prime appeal

3. Rewriting Your Draft for Greater Impact

Assume you are a state governor presenting the next fiscal year's budget. You have drafted opening paragraphs of the talk as given below. Rewrite and edit that draft for greater impact, applying rules given in the chapter (short words, short sentences, and personal words). The draft opening paragraphs to improve are as follows:

This budget is in essence a product of an effort to reexamine our priorities and to make choices consistent with our resources. The total budget I present to you shows an expenditure increase of 6.8 percent—40 percent below the projected rate of national inflation for the year ahead. In total, it is an austere document. But it is a document that discerns between those public services which fundamentally require additional resources and those that do not. It spends less on general government and more on direct human services. It does not provide for increased state employment, but it redeploys manpower to meet critical human needs. It recommends resources for capital expansion, but it spends not a dollar more to house bureaucracies.

This budget continues the discipline we have imposed upon ourselves over the past six years, a discipline we have learned is necessary if we are to make intelligent decisions about public priorities while annually reducing the real cost of government.

Illustrative Solutions to Practice Activities

Among many possible ways in which the three foregoing activities could be carried out, here are three that illustrate satisfactory solutions for each activity.

1. STARTING NOTES FOR A TALK IN YOUR COMPANY

Beginning notes for your talk announcing the flextime plan could be as follows:

- Central idea: Flextime lets you adjust your own workday.
- Prime appeal: Flextime gives you more freedom.
- Connection: First-person stories telling of changeovers to well-liked flextime plans in other companies.

2. STARTING NOTES FOR A TALK IN YOUR COMMUNITY

Beginning notes for your talk on the proposed solar-energy program for the local high school could be as follows:

- Central idea: Program builds for the future, at no cost.
- Prime appeal: Program involves sound and relevant learning while also helping future homeowners save money and the country save energy.
- Connection: Enthusiastic endorsements by students, teachers, and administrators at the school, coupled with low program cost projections.

3. REWRITING YOUR DRAFT FOR GREATER IMPACT

One way in which you might have edited and rewritten the draft of your opening paragraphs is as follows:

Your state budget strikes a balance in the best way possible. On one side are the priorities we all have for meeting the needs of our state—priorities we have carefully examined and reexamined. On the other side are our resources.

I can present to you as a result a total budget that shows an increase in spending of only 6.8 percent. That increase is much less than the projected rate of inflation nationwide for the year ahead. It is, in fact, 40 percent less.

Your budget, then, is an austere document. One with no fat and no frills. It reduces spending for general government, at the same time increasing spending for valuable human services. Your budget does not provide for more state employment. Instead it redeploys manpower to meet critical human needs. Your budget recommends resources for capital expansion. But it spends not a dollar more to house bureaucrats.

Once again, your budget shows an annual reduction in your real cost of government. In doing so, it continues the discipline that this administration has maintained for the last six years. That discipline, we will all agree, is needed if we are to make wise decisions about public priorities while still cutting the real cost of government.

Incidentally, the opening paragraphs as originally given (without illustrative rewriting) were part of the 1981 budget message of Hugh L. Carey, then governor of the state of New York, to the legislature.

CHAPTER 11

Using Skills of the Experts in Giving Prepared Talks

That casual, witty, forceful talk you have written on the basis of the advice given in the preceding chapter is about ready to be delivered. In this chapter we show you how to ensure success in giving the talk. We tell you how to apply the prime skills used by expert speakers of the past and the present to achieve greatest impact.

Perhaps the most important thing of all for you to remember in giving a talk is this: Make your talk as natural and conversational as possible.

The importance of such an aim was suggested by Mark Twain when he said, "It usually takes me more than three weeks to prepare a good impromptu speech."

Informality and ease in delivery are even more important today. Television anchormen and anchorwomen set the ideal for today's speakers, ranging from business executives to Presidential contenders. And the leading TV news commentators deliver their very elaborately prepared talks as informally as if they had dropped in on you for a chat.

Natural ease in giving your talks should complement all the specific skills we recommend for you here. Those skills concern, first, the general way in which you decide to give a talk, whether from a written text, or as an extemporaneous talk or an impromptu talk. Additional skills or personal techniques apply to your overall manner and specifically to eye contact, use of your voice, and your gestures and movements. Let's see now how you can benefit from using all these skills.

Expert Ways for Giving a Prepared Talk

You have three broad alternatives from which to choose in selecting a method for giving a talk you've prepared in advance. The alternative you select effects the kind of material on which you will draw when you deliver the speech. As you'll shortly see, much or all of this material consists of thoughts, facts, and actions you learn so well that they become almost second nature to you. But the material may also include a written text, extensive notes, or other memory prompters.

Most Popular High-Level Method: Delivery from a Written Text—but NOT Read

Almost all major addresses given by leaders in business or government today are made from texts that are completely prepared word for word. Many persons who admire the brilliant, text-free orators of the past deplore present widespread reliance on written-out texts. But this approach has become the most popular method for delivering speeches on high-level occasions—and for a number of compelling reasons.

Perhaps the most compelling is that using a written-out text often saves the preparation time of the speaker. Many business executives and government leaders are not accomplished speakers, and would need far more time to prepare to give a speech *without* a text than *with* one.

Moreover, these business and government speeches are official policy statements. Any unfortunate slips or slurs they might contain could conceivably be flashed by our modern news media around the world—or, in our legally contentious society, could even draw a lawsuit. On the positive side, time and length for presenting these policy statements are almost always sharply limited, and a written text is relied on to help make sure of including all the essential points.

Then, too, as a byproduct, speaking from a written-out text

makes it feasible to provide texts of the address for publicity use. Securing such publicity for a talk often represents a result far more important than presentation of the address to the original audience. As you'll see, though, you would not distribute to the press duplicates of the written-out text that you actually used in giving the talk.

HOW PRESIDENTS HAVE USED THE TECHNIQUE OF DELIVERY FROM WRITTEN-OUT TEXTS. It is to Woodrow Wilson, President of the United States from 1913 to 1921, that we may owe today's widespread practice of giving speeches from texts. Thomas Jefferson had begun the Presidential practice of merely sending messages to the U.S. Congress and having them read by a clerk. In this he departed from the earlier examples of George Washington and John Adams, who had read their messages in person. But Presidents after Jefferson had clerks read their Congressional messages aloud, and this practice continued down to the time of Wilson.

Highly skilled as a speaker, Wilson easily could and often did give speeches without any text whatever. (He used skills that we'll discuss shortly.) But his reintroduction of the practice of personally delivering his messages to the Congress from written-out texts set a distinguished and famous example for the practice. Later Presidents and other prominent speakers followed Wilson in delivering speeches from texts. Still, admiration continued for old-fashioned oratory without anything to read from—isn't eye contact the basic reason? Apologies for speaking from a text were heard often for another two or three decades. In time, though, such apologies almost entirely died out.

METHODS OF WILSON, THEODORE ROOSEVELT, AND LINCOLN. Woodrow Wilson appears to have been one of the last Presidents to write his own speeches while holding that high office. For about a half century now, speechwriting has been a top-priority function of White House staff members. Wilson once explained how he wrote his own drafts. He would begin writing a speech by making a list of the topics he wanted to cover, "arranging them in my mind in their natural relations—that is, I fit the bones of the thing together." Like playwright George Bernard Shaw, Wilson wrote in stenographer's shorthand, which he found "a great saver of time." He would write the entire speech out in shorthand. Then, he said, "I copy it on my own typewriter, changing phrases, correcting sentences, and adding material as I go along."

You yourself might prepare the texts from which you give your speeches in much the same personal way—except, probably, for the shorthand stage.

Theodore Roosevelt, who was U.S. President from 1901 to 1909, used a more modern method than Wilson to develop prepared texts. He began by assembling his thoughts, facts, and key phrases on a note pad. Then he dictated a first draft to a stenographer—rapidly, to give it the rush and flow not only of speech but of his own vigorous, hard-driving style. He next revised the typed draft himself, and dictated from it again. Often he would go through several such revision cycles, at times asking an advisor to listen to him dictate or read one of the drafts. The final version would go to the newspapers. His spoken version would frequently be one he delivered extemporaneously, without a text and using skills we shall describe soon.

In an earlier era, even so formidable an impromptu orator as Abraham Lincoln wrote out all of his talks as President of the U.S. He would compose a speech in his head for days as he went about his other activities. Notes of phrases, facts, ideas, and points would be jotted down as they occurred to him and would be stowed under a band inside the tall top hat he wore. He would then arrange and work with these notes once he sat down to write out the address for delivery and, possibly, for publication. For example, his first inaugural address as President was written in a room over a store in Springfield, Illinois, where he locked himself away to draw on just such notes plus copies of the U.S. Constitution and of three speeches he had given earlier.

Lincoln would also revise his speeches again and again. He thought about what to say in what would become his immortal Gettysburg Address for days in advance, even though the address consists of only ten sentences. He apparently went on revising it right up to its delivery. To a friend, Noah Brooks, he confided on the Sunday before he delivered the speech, "It is not exactly written. It is not finished anyway. I have written it over two or three times, and I shall have to give it another lick before I am satisfied.''

HOW MODERN PRESIDENTS AND MAJOR BUSINESS EXECUTIVES USE THE TECHNIQUE OF DELIVERY FROM WRITTEN-OUT TEXTS.

Speech content and delivery style today represent crucial elements in the broad range of communications techniques employed by candidates to win the office of U.S. President. Certainly the individual candidate makes the ultimate decisions about what to say and how to say it. But speech preparation and coaching in style of delivery are substantially the work of a large, highly specialized team on the campaign or White House staff. That speechwriting team provides written-out texts from which to deliver talks for every possible occasion. Talks without texts are held insofar as possible to safe statements with which the candidate or President is completely familiar. Similar techniques and approaches are used by government officials holding almost any of the more important posts today.

Major business executives commonly take the same approach by having the texts of their addresses prepared by specialists. In their case, speechwriting is a specialty in the elaborately developed field of corporate public relations, or communications. Business firms of any size today are served in virtually all cases by outside public relations consulting firms or by internal public relations departments, if not by both. The largest corporations—Exxon, GM, GE, IBM, and others—usually have PR or communications groups at all their major management and plant locations. As a result, addresses of any importance given by executives inside or outside their corporations are almost all speeches delivered from written-out texts drafted by speechwriting specialists in corporate PR or communications.

How You Can Best Give Speeches from a Written Text

Even without the help of a speechwriting staff, you can be as professional in giving your talks from prepared texts as many business executives and government officials. We explain here how you can accomplish this. The guidelines we give you cover, first, the main ways of achieving the vital result of making your delivery from a text completely natural and appealing. Our guidelines go on to show you the key differences between the two main types of copies of your talk you would use. One copy is only for you to use on the platform. The other copies you prepare are intended for distribution to editors and reporters for publicity.

KEEPING DELIVERY FROM A TEXT NATURAL AND APPEALING. Most vital of all in giving your talk from a written text is to have your audience as unaware as possible that you're using a text. But how can you do this?

Two practices can lead your audience to forget you have a text. One is to rehearse your talk ten or more times, long enough almost to put it in your memory verbatim. (Do *not*, however, memorize the talk, for reasons shortly explained.) Long-repeated practice enables you to work with the talk until its thought and wording feel absolutely natural to you. Long practice also enables you to develop until thoroughly natural the many expert ways to use your voice, to gesture, and to move that we will soon discuss.

In addition, repeated practice makes possible your second vital approach to natural delivery. The main technique in this second approach is to look at your listeners as much as possible, and at your speech text as little as possible.

In doing this, you glance at the copy of your speech only at the start of sentences, or paragraphs—and you make these glances very brief. You don't read the material you are about to give while taking one of these quick glances. You merely remind yourself of the thought and essential phrasing in the sentence or paragraph. The thought, phrasing, emphasis, and other elements in the sentence became completely familiar to you through practice, so the quick glance jogs your memory. While actually delivering a sentence, you are looking a member of the audience right in the eye. While delivering the next, you look another member of the audience right in the eye. You're applying our very first secret for speaking with impact: *maintaining eye contact*. Each quick glance at your text reminds you of the next sentence. That glance lasts no longer than a sweep you make in shifting your eyes from one member of the audience to another.

Know your talk—and know your thinking in it and expression of it—so well that you can improve on its wording and its emphasis while you are giving it. The human contact with your audience can be counted on to give you fresh wording and improved delivery. Your text is there not only to back you up should you need it. It's there to give you a springboard for possibly adapting your talk as you watch the living response of your audience.

How should you try to appear to your listeners when you give a talk from a text? A helpful image for you to keep in mind is readily available. It's the image of TV newscasters or government officials giving broadcast talks. President Reagan looks right at you out of the screen of your TV set whenever he gives a talk, and he does it all the time. Of course he has a TelePrompTer device just above the lens of the TV camera, so he's able to read his speech word for word while still seeming to look squarely into the camera—and hence at you. But you don't have to match him.

Although you probably won't have a TelePrompTer for your talks, active practice will enable you to speak much more naturally than you can now.

HERE'S THE IDEAL WAY TO PREPARE THE TEXT FROM WHICH YOU GIVE YOUR TALK.

As you might expect, the text from which you give your talk can be prepared in ways that make delivery of the talk easier for you.

Experts usually prefer to have the text from which they speak put on small, loose-leaf sheets, about 5 by 8 inches or 6 by 9 inches in size. Sheets can then go safely into a binder. You will find it useful to do the same in preparing your text. Here's the way to proceed.

First, type or print in big letters, perhaps capitals. Professional speechwriting departments often use what they call "speech typewriters," which print in very large capital letters of a size and style that one typewriter manufacturer calls Orator. But you can get results just about as good for all practical purposes by typing in all capitals on any conventional typewriter.

Space between the lines of your text widely—at least double-spaced if typed, and preferably triple-spaced. When there's a pause within a sentence, you might write (PAUSE).

You should also indicate longer pauses after a sentence when you anticipate the need for such pauses. You'll need these at high points, for laughter or applause. You can show these by writing (PAUSE) on a separate line with extra lines of space above and below the word. Some speakers instead use slant-line marks to note pauses—a single mark for a short pause, like this /, and multiple marks for longer pauses, like // or ////.

By all means, mark up your text in any other ways you find helpful. One of the commonest would be to underline or double underline words and phrases you want to emphasize. Make any other notes you find helpful, perhaps for facial expressions, or loudness of voice, or gestures. Feel free to rewrite phrases and sentences as you practice more and more with the talk. Experts often find better phrasings as they practice. It was apparently through practice that Lincoln came upon the immortal phrase, "A house divided against itself cannot stand."

HOW TO REHEARSE, REVISE, AND POLISH YOUR TALK.

Once you have a first version of the text from which to deliver your talk, start practicing it. Try rehearsing it in any or all of these ways. With a tape recorder. Before a mirror. With a friend, or ideally, with an expert teacner, speaker, or speechwriter.

As you rehearse, you will almost certainly mark up and change the text as the speech improves. You may find yourself making minor or possibly major revisions. Such major revisions may lead you to make one or more completely clean, fully revised texts for delivery. In time, your changes should become fewer and smaller as you add or as you alter this or that touch while you give your delivery of the talk its final polish.

Try not to cut short the time you give to rehearsing, revising, and polishing. These all take much time. However, by and large, the more expert the speaker, the more time he or she spends rehearsing and changing until the talk is just right.

WHY TO AVOID MEMORIZING.

You might think that, with all the time you spend practicing the speech, you could simply go ahead and memorize it straight-out in much the same time anyway. But almost all expert speakers would advise you not to memorize. Such experts can often give a prepared speech running as long as twenty or thirty minutes without a text by speaking extemporaneously, as recounted in the next section. They are careful, though, not to memorize an extemporaneous speech.

Delivering a speech from memory has two main drawbacks. First, memorized delivery tends to be mechanical. It usually lacks the vital spark of transmitting live emotion from speaker to listener. Second, memorized delivery turns into an absolute disaster should the speaker block at some point and realize that the mind has gone completely blank.

Delivery of a completely memorized speech might possibly work well for you if you had previously developed advanced skills in acting over a number of years. Actresses and actors do, of course, deliver memorized speeches. They do so, though, only after years of training and practice, plus, of course, native talent. Most speakers, however, don't have sufficient background in acting, and generally should avoid memorizing their prepared talks.

FOR PUBLICITY, MAKE SPEECH COPIES OR NEWS RELEASES LIKE THIS. If you want your speech publicized, you would want to make the kinds of copies needed for publicity once you had thoroughly worked out the final wording. At that point you would take your special marked-up delivery copy and from it produce a typed copy, double-spaced, and without the messages you added to your speech delivery copy.

A few touches would give that conventionally typed copy a professional public relations finish. If possible, have the first page start on the printed letterhead of an organization (your company, perhaps, or the organization you're addressing), or of an individual (you). At top left, near the letterhead, add a line saying: *For further details, contact*. This would be followed by the name and telephone number of an individual. This could be you, an associate of yours, or an officer of the organization you're addressing. A few lines lower, put in a centered, single-space statement saying that this is the text of an address delivered by you (identified by name and whatever title and organizational affiliation you wish) before the such-

and-such meeting of the such-and-such group. Then, several lines farther down and to the right of center, put either FOR IMMEDIATE RELEASE or FOR RELEASE, followed by a weekday and date or by a designated hour, weekday, and date.

Duplicated copies of such an original can then be given to reporters at or after the meeting, and can also be mailed to local newspapers, general or special magazines, radio stations, and other sources of coverage. Copies can even be sent to dailies or weeklies long enough in advance to enable them to carry a report very soon after you've given the talk.

With the help of a skilled journalist, you may instead prefer to issue only a news release on your talk, reporting it as a news story with quotations selected to emphasize the key facts you want covered. However, it is often simpler and more effective to provide a full text. Both news release and full text are sometimes issued.

Popular Method for Giving Prepared Talks: Delivery Without a Speech Text

Delivery of a prepared talk without use of a complete text of the speech remains a popular method for giving talks today. This is true even though most of today's more important speeches are given with a text at hand.

Expert speakers today may recommend delivery without a text (though possibly with notes), primarily because it permits use of a completely natural manner and because it reflects impressive confidence and skill on the speaker's part. Their thought is not unlike a viewpoint once expressed by Abraham Lincoln. While Lincoln used extensive notes for virtually all his talks in Washington, he would not use notes of any kind when giving speeches back in his home state of Illinois. Explaining why, he said of notes that "they always tend to tire and confuse the listener."

From what you have already learned about giving a prepared talk from a full text, you can readily see how you might prepare yourself to deliver the talk without a text. As you'll recall, you rehearse with a text some ten or more times until the essential thought and expression of the speech are deeply fixed in your mind. At this point, you may need only to glance at your marked text very briefly from time to time.

At such a point of readiness, you could shift to delivery without the text as follows. First, make up a set of cards on which you put only brief notes for the speech, like major points to make or key statistics and other facts to give. Then, practice the speech enough times more to enable you to set the text aside and give it just with the notes at hand.

Should you then want to equip yourself to give the talk without the notes, continue practicing with the notes, rehearsing the talk over and over. You'll find that you're increasingly able to speak without relying on the notes and that eventually you can put them aside. Again, resist any urge merely to memorize your talk. It should live in your thought and emotions as you give it.

Two broad conclusions probably occur to you on thus seeing how you can indeed learn to deliver a prepared speech without a text or without notes. You can understand how almost anyone can become skilled at extemporaneous speaking if he or she invests sufficient time in the effort. And you can appreciate how speaking from a text does indeed save preparation time.

Still, extemporaneous speaking has a grand, moving cadence to it when employed by expert speakers of talent and experience. Here is a somewhat old-fashioned example of this live, majestic quality of extemporaneous speech. It was given some sixty years ago in the U.S. Senate, at a time when decisive addresses were still made on the floor of Congress. This one, by Senator William E. Borah of Idaho, spelled defeat for President Wilson's draft treaty to bring the U.S. into the old League of Nations, the ill-fated predecessor of the United Nations. In speaking against the treaty on November 19, 1919, Borah said:

> Sir, we are told that this treaty means peace. Even so, I would not pay the price. Would you purchase peace at the cost of any part of our independence? We could have had peace in 1776—the price was high, but we could have had it. James Otis, Sam Adams, Hancock, and Warren were surrounded by those who urged peace and British rule. All through the long and

trying struggle, particularly when the clouds of adversity lowered upon the cause, there was a cry of peace—let us have peace.

We could have had peace in 1860. Lincoln was counseled by men of great influence and accredited wisdom to let our brothers—and thank heaven, they are brothers—depart in peace. But the tender, loving Lincoln, bending under the fearful weight of impending civil war, an apostle of peace, refused to pay the price, and a reunited country will praise his name forevermore—bless it because he refused peace at the price of national honor and national integrity. Peace upon any other basis than national independence, peace purchased at the cost of any part of our national integrity, is fit only for slaves. . . .

Speeches with such an inspired, impassioned quality of extemporaneous delivery continue being given today. That quality is evident, for instance, in an address given in November of 1980 by Oscar Dystel, for many years the chief executive officer of Bantam Books, Inc. Talking of the most essential element needed in book publishing management today, he said:

I am not, of course, suggesting that we allow every bright person in our publishing houses to run wild with earnest and probably unsalable ideas. Rigorous analysis of any publishing project is mandatory. But the real challenge to publishing management today lies in allowing the restless, roaming, searching editorial mind to create something exciting from the sum total of our analysis of trends—ideas which fire the whole publishing process that begins with the visceral reaction to a piece of writing when editor and author work together, a process that reaches its zenith when the book arrives at the point of sale.*

*The passage is from Mr. Dystel's Eighth Annual Richard Rogers Bowker Memorial Lecture [New Series], the text of which appeared in *Publishers Weekly*, Dec. 12, 1980, pp. 18–25.

Force and eloquence along these lines can be open to you in extemporaneous speaking of your own, if you want to achieve them, but be prepared to invest much time and deep conviction in doing so.

Impromptu Delivery for Talks Either Completely Unexpected or Completely Familiar

Impromptu delivery normally has no connection with a speech prepared in advance. It's the style of giving a talk that you deliver presumably without advance warning or preparation, on the spur of the moment. Most of the early chapters concerned giving talks in just such an impromptu style.

People who have occasion to speak in some regular capacity actually may prepare some of their impromptu talks in advance, contradictory though this may seem. Winston Churchill, Great Britain's prime minister during World War II and one of the historic orators of this century, illustrated how this can happen. Early in his parliamentary career, Churchill felt unsure of his skills in impromptu debate. Accordingly, on important issues of the time, he prepared a number of short speeches in advance so that he could give them as apparently impromptu talks whenever occasion arose.

Frequent speakers find it rather simple to give another kind of impromptu talk. These are talks on matters completely familiar to the expert speaker. Since the individual has spoken often on the subject, it's usually quite simple for her or him to give an impromptu talk on the basis of general preparation.

Expert Techniques Essential in Giving a Prepared Talk

TOTAL IMPRESSION—NATURAL, ASSURED, ENER-GETIC. You'll find it helpful in using effective techniques when you give prepared talks to have a sense of the total impression you make on your listeners. The image or overall effect you communicate should at all times be natural, assured, and energetic. In consequence, when applying the expert techniques we explain in this section—techniques for holding attention, varying your voice, gesturing and moving—take care that the techniques make you seem more natural rather than artificial and forced. Blend in your use of these techniques until they function as part of your natural self.

As you do this, you should also find your manner becoming more assured, more poised, more confident. And you will want at the same time to keep your style of delivery energetic—alert, alive, full of vigor.

Remember Always to Use Eye Contact

Whatever else you do or don't do in giving a talk, make sure to look your listeners squarely in the eye as much as possible. Forgive us if we repeat this once again here, but it can hardly be stressed too much. Maintaining eye contact is the single most important thing you can do to hold the attention of your audience, and to appear natural. And failing to look your listeners in the eye is the surest way to make them indifferent—while also making you seem awkward, artificial, and amateurish. It's also one of the commonest failings of beginning or infrequent speakers. Accordingly, be sure to use eye contact as the foundation of your technique all through your delivery of a talk.

Keep Your Voice Deep, Slow, Loud Enough, and Expressive

Here are two ways of using your voice that can go far to make your speech sound important and impressive. First, when you start giving the talk, make the pitch of your voice somewhat deeper than its usual level in conversation. And all through the talk, keep your voice on a level that, for you, is deep.

You can see in a moment what this accomplishes, especially when combined with the second way of using your voice. This second way is to slow down as you talk. To speak more slowly is also one of the original key secrets we gave you for speaking well, you'll recall. But it's worth reemphasizing here as a fundamental technique for delivering a prepared talk.

At this point, in a little experiment, suppose that you say the following line aloud in your usual manner: "Ladies and gentlemen, I am very pleased to be able to speak to you tonight."

A statement like this could be a very ordinary beginning of a very ordinary speech.

However, get ready to deepen your voice. Also, get ready to state that sentence with the pauses indicated by slash lines (//). All right—say it now, deeper, more slowly, as follows:

"Ladies // and gentlemen // // //,

I am very pleased // //

to be able // to speak to you // tonight."

If the experiment worked, you should have noticed several things as you spoke even this simple phrase deeper and more slowly. In a deeper tone, your voice was probably fuller, richer, rounder, more resonant, more relaxed, mellower, and stronger in the distance it could carry. Speaking more slowly, with pauses, enhanced this richer quality of your voice. Speaking more slowly made it possible for you to speak with greater expression. Speaking slowly also showed that you gave importance to what you were saying. Anyone hearing you would give it importance as well.

Our other two suggestions for effective use of your voice should be easy for you to adopt once you speak deeper and more slowly. These two further suggestions for expert technique are to speak loudly (again, a key secret), and to keep your voice richly expressive as you speak by appropriately varying the speed, the intonation, and the pitch of your words and phrases to bring out their meaning clearly. The point is to avoid becoming that all-too-familiar kind of speaker who mumbles on too quietly to be understood and whose voice drones along in a singsong that ignores any meaning that should be conveyed by the words being said.

All four ways of using your voice for greatest impact in a speech reinforce one another. Speaking more deeply and slowly gives you the breath for speaking more loudly. Talking slowly, with pauses, enables you to think about and bring out the meaning of what it is you're telling the members of your audience as you tell it to them.

You need make only minor adaptations in these ways of using your voice when you speak into a microphone over a public-address system. With a mike, you'll want to restrain some of the loudness or volume of your voice. But you will also want to speak even more slowly in order to avoid amplified reverberations, and to speak more deeply and more expressively.

On the other hand, if you're in a small- or medium-sized room, speak without using a microphone and public-address system whenever you can be heard clearly without those aids. You'll find that speaking without a mike is more flexible and natural.

Make Sure to Gesture and Move Naturally

Gesturing and moving in ways that further express the emotion and meaning of the speech are also hallmarks of expert speakers. Include techniques of gesture and movement in your delivery, by all means. But let them grow out of the meaning you are trying to convey and the gestures and movement you would normally use to convey that meaning. In addition, you may want to develop your skills with gestures by paying close attention to how famous speakers and actors use gesture and possibly by trying new kinds of gestures for yourself.

Gesturing with your hands and arms at appropriate parts of your talks may come more easily to you if you think of common gestures that speakers often use.

POINTING. Pointing with your finger stabbing at the air or in some meaningful direction is one of the most common and direct of gestures used in all kinds of speech. You can of course use it whenever you're pointing something out, or in some direction—back, forward; or up, down. You can also use it for emphasis, as with: "Mark my words: closing this factory will prove to be a colossal mistake!"

OFFERING. Holding out your hand with the palm open and up and moving it toward the listener would represent another very common gesture, one of offering. It can be done with both hands too. You might use it when you are proposing an idea or a course of action to your listeners.

REJECTING. Holding your hand up and pushing away with it clearly signifies rejection. You would apply it perhaps when advising an audience of some alternative the audience should avoid or oppose. A gesture like this can also be used to express caution.

DIVIDING, OR DISTINGUISHING BETWEEN. Any audience of yours would similarly understand a gesture of yours in which you started with your hands together, palms facing out, and then you moved your hands apart as if dividing some substance with your hands. Such a gesture signifies you are dividing or clearly separating one thing from another.

DEFIANCE, OR OTHER STRONG EMOTION. Raising a clenched fist universally carries powerful meaning. You would use it to express defiance, or some other emotion of highly unusual intensity. It might come at a climax of a speech.

Still other kinds of gestures will occur to you in thought or action. One might be the granting of a kind of benediction or blessing in a priestly raising of your hand with the palm facing your listeners. Another for use only at times of great exuberance would be holding up both arms out straight in a V—which has become a traditional victory symbol. Some speakers hold up their fingers to enumerate, as with "first," "second," and "third." Folding the hands together as if in prayer is a gesture expressive of fervent belief or earnest plea.

In your own talks, gestures of any kind will heighten the impact of what you say if the gestures truly fit you, your meaning, and your audience.

BODILY MOVEMENTS TO HELP HOLD INTEREST. Similarly, you will want to move by changing your posture and the place where you're standing in ways that fit your meaning as well as shifts you make to new parts of the talk. You can and should move at appropriate points in your talk even if you prefer to remain near a lectern (with, possibly, a microphone) from which you're speaking.

Movements of your shoulders, trunk, head, or feet can be slight but, like the natural changes of facial expression you'll make as you speak, they will help you continue to capture the eye and the interest of your listeners.

Movement catches the eyes. Use it most assuredly. Holding still dulls the eye and lets attention wander.

Paradox for Success: Practice to Be Spontaneous

By now you know all the basic techniques for giving prepared talks that are essential tools developed by expert speakers down the centuries. Applying them successfully yourself involves a paradox. Let us explain.

You saw from the start of the chapter that the most vital quality of speaking well is utter naturalness in your delivery. We hope we've convinced you that you'll be your most effective when you seem completely unstudied, conversational, and spontaneous.

But in order to be absolutely spontaneous in this way, you can't simply step before an audience in your natural state of no preparation whatever. Therein lies the paradox. An unprepared amateur speaker is most often awkward, stiff, and artificial. It takes very thorough preparation and very long and diligent practice to be truly relaxed and spontaneous.

Preparation and practice equip famed speakers to make striking spontaneous remarks when they're on their feet. Woodrow Wilson suggested this when asked how long it took him to prepare a ten-minute speech. "Two weeks," Wilson fired back. The questioner asked how long for a one-hour speech? "One week," said Wilson. And a two-hour speech? Wilson had the long-developed presence of mind to say, with a twinkle in his eye, "I'm ready now."

And it was long practice and preparation that enabled Winston Churchill to be memorably spontaneous in an address early in this century to members of the British House of Commons. News of completion of the lines to transmit telegraph cablegrams to Africa interrupted proceedings in the

House, and was met by cheers. As the applause subsided, Churchill rose to address his fellow MPs. "Excellent, excellent," he declared. "Now, what shall we tell the Africans?"

This, then, is the one last secret behind the skills of the experts in giving talks: practice as much as you can in order to be both effective and spontaneously yourself. As you can appreciate, the greatest speakers practice all through their careers.

For instance, an admirer questioned Daniel Webster about the length of time he had worked on an address regarded as one of the greatest of that time, Webster's celebrated "Reply to Hayne." The senator said simply, "Twenty years."

Practice Activities

1. A few paragraphs from an interview address by Edmund S. Muskie, when he was U.S. Secretary of State, are given below. The interview concerned the American hostages in Iran. The secretary's remarks were made after he was asked if the U.S. Government at that time (December, 1980) ruled out military force as a means of securing the release of the hostages (who by then had been held in Iran for more than a year).

For practice, take these paragraphs and assume they are draft remarks in a speech you will be making. Mark the draft with the notations you would make in readying it as the speech text you would use on the platform for actually giving the talk. Notations would include pauses, emphasis, gestures, and loudness or softness of voice. Feel free also to revise the wording in ways that you think would be more effective.

Text of Address on Using Force to Release Hostages

Well, we tried a form of military force in the rescue effort which failed. And that effort did not succeed and, in addition, making the effort, I think, prolonged the agony of the problem.

Now, it is not easy if one looks at a map of Iran to

consider military options, unless one were to consider options with consequences that need to be carefully weighed, for our other national interests, before making it.

I mean, an automatic military response is not an easy thing to devise, or an easy thing to execute, or one that one easily contemplates when one considers other national interests that might be impacted.

But the President has made it clear for a year that we will hold Iran accountable for the safety of the hostages, with whatever that implies for the circumstances that may arise. I don't think it is helpful to try to hypothesize what circumstances may arise. . . .

2. The following activity presents a nobly stated prose passage which you almost certainly know by heart. Your aim in the activity is to deliver this prose passage in the manner you would use when giving a talk from a complete speech text, and in particular to practice maintaining eye contact with your listeners.

In other words, glance only briefly at this passage as a speech text. Almost all of the time you deliver the passage, look up and out, as if at an audience. You may want to try the activity while standing before a mirror, in order to see for yourself just how effective it is to maintain eye contact. (Mark the passage first for delivery, if you wish.)

The passage follows. It is the "Pledge of Allegiance," with which public school classes have opened throughout this country for many years.

I pledge allegiance to the flag of the United States of America, and to the republic for which it stands, one nation, indivisible, with liberty and justice for all.

CHAPTER 12
Using Visual Aids for Maximum Impact in Your Talks

You can greatly increase the impact of your prepared talks by using one or more kinds of visual aids—but only if you use them well. With the very first suggestion to use visual aids, you need to know the very first rule for them: don't botch, please. No use is better than wrong use that makes you look ridiculous. We explain right and wrong uses of visual aids here in this chapter.

Visual aids from which you might choose range from the very simple to the very technical. Some of the highly technical ones available, like tape-programmed multi-slide displays with music, can achieve impressive effects indeed. But some of the simplest, like an ordinary blackboard or a flip chart (which is really just a wall-size writing pad), can be quite effective. We explain in this chapter essential points about using all the major kinds of visual aids.

Three More Basic Rules with Any Visual Aid

That "don't botch" we just mentioned is the supremely important *first rule*. Granting that you'll be flawless in handling your visuals, let us give three more working rules that can apply to any kind of visuals you use. These are:

2. Present your visuals in such a way that you're in a position to look at your audience almost all the time. Among other things, this means no slide lectures from the back of the room—get a long cord and stand up in front of your listeners and face them as you talk. It also means facing your listeners at any time you are pointing out something on a flip chart or slide. DON'T TURN YOUR BACK TO THE AUDIENCE WHILE POINTING. You must maintain eye contact.

3. Stay in control of your visuals at all times, and direct the attention of your listeners to what you want them to notice. Visuals should always reinforce what you're saying. They should never distract from your message. We cover detailed rules for staying in control as we go along in the chapter.

4. Mark on the text or script (when you use one to deliver your talk) all the cues for the visual aids you present. Notes like this would read something like "Slide number 3 on" and "Slide number 3 off."

Guidelines for Speaking with a Blackboard

One of the simplest and commonest of visual aids can also be one of the most effective when used properly. It's the blackboard or chalkboard that you have watched through years of education. Familiar though the chalkboard itself may seem, the few cardinal rules for using it well are often not known by a great many speakers who work with it. Let's look at chalkboard fundamentals, including those helpful rules.

Chalkboard techniques are the same whether you're using a traditional blackboard, a more modern greenboard on which speakers also write most often with white chalk, or a whiteboard of the type frequently used in business firms and written on with special color markers that wipe off with a cloth. Chalks or markers of different colors naturally prove helpful for underlining or otherwise giving special emphasis or identity to certain material. (Incidentally, break any long, new pieces of chalk in two and write with a broken end to prevent the chalk squeak that sets the teeth on edge.)

In advance, jot down on cards essentially what you plan to put up on the chalkboard, at least in note form. Do this to help you make sure that you'll put what you want on the board in the right order.

Also in advance, go into the room where you'll talk and, from the rear, estimate or set by actual tryouts the right size of letters to write in order to be seen clearly at the farthest points from the board. Make sure, too, that there will be enough light on the board for legibility. You should also plan ahead of time to have about two spare pieces of each color of chalk or two spare markers that you plan to use.

Plan to write on the board while you give your talk, if possible. Try to avoid filling the board with your writings beforehand. If you do fill the board first, the audience will tend to ignore you and read the board ahead of you while you speak.

Then, when you write on the board at times during your talk, try to turn only sideways so that you can glance from the board to your audience at the same time as you write. Say what you're writing as you put it up. Of course, make your writing as legible as possible. You may want to use hand-printed block letters for clarity.

From time to time, when writing on the board, look up and ask, "Can you see this from the rear?" Doing this provides some modestly stimulating interaction for your listeners.

You may find it helpful to put up one or another kind of blank form on the board before you speak. One type of blank, for example, could look like this:

MAIN IDEA: _____

    SUBORDINATE IDEAS:

    1. _____

    2. _____

    3. _____

    4. _____

With such a blank, you would then fill in the words while actually giving your talk.

Any diagrams or drawings you plan to put up on the board require special care. Make a diagram or drawing first on a note card, with every part of it worked out on the card. Label parts of the diagram or drawing sufficiently so that the audience will be able to understand what it represents. Be prepared also to keep talking in a regular, interesting way as you draw and label at the board. Talk about the drawing and say the labels aloud as you write them.

Unless you are well experienced with talks at the chalkboard, it would probably also be a good idea for you to practice putting up each drawing or diagram with labels in advance. You can practice continuing to talk at the same time. Advance practice with chalkboard drawings can be important. Speakers who neglect it risk embarrassing, annoying silence as they make their drawings. Worse, if they make mistakes, the result is badly flustered confusion.

Practicing the whole talk while making all the chalkboard writings for it would probably be advisable unless you are an experienced lecturer or teacher. Practice should help you find ways to improve your talk. A friend or co-worker could listen to you practice and make additional suggestions for improvements.

Having large chalkboard panels on which to write may enable you to make all your notes during the talk without having to erase any earlier notes as you go along. Doing this has an advantage you may welcome. At the end, you are able to return to the start and then go through all the notes on the board, pointing out the most important items as you make a concluding summary.

On Flip Charts, Try to Write as You Go Along

Flip charts consist of large sheets of paper padded together across the top. Sheets are the size of full newspaper pages or larger, about two feet wide and four feet deep. Flip-chart pads are held at about standing eye level on boards or stands so that each sheet can be flipped over to the back of the pad, revealing the sheet underneath. Because of their limited size, flip charts tend to be used with small groups, no more than a hundred or so persons in number, and not in large auditoriums or lecture halls.

Corporations widely use flip charts for their own internal conferences. For instance, IBM has equipped most of its managerial offices and conference rooms with flip charts.

If you are ambitious about getting ahead in a corporation, you might take special interest in becoming adept at giving talks with flip charts. As you can appreciate, any talk engenders support and enthusiasm not only for the ideas or actions it concerns but for the speaker as well. Ambitious individuals in business firms are often eager as a result to give talks to management, because persons who do so usually win backing and interest and tend to get ahead.

Features of two other kinds of visual aids are combined by flip charts. As with chalkboards, flip charts can be written on. And as with slides, they present one image at a time for viewing by the audience. Guidelines applying to flip charts thus tend to be like those you would follow for chalkboards or for slides.

Two broad approaches to use of flip charts have correspondingly developed. The more commonly used is to prepare the flip charts to be used in the talk in advance, in much the way that slides are prepared in advance. What we believe to be the more effective use, albeit more demanding, is to write out each flip-chart sheet as you give the talk. (This kind of use parallels good chalkboard technique, you'll recall.)

Whenever possible, we think you should try to write out your flip-chart sheets as you go along, instead of having them all written out in advance. Prewritten flip charts usually distract from the speaker, especially if the message is all given in condensed form on the sheets.

However, when you write out a sheet as you go along, your listeners will feel you're not just parroting a canned address but thinking as you speak. Giving such an impression of spontaneity as you talk proves very effective in generating appreciation from an audience.

Specific points to observe in using flip charts effectively are as follows. First, before you talk, look into two matters. Inspect the stand or mounting that will hold the flip chart with which you'll be speaking. Make sure it won't tip over as you work with it, or that you know how to hold it so it won't fall. Also, try out the broad, felt-tip marker pens you will use to write on the flip chart. See that the ink of the pens you have does not soak all the way through one sheet and mark on the next sheet or sheets. If it should soak through, get a drier pen or pens, or else change the paper.

As an extremely important second point, be careful not to write too low on the flip chart. In a room with a flat floor, listeners sitting a distance away from you and the chart will almost certainly have the bottom part of the flip chart blocked by the heads of the people sitting in front of them. For this reason, keep your writing or drawing on the flip-chart sheets well above the bottom part of the sheets. Be sure to remember this precaution not only for flip charts, by the way, but also for any other kind of visual aid that might similarly have its bottom portion obscured for some of your listeners, as with, for instance, a chalkboard or overhead viewer transparency of the type discussed next.

Third, as with a chalkboard, write in different colors to emphasize, distinguish, or enliven what you write or draw on the flip chart.

Fourth, if you do write on the sheets as you talk, rather than prepare them in advance, be sure to rehearse the talk and your sheet-writing enough times to make your delivery smooth and spontaneous.

Fifth, if you instead prepare your flip-chart sheets in advance, try to sequence the sheets to stir the interest of your audience as much as possible. As an example, suppose you want to cover three points in some part of your talk. You might do this by having the first flip-chart sheet give only point 1. On the next sheet, give only point 2. And on the next, give just point 3. Then, on the last sheet of this sequence, supply all three points by way of review.

Finally, for the end of your talk, you can take advantage of the flip-chart form and go back to cover selected sheets or all sheets in giving your conclusion.

An Overhead Projector Can Be Better Than Slides

Overhead projectors beam an illuminated image on a screen, as do slide projectors, but can provide some advantages you don't have with slides. Perhaps the main advantage is that the lights in the room in which you're talking do not need to be dimmed in order to make overhead projector transparency images visible. Another possible advantage is that, with an overhead projector, you can write or draw on a transparency while it's being projected and while you are still facing and looking at your listeners. It's also extremely convenient to point with a pencil to any part of the transparency you are using.

An overhead projector is in essence a box beside which you stand or sit at the head of the room, while facing your listeners and talking. On the top of the box is a lighted glass window the size of a sheet of paper. Over the window you put the transparent plastic sheets, or transparencies, with writing and/or drawings or graphs you want projected. An arm on the box holds a small projecting head a foot or so above the window, and this head projects a large image of each transparency on a screen or wall behind the speaker. The size of the image can be adjusted by moving the projector. Projectors are made in sizes varying from portable up to jumbos for large auditoriums.

As with flip-chart sheets, you can write and draw directly on the transparencies as you go along. Doing this gives your talk more spontaneity than you will achieve with transparencies made ahead of time. (Writing words backward—right to left—is not needed for an overhead projector, by the way. In writing on a transparency, simply put down the letters from left to right, just as you would on a sheet of paper.) You can write or draw on a transparency with felt-tip marking pens of different colors; the inks of these pens are translucent and project in color.

Interesting special effects can be gotten with transparencies if you want to become especially proficient with them. The transparencies can be made up in advance as a series of overlays, which can show successive stages of development, for example, the progressive westward settlement of the U.S. A transparency can be partially covered by a card while you use it, so you can show only part of it at a time. Then you can progressively uncover the transparency to present more and more of the full image. A transparency can carry a basic image or message prepared in advance, and can then be added to while you are giving your speech. (Additions like this may be drawn on a separate clear plastic sheet over the original transparency.)

As with any other visual aid you use, practice with transparencies and an overhead projector ahead of time until any possible snags or troubles have been eliminated.

Be careful not to confuse an overhead projector with a related device, the opaque projector. Opaque projectors display images on opaque sheets, such as pictures from books or magazines. Opaque projectors tend to be used far less than overhead projectors. One main reason for this is that, with an opaque projector, you would have to make the room almost totally dark in order for the projected image to be visible.

For the Largest Impact with Slides, Keep Them Down to the Smallest Number Possible

Color slides of the 35-millimeter size, so popular for personal snapshots in millions of family homes, are also very popular as a visual aid for speeches delivered in business and professional meetings. Slides used with such speeches include not only photographs of scenes but slides giving just words or drawn diagrams, graphs, or pictures. These word or diagram slides are best prepared by commercial artists skilled in making them up in commercial art departments of companies or in independent commercial art studios. Word or diagram slides drafted by inexperienced persons may look amateurish and crude.

Because slides are often so very attractive and professional looking, you may need to guard against the frequent mistake of using them to damaging excess.

In general, you will have greatest impact when you use as few slides as possible. The main reason for this is that listeners primarily respond to and believe in the live speaker communicating with them. Another important reason is that no effective talk should have more than one central point and about three or four important subordinate points, because that's as much as people are able to remember. And putting only those central and important points on slides helps your listeners fix them in mind.

A third reason for using fewer rather than more slides is that an audience cannot help but give each slide equal emphasis and attention. In consequence, showing some fifty slides in twenty minutes will usually leave your audience with only a pleasantly confused blur. However, your audience will clearly grasp the basic points if it sees only about six significant slides in twenty minutes.

One of the coauthors of this book, when beginning to work with an executive giving a speech, will first ask: "All right, what's the main point you want to get across?" The executive gives it, and that's the central point.

"Now, what three or four things do you need to show in order to prove that main point?" And the executive will give them. By asking these questions, we know we have identified the very few all word slides that we'll use with the talk.

Limit Your Slides to Only Two Types of Content

You will realize greater impact from slides with your talk if you keep their content as well as their number down to essentials. In deciding what content your slides should have, keep in mind that slides should really be restricted to just two types of essential material.

First, content most easily understood when shown rather than described in spoken words. Such content would include things such as plans for the division's new factory, main sources of company revenues as shown in some visual form, perhaps a pie chart, or the firm's line of revolutionary new power lawnmowers.

Second, content consisting of any message you want your listeners to remember in words. Content of this kind would usually be the briefest and most memorable phrasing you can devise for your central point and several most important supporting points. As an example, a central point in which you were urging your corporation to invest in a demonstrably profitable new petrochemicals plant might be stated most memorably on a slide:

HOW TO TURN $500 MILLION INTO $6 BILLION

Limiting your slide content only to essentials like these will keep your audience alert, absorbed, and convinced.

Put Few Words on a Slide—and Use Color

Keep the wording on any one slide brief, down to just the essential message you want the audience to remember. A rough rule of thumb might be to give no more than ten words on an all-words slide. That's about as many as listeners will remember. Fewer words are better (as these four words themselves illustrate).

Above all, don't put any substantial chunks of your speech text or outline up on a slide, and then read from the slide as if it were a sort of cue card. Reading part of your talk from slides breaks your direct communication with your audience. It marks you as an amateur.

Of course, using color on any word slide or diagram slide gives it liveliness and interest. Adding color should be worth the extra time and expense it involves. Words in black-and-white letters might be given against color backgrounds. Some speakers like to use light-colored letters in a yellow or green or blue against a black background on slides.

Spotlight on You—and on How You Stand and Point

Lighting in a room where you give a talk with slides should be carefully arranged in advance. You will of course want to make sure that the room can be dimmed enough for your slides to be easily visible. Try for dimness, incidentally, in preference to blackness. Dark rooms tend to put listeners to sleep.

You might overlook a second kind of lighting that's just as important. You as the speaker need to continue to be seen by your audience after the lights go down for slides, and you yourself should be illuminated by some kind of spotlight.

Stand at all times facing your audience during a talk with slides. Only glance now and then at the screen, as you gesture or point toward a slide. If you're right-handed, you'll want to stand at the audience's right-hand side of the slide screen so that you'll be able to point with your right hand without turning your back on your listeners. (You'd stand on the left if you're left-handed.)

Point to particular parts of graphic or pictorial slides to be helpful or dramatic. A stick or telescoping pointer might be suitable for this. In a larger auditorium you might instead use a light pointer, which projects a bright, white arrow on the screen. With a light pointer, a slight shaking of your hand while you are pointing can wobble the white arrow quite a lot. Avoid having this happen to you by pointing briefly with the white arrow and then turning the light pointer off.

After making direct references to a slide you show, don't leave it on the screen while you go on talking about other matters. Project a pleasantly colored blank slide instead, or turn off the slide projector and turn up the lights in the room until the next slides are due.

Final Checklist for Using Slides

Several last points to check before giving a slide talk will help ensure a smooth, impressive presentation.

- Comb through the finished slides for any errors, especially any misspelled words, in time to have them corrected. Don't use any slide if you can't have it fixed.
- Rehearse with the slides in advance, perhaps in your hotel room if you're on the road, or preferably in the room where you will be speaking. In your last rehearsals, adjust the cue or timing for each slide to the precise points or words at which you will want the slide to come on and go off. Mark those cues on your script or speaking text, and possibly on a duplicate copy being followed by a person running the slide projector for you. (By all means, rehearse with such an aide if you use one.)
- Make sure that the slides are in the right order, and are right side up. It's hilarious whenever an upside-down slide or a wrong slide flashes on—for everyone except you, the speaker. Do not let this happen.
- If you're providing the slide projector, make sure you have the right electric current in the room where you speak. Carry your own extension cord. Carry a spare light bulb for the projector, and *know how to put the bulb in*.

Use Films in a Talk Only for Special Purposes

You would probably not use motion-picture film as a visual aid in a talk, as film is expensive to make and is suited only for quite limited uses with a speech. With a short segment of silent film, for example, you might speak while it runs to show such things as a test of new equipment, perhaps an aircraft or an experimental auto, or the operation of a new steel-rolling mill or other industrial equipment. You would use such film segments as these in much the same way as with illustrative slides.

Conceivably you might want to show a sound film at some point in, or in connection with, a talk you give. (Or, if for viewing by a smaller group, it could be a sound videotape run on a tape player.) Doing this can be highly effective, depending on the aptness of the film for your talk. However, the film in this case functions not as a visual aid in your talk but as a different kind of presentation given in conjunction with your talk.

Practice Activities

1. Using a pointer while maintaining eye contact. Pick out a picture or poster on the wall of your home (or one you can put up on the wall) showing an outdoor landscape. Then, imagine some business development project that could fit your scene. For instance, if the landscape is hills and valleys, perhaps an electronics plant to make calculators, or an airport for corporate small planes. If a river, your project might be a line of excursion boats. A beach? Perhaps plan a resort hotel and marina. If mountains, think possibly of ski lodges and trails. Imagine the project so that parts of its buildings, phone and power lines, connecting roads and other features connect with various parts of the landscape you've selected.

Next plan a short segment of a talk for which you would

use this scenic landscape as though it were a slide. Your talk segment would explain how the features and operations of your project would fit specific features of the landscape pictured. Assume you are giving the talk as a leading executive to twenty or more fellow executives of your company. Assume, too, that your company is in the business of investing in projects like the one you're proposing, and that you are giving the talk to recommend this project for investment by the company.

Once you're all set with the picture/poster and short talk segment, get a pointer (a yardstick or other ruler should do). Stand beside the picture so that you can point to parts of it without turning your back on an imagined audience facing the picture (that is, you would stand with the picture on your right as you face the audience, if you're right-handed).

Then give the talk segment as you point out salient parts of the landscape. Be sure to keep facing your assumed audience and maintaining eye contact with the twenty imaginary people in your audience. Give only an occasional glance at the landscape to check where you're pointing.

As an example, your talk segment might go: "Here, at Smith's Bend in the river [point], we would build the main dock from which two million passengers a year would board our excursion boats. Each boat ride would head first for the scenic wonders upriver [point along the river]. Interstate Highway 62 dips down near Smith's Bend right here [point], and from this spot we would run our access road down to the main dock [point]. Beside the dock, in this beautiful site on Smith's Bend, we would build and operate our resort motel [point] with indoor and outdoor pools, tennis courts, and a health spa. Cottages for year-round vacation rentals would be nestled privately in the countryside nearby along here [point]. . . ."

Once you've become adept through practice, you might want to have a friend or family member listen to you while you give the presentation, point effectively to the visual aid, and maintain actual eye contact.

2. Flip chart technique. For this activity, get several large sheets of wrapping paper or drawing paper, and two different-color broad-tipped marking pens that don't soak through the paper. With transparent tape, fasten the tops of the sheets near

the top of your kitchen refrigerator, on the front or side. Tape the sheets so that you can flip them up onto the refrigerator top.

Next, go back to your business development project of the first activity. Plan a summary segment to come later in the same talk, to cover total income, costs, and profits, and to cite business advantages. Make the figures attractive. Decide which label terms and financial figures you would present in giving this summary segment with a flip chart. Write those terms and numbers down on cards you can hold inconspicuously in your hand.

Then, stand beside the flip-chart sheets fastened to the refrigerator. Give the summary talk segment as you've planned it. However, when you come to a term and dollar amount you want to show for your assumed listeners, write it on a flip-chart sheet (from the note card in your palm, if you need the reminder).

This talk segment of yours might run, for example: "As a business venture, Smith's Bend Excursion Boat Line looks highly profitable. With two million boat passengers annually paying an average of five dollars a head, gross income would total ten million dollars." (Write on first sheet as you are talking, and glancing only occasionally at the sheet and away from your assumed audience: TOTAL INCOME: $10,000,000.) "And remember, that's a very conservative figure. Total gross income a year could run easily twice that ten million dollars." (Flip the first sheet back.) "Now, as we have seen, our total operating and capital costs for the year come to only some six and a half million dollars." (Write on second sheet, while talking: TOTAL COSTS: $6,500,000.) "Once again, that's figured conservatively. Total costs could run much lower, as low as five million dollars a year." (Flip sheet back.) "However, let's stick to the conservatively figured amounts. When we do, we get a remarkable gross annual profit." (Write on third sheet, while also talking: "GROSS PROFIT FIRST YEAR: $3,500,000. Underline it with your second-color pen.) "Our minimum gross profit on the Boat Line, as you see, would be three and a half million dollars. These days, that's very handsome indeed. . . ."

Again, once you have gotten skilled at this by practice, you could have someone listen to your presentation as a member of your audience.

CHAPTER 13

Humor and Jokes: Handling These Vital Ingredients in Your Talks

"Man was made at the end of the week, when God was tired."—Mark Twain

• • •

General George C. Marshall went to President Roosevelt with plans to strengthen the ground forces of the Army. Every time the general made a point, however, he met with much resistance from the President, whose sympathies lay with the Navy.

Finally, Marshall said, "At least, Mr. President, you can stop referring to the Navy as 'us' and the Army as 'them.'"

• • •

"Remember," said the teacher to the class, "you can't always be first. Even great men come in second sometimes."

A wiseacre in the back row piped up. "But what about George Washington? He was the first President and the first commander of the Continental Army. That made him first in war, first in peace, and first in the hearts of his countrymen."

"True," the teacher answered, "but don't forget—he married a widow."

• • •

A few weeks after the death of a prominent composer, an ill-informed man asked W. S. Gilbert, of Gilbert and Sullivan, if he knew what the *maestro* was doing with his time.

Gilbert answered with a straight face, "He is doing nothing."

"Surely he is composing," said the other man.

"On the contrary, he is decomposing," said Gilbert.

• • •

"Insanity is hereditary. You can get it from your children."—Sam Levinson.

• • •

Business is like sex. When it's good it's very, very good, and when it's bad it's still pretty good.

• • •

"A conservative is a statesman who is enamored of existing evils, as distinguished from the liberal who wishes to replace them with others."
—Ambrose Bierce.

Why You Should Use Humor in Your Speeches

There are many good reasons for incorporating humor in your speeches—mainly, to capture attention, to win the sympathy of your audience (dispelling your own nervousness in the process), and to make your argument clinching and memorable.

A well-told joke, anecdote, or quip will enliven and enrich

any talk, even a very serious address. After all, it is the mark of exceptional people to be able to see humor even under adverse conditions. We remember and admire great men for their *wit* as well as their *wisdom*.

But Please Use Humor Judiciously

Humor, like any other speech tool, should be used judiciously. And some people shouldn't try to use it at all.

Professional speechwriters are very clear on this point. "Humor must come naturally to the speaker," says Jan Van Meter, a writer for a large New York public relations agency who has written speeches for some of the most prominent men in corporate life. "If an executive can't tell a joke to his friends, he'll never get away with it in public."

As anyone who has suffered from stage fright can attest, it doesn't get any easier to be yourself when you step in front of an audience.

Even if your timing on jokes is inept, however, and you think a punch line is something you stand in to get a drink at a party, take heart.

There is more to humor than just telling jokes. In fact, some of the wittiest speakers don't tell jokes at all; instead they master the art of the incisive anecdote, a funny story that sheds light on the subject.

The big difference is that with a joke you are looking for laughs, and if you don't get them, you may throw your whole speech out of kilter. The anecdote is intended to evoke not laughter but, rather, a knowing grin. Laughter is a bonus.

A speech is not a nightclub performance. You don't want them rolling in the aisles. The minute you start telling jokes that are "hah-hah funny" you are in danger of losing your audience.

At worst, your joke will be received with silence, or groans, or "I don't get it." Such a reaction will cause you to lose confidence and falter.

The best way to cope with this kind of disaster is to chime in quickly with a throwaway line like "If I lay another egg like that, I'll make a soufflé," and move on. Or just move on.

Don't let your disappointment at not setting the world afire throw you.

If you do set them roaring with laughter, you are also in trouble. For while you are trying to shift to the more serious business of your talk, some people in the audience will maintain their taste for merriment and start telling jokes among themselves. You have, in effect, challenged them to top you.

Furthermore, performing is intoxicating. That's one of the reasons why comedians and actors put up with the stress of life on the road. They live for laughs and applause. You may find you like the laughter so much that the rest of your speech is an anticlimax. When you become bored, the audience will also become bored. Pace yourself. One funny remark every five minutes is more than enough.

Aim for Chuckles Rather than Guffaws

With anecdotes, quips, and funny definitions, however, the risks of failure can be minimized. Instead of laughter, you expect a nod and a smile.

An anecdote can be much more easily adapted to amplify the point you want to make. And that is, after all, the most important reason to use humor in the first place. Every joke must be relevant to some larger point.

You are not a comedian.

Starting with Humor Puts Everyone at Ease

You have greater latitude for being funny at the start of your speech than you do in the body. If you are going to play for a big laugh, do it then and forever hold your peace.

One of the best reasons to use a joke at the outset is to put both you and your listeners at ease. You can win them over with a good joke, but again, don't make it too good.

Many speakers try to defuse their nervousness by making a joke at their own expense. This is called self-deprecating humor. Here again, many professional speechwriters sound a warning.

Use a self-deprecating joke only if you are secure enough so that it doesn't sound as though you are demeaning yourself. If you demean yourself, your audience will lose respect for you at the outset, which is the worst thing that can happen.

Here's an example of a self-deprecating joke that strikes a safe balance. (Like any joke, you can easily adapt it to your own purposes.)

> "I had the pleasure of meeting our hostess, Miss McGillicuddy, just before the proceedings began. She asked me what I was doing here.
> "I'm here to address the company."
> "Do this often?" she asked.
> "Fairly often."
> "Nervous?"
> "No. Why?"
> "Then what are you doing in the ladies' room?"

Being Unoriginal Is Not a Sin

Don't worry that your jokes are old. Just make certain that they sound fresh when you tell them.

Even old, corny jokes, known to everyone in your audience, can be effective if told with imagination. It is always more important to be in control of the joke and its meaning than it is to be original.

Don't be afraid to use material you've heard before. Even if your remarks are recorded for the future, no one is going to care much. And old jokes that stand the test of time are often better than untried new jokes.

Professional comedians are constantly raiding the past for jokes and updating them. They even steal from their contemporaries. One top TV actor, Robin Williams, was barred from Los Angeles nightclubs a few years ago because younger, less prominent comics often saw their new routines incorporated into the TV shows of their famous colleague.

There are dozens of useful books. As one writer put it, if you steal one story, it's plagarism, but if you steal a hundred, it's research. (See the list at the end of this chapter.)

And don't hesitate to use television humor.

Try to repeat a joke just as it was told by Johnny Carson or Bob Hope—right down to the last pause. Those pauses help build dramatic effect. You might think of a throwaway line as a one-act play, and of longer jokes as plays having two or three acts, each with a specific function.

There is an innocence to any good humorist's delivery. A good humorist is discovering the material with you instead of letting you in on a secret.

Instead of saying, "Did you hear the one about . . . ?" experts will say, "Did you hear about . . . ?" or "What do you think of . . . ?" as if it were any ordinary story. Their faces are childlike, not cynical or laughing in advance of the punch line. Smiling, perhaps, but always in control.

Let the Subject Guide You

How do you choose where to use a joke or an anecdote? Part of it is inherent in the nature of humor and what a chuckle can do for your listeners. You want to kindle or rekindle interest; you want emphasis; you want vivid illustration—all in the context of the subject.

To make the proper choice, let the subject guide you. One very effective way to add humor to the body of any speech is to take a key word or point and draw attention to it with a funny definition or anecdote. You can make these up yourself or consult one of the many books on the subject that provide ready-made material alphabetically by subject.

For instance, if you thought that a group you belonged to was making a crucial mistake in policy despite evidence favoring another course, you might add a line like this:

As Winston Churchill put it, "Man will occasionally stumble over the truth, but most of the time he will pick himself up and continue on."

How does a professional speechwriter come up with original humor?

Let's follow the progress of one young pro in the development of a humorous and engaging introduction to a speech.

The assignment was to write a twenty-minute speech for a Dutch trade official who was trying to encourage Americans to invest in his country. In addition, the speech had to have a statesmanlike air, since it was going to be given before a public forum, and the hard-sell approach that characterized the official's usual speeches was inappropriate. (Such intricate instructions are quite common for speechwriters.) The audience was a conservative group in a Western state of the U.S.

"In my reading," said the speechwriter, "I came across the fact that Holland had made the first loan ever to the United States Congress back in the eighteenth century and that Dutch banks held the entire external debt of the U.S. Government for many years afterward.

"Currently," continued the speechwriter, "our historic ties with Holland are very strong. Holland is the largest single investing nation in U.S. business. Now, however, we are the largest investors in their economy as well."

How does such information lend itself to humor?

Here's what the speechwriter did with the information:

It gives me great pleasure to represent one half of one of the oldest and most productive business alliances in the world, that between the United States and Holland. In 1782, three Amsterdam banks made the first loan ever to the United States Congress. Twelve years later, Holland held the entire foreign debt of your country— thirty million guilders.

Today we live in a much more complex world and our business relationship is not so one-sided. You are the largest foreign investors in our economy and we are the largest foreign investors in yours.

I have been in the United States on and off for the last ten years, until quite recently employed exclusively

in private enterprise. That is long enough to have
learned that in the United States when a boy and girl
each pay their own way on a date, it is known as a
"Dutch treat." I think that it is only fitting that in the
two hundred years in which we have been doing business we have come to a similar arrangement. I propose
that as our romance goes on we each continue to pick
up our own checks."

Not only was this an amusing twist on an institution that
Americans could appreciate—the Dutch treat— but it incorporated history and the idea that democratic countries can
participate in one another's economies without political domi-
nation of one by the other.

It was also the kind of joke that could be told by a
non-native English speaker. (You wouldn't expect such a
fellow to have a delivery as good as Johnny Carson's.)

Some Tips on Making up Your Own Humor

What makes something funny?

Wit and humor are most effective when they crystallize or
enhance some truth which the members of an audience already
recognize, but which, perhaps, they have never put into
words.

You cannot usually convert people or inform them in great
depth with humor, but you can increase their awareness of
things they have partially perceived.

For example, if you tell an audience that advertising is
good for business because it lets people know that the
products are available, you will be greeted with a big yawn.
"So what?" they will say. "We know that."

However, by conveying the same idea in a joke, you will
get the message across to a much more receptive audience:

Doing business without advertising is like winking
at a girl in the dark. You know what you're doing
but nobody else does.

Humor is paradoxical. On the one hand, it depends on the familiar. You must gear your humor to your audience as you do every other aspect of speech, including diction and point of view. If the joke involve a play on words, ideas, or situations, the audience must be familiar with these things.

At the same time you depend on familiarity, there must be an element of surprise. The punch line of any joke should be unexpected. You know what a corny joke is—it's one that seems so obvious that you can't possibly laught at it. It breaks no new ground at all but merely replows the sme old cornfield.

If you look back at the beginning of this chapter you will see a variety of jokes, from one-liners to a rather sophisticated literary anecdote. Some of these are old while one is brand-new. Yet all of them maintain a degree of freshness because they contain the dual elements of familiarity and surprise.

Finally, all of them are concise. There is no excess verbiage. There's an old saw: Brevity is the soul of wit.

The fact that this phrase is hackneyed does not detract from its truth. All humor is best told when it is terse. Even a bad joke will be appreciated if it is mercifully brief.

Different jokes are funny for different reasons. Some are bawdy. Other jokes are funny because they are clever plays on words, because they are ridiculous, or absurd. All of them, however, force us to look harder at the subject matter. They are often wise and finely observed portraits of life in miniature.

Here are two brief examples, both from joke styles that were current a few years ago. (It is acceptable, by the way, to use fad jokes when they are current. The standard introduction immediately alerts the audience that what follows will be worth listening to.)

"How many Californians does it take to screw in a light bulb?"

"Ten. One to turn the bulb and nine to share the experience."

This simple joke embodies the popular stereotype of California as a community of single-minded seekers after pleasure disguised as spiritual values. Such a joke could be used to defend as well as to ridicule such behavior.

Anyone who has ever been punished as a child will sympathize with the "Three biggest lies told by parents to their children":

I'm doing this for your own good.
This hurts me more than it hurts you.
I'm doing this because I love you.

Some Tips on Telling Jokes to Crowds

Don't beat a dead horse.
And never explain a punch line.

BE NICE. In the privacy of your own circle of friends you can make any kind of joke. You may poke fun at any group, perhaps, but when you go before an audience, this kind of humor is bound to offend someone. Don't take a chance on hurting their feelings. Once you begin to lose sympathy in this fashion, you will seldom retrieve it.

BE SOBER. This applies to all speechmaking, but particularly where your speech demands something as elusive as timing, the way being funny does. A tipsy person is more likely to laugh at his own punch lines, even before he has given them. The temptation is to drink for relaxation on the theory that a relaxed delivery is more effective. But this is false relaxation. Disarm them with a little self-deprecating humor instead.

One speech expert advises you to drink a little less than the average person in the room unless the speech comes at the end of a two-hour dinner, in which case you should drink a lot less.

BEWARE OF PUNS. Puns have a bad reputation. They have been called the lowest form of humor, and in fact there is nothing more obnoxious than someone who puns incessantly. For every good one, there will be dozens of groaners.

Puns can be sublime, but for public speaking, appreciation of all but the least sophisticated pun will require a very sharp audience. Professioal speechwriters stay away from them. An after-dinner audience or a business audience is usually not attentive enough to laugh at a pun, even a good one.

THE GREAT OUTDOORS. Should you ever have the occasion to speak outdoors, better skip the idea of jokes. Laughter ripples through a hall. The noise echoes off the walls and feeds itself. Outside not only are you subject to more distraction from extraneous noise than inside but you don't have the echo effect you can get indoors.

SARCASM. Sarcasm is derived from a Greek word meaning flesh-rending, teeth-gnashing and speaking bitterly. Like jokes made at the expense of someone in the room, sarcasm reflects badly on a speaker. Stay away from it. It may make you feel clever and powerful but it will drive your listeners into sympathy with the other side of the issue.

LISTENING TO OTHERS. One of the most embarrassing moments in the history of speech humor came at a political event where then-President Ford was scheduled to be the last speaker. The speaker before Ford used a joke and received a good response. When the President rose, he used precisely the same joke. Let this be an object lesson. Listen to others before you go on, lest you duplicate this mistake.

Practice Activities

One of the most useful types of humor for public speaking is the funny definition.

Golf—a good walk spoiled.

England and America—two countries separated by a common language.

City life—millions of people being lonesome together.

Each of these combines the elements of humor—the familiar, the twisting of some element of the familiar, and brevity. These three were written by great writers: Twain, Shaw, and Thoreau. But you can make up your own funny definitions. Study those above and then work on the following words:

Expense account
Presidential election

Try these answers on for size:

Expense account—a device that allows you to eat, drink and be merry after which someone else gets the hangover.

Presidential election—a day on which the bars are closed every four years to punish us for the extra day in February on which they are open.

Here are some more of our favorite definitions:

History—fiction with the truth left out of it.

Inflation—when everyone is so rich no one can afford anything.

Conservative—a liberal with grandchildren.

Liberal—someone who wants to spend conservatives' money.

Zeal—what's left when ability runs out.

Try making up a good introductory joke for yourself to break the ice and establish a bond between you and an audience. Remember that one good line can say more about you than all the biographical material in the host's introduction.

Now turn back to the beginning of the chapter and study the examples of humor with which we opened. Most of these are culled from the pages of standard sources for jokes— magazine articles and anthologies of humor. See if you can figure out ways of working them into the introductions of speeches.

Here are some ideas we had for using these jokes:

It's late in the evening and everybody who's anybody has already had his say. Holding me until the end like this was probably a mistake. I'm tired and I do my worst when I'm tired. I'm not the only one, of course. As Mark Twain pointed out, "Man was made at the end of the week when God was tired."

• • •

Thank you for the kind introduction. Of course, you may not feel so kindly when you begin to listen to what I have to say.

Then again, I've never had a really hostile audience. Now you take General George C. Marshall going to ask President Roosevelt to strengthen the ground forces of the Army. There's a hostile audience. . . . Every time the general made a point, he met with much resistance from the President, who had loved the Navy since childhood and had served as Secretary of the Navy in the old Department of War.

Finally the general said, "At least, Mr. Prsident, you can stop referring to the Navy as 'us' and the Army as 'them.'"

• • •

I hate to have to follow all that's been said up here tonight. Now that you've heard all the important business of the evening, it must be a drag to have to listen to me. If I had my way, I'd just get up, speak my piece, and leave you to get on with your meeting.

It reminds me of a story about a teacher who once told our class, "You can't always be first."

Of course, there's one wiseacre in any crowd. Our class clown said, "But what about George Washington? He was first in war, first in peace, and first in the hearts of his countrymen."

The teacher, to her credit, said, "Yes, but he married a widow."

• • •

Try adapting any of the quips, definitions, anecdotes, or jokes in this chapter, or any you come up with on your own, to situations in which you might have to speak soon.

Keep a clipping file of material you come across in newspapers and magazines (with notes on humor from TV and books). Also write down anything you hear which you feel might be adaptable to your own style of humor.

Such a clipping file will help you develop a repertoire that will be useful in public speaking.

Compiling your own joke anthology will help you cultivate a personal style of humor, but it can also save you money. Joke newsletters for speakers cost about seventy-five dollars per year, yet they often are not very funny. Your clippings could even have intrinsic monetary value. Leopold Fechtner, an immigrant from Austria, has collected almost two million jokes, gags, cartoons, limericks, anecdotes, and books of humor. His collection has been valued by a university library at more than one hundred thousand dollars.

If you run across a new joke that you think will be useful, try it out six or seven times on varities of your friends. If it doesn't work with them, forget it.

Source Books for Humor

The entries in most of the humor source books are classified according to subject in alphabetical order so that you may turn to the entries for the precise point you wish to make. Relevant material can be found in all of them. In some cases you may find the wording a bit difficult, either because they were written many years ago or because you have a verbal style that conflicts. In either case, feel free to adapt the language to fit you.

Bierce, Ambrose. *The Devil's Dictionary*. Many editions in the public domain. The most original and elegant definitions, most of which are contemporary even now.

Fuller, Edmond. *2500 Anecdotes for All Occasions*. New York: Dolphin. A classic, published many years ago. Still useful.

Humes, James C. *Speaker's Treasury of Anecdotes About the Famous*. New York: Harper & Row, 1978. Stories about famous people are good attention getters. They also make you sound quite learned.

Levinson, Leonard L. *Left-Handed Dictionary*. New York: Collier, 1964. Same as below.

Levinson, Leonard L. *Webster's Unafraid Dictionary*. New York: Collier, 1967. Funny definitions gathered from hundreds of sources. Arranged like any dictionary, in alphabetical order.

Prochnow, Herbert V. *The Complete Toastmaster*. New York: Prentice-Hall, 1960.

Prochnow, Herbert V., and Prochnow, Herbert V., Jr. *The Public Speaker's Treasure Chest*. New York: Harper & Row, 1964. Stories of all kinds, anecdotes, sayings, and jokes.

Simmons, Sylvia H. *The New Speakers' Handbook*. New York: The Dial Press, 1972. Pages from the notebooks of an old master speechwriter. Wit and wisdom for every occasion.

Your public library will have books you can use for humor. They are listed in the card catalog under the numbers 808.8 and 808.88 of the Dewey Decimal System.

Every month *Reader's Digest* has a feature that is a good source of jokes and anecdotes.

And remember that public speaking is very much the same as what Sir Ralph Richardson said of acting:

"The art of acting consists in keeping people from coughing."

CHAPTER 14

Effective Speech According to Parliamentary Rules

If you've ever been elected presiding officer of a club or organization—or if you hope to be—you've probably felt the way Erica Walters did when she became president of her school's PTA a few years ago. Excited, of course. And also overwhelmed.

Erica had been going to meetings for years, and she'd even been treasurer before becoming president. She knew the procedures for making motions and voting so well that she sometimes felt as if she could recite Robert's Rules of Order in her sleep. But when it came to sitting in front of the group and calling the meeting to order for the first time, the responsibility of her position suddenly hit home.

She was on the spot.

If people started getting worked up and argument threatened to rage out of control, she was going to have to keep things in order.

If the meeting got bogged down in an endless discussion, she was going to have to get the action moving.

She had to know how to use the rules of parliamentary procedure well enough to make sure everything was done properly, without being so formal that the meetings would become boring. She had to try to lead the group to get things done, without taking sides in any disputes.

For a long moment, Erica wondered how in the world she could ever manage.

She took a deep breath. Rapping her gavel firmly, she declared, "The meeting is called to order." Then she gave the group a smile.

"You all know this is my first meeting as president," she began, "and it's going to take me a while just to get used to sitting up here. In fact, it may take a few meetings before I realize that when you say 'Madame Chairwoman,' you're talking to me." The group laughed. "But," Erica went on, "the most important part of our organization is you, not me. You're the ones who decide what we're going to do and whether we're going to accomplish anything worthwhile this year. My job is just to make sure we have the kind of meetings and the kind of organization that can accomplish those goals you choose. And I promise I'll do that job."

The group applauded. And Erica gave a sigh of relief.

Erica was off to a good start because she understood the most important aspect of running a meeting effectively.

It's not just knowing the rules of parliamentary procedure—though you have to know them.

It isn't even knowing the tactics of how to use the rules to get done what you want to get done—though that's important too.

Most of all, what makes a good leader is a combination of the effective speaking skills we've talked about already in this book plus an understanding of the *meaning* of parliamentary rules.

It may involve persuasive speaking skills, group rapport, tact, common sense, firmness, and fairness. And, in addition, you have to understand the spirit—not just the letter—of Robert's Rules.

Sure, there are rules of parliamentary procedure for just about everything that happens in a meeting, and you can stick blindly to those rules. But unless you're involved in an official government body, such as a city council, your organization probably doesn't follow the procedures formally. What's more important is to realize the purpose of the procedures. Robert's Rules weren't thought up merely for the sake of having rules. They are supposed to be tools for making meetings run smoothly. And they are intended to help the democratic process work—to make sure the group recognizes majority wishes while protecting the rights of the minority and allowing a full discussion.

As presiding officer you are supposed to enforce the rules.

But even more, as leader, you must have the trust of your group.

Erica understood that. In her speech, she reached out and did some things that weren't in the rules. She established rapport with her group. First, she used a little humor to create a bond by admitting that she was new at the job. Then, she showed that she respected the group's rights and responsibilities. Finally, and firmly, she told them her goals as president.

In this chapter, we'll show how you can use effective speech to run meetings effectively.

Though you probably know at least something of Robert's Rules, we'll give you a quick refresher course first. We've also included a chart you can take to your meetings that lists the main rules you need to know about most kinds of actions or questions.

We'll also show you some of the best tactics for using the rules.

And, since you may not always be presiding officer, we'll show you how to be effective as a member of an organization as well.

The Basics: Motions, Debate, and Voting

Most meetings follow an agenda similar to this:

- Call the meeting to order
- Read and approve the minutes of the last meeting
- Reports of standing committees
- Reports of special committees
- Unfinished business
- New business
- Miscellaneous
- Adjournment

To bring a topic up for discussion, one member of the group must make a motion, and another must second it. (The

exceptions are summarized on our chart.) The way to do this
is to ask the chair for permission to speak and then say, "I
move that. . . ."

If you follow the formal parliamentary rules for debating a
motion, members of the audience must always address the
chair, not each other. Every time anyone wants to speak, that
person must first request permission from the chair. Even if
someone just wants to ask another person a question, the way
to do it is to say: "Mr. Chairman (or Madame Chairwoman),
I would like to ask the previous speaker. . . ."

In fact, in the most formal settings, no one even refers to
another person by name. You may have seen sessions of
Congress in which the members talk about "the senior
senator from California" or "my colleague from New York,"
never "Senator So-and-So."

The idea of these formalities is to keep members of the
group from arguing with each other and to emphasize that the
chairperson is in charge. Organizations you belong to will
probably not be that formal. But even if your group is strict,
it's not too hard to follow the rules. Once you get past the key
phrases, you can use your own words.

Otherwise, the main rules of debate are concerned with
giving everyone a fair chance to speak. Generally, the person
who asks for the floor first should be recognized to speak
first. To give everyone a turn, no one can usually speak a
second time on a motion until all the people who want to talk
have spoken once. In addition, Robert's Rules set certain
limits on how long and how many times people can speak.
However, your organization may set its own limits. And the
group can vote at any time to change those limits.

Now, what about a time when someone interrupts debate
with another motion or question?

This, of course, is where Robert's Rules get sticky.

It is just about impossible to memorize all the rules
regarding which motions can be amended, which can be
debated, which have what priority, which can interrupt others,
and all the assorted details that make parliamentary procedure
seem so complex. Even as chairperson, you are not expected
to memorize them. That's what our chart is for.

What you should understand, though, are the general reasons behind the rules.

Main motions are the actual resolutions your group acts on. When Congress approves or votes down a bill, or your city council approves or disapproves a proposed ordinance, or your PTA votes to ask the school board for a crossing guard, the resolutions are in the form of main motions. They are the most important motions an organization considers.

Because they are so important, the group must have the opportunity to debate them fully and amend them. It also means that they must give way to any other type of motion that is brought up. If that doesn't seem to make sense—why should these important motions have lower priority than any other motion?—look at it this way: All the other motions are actually part of the debate on the main motion.

Privileged motions have the highest priority. Basically, they deal with questions of the order of the agenda, adjourning, and emergencies.

Incidental motions are the next priority. They mainly concern rules and procedures, although they can also relate to a main motion.

Finally, there are *subsidiary motions*, which deal directly with the main motion. They are attempts to change, postpone, or vote on the main motion.

There are also a few motions that are called either main or *unclassified motions*. Like main motions, they involve significant actions, such as rescinding a previous vote. So they have the same general priority as main motions.

Some of the orders of priority should make sense to you. You may even be able to memorize those that seem the most reasonable. For instance, a privileged motion that has to do with an emergency should take precedence over just about everything else.

Again, your organization may not be strict about these rules anyway. So don't get too bogged down worrying about them.

At last you're ready for a vote. There are five basic ways you can do it.

The fastest and most anonymous is voice vote—asking

everyone in favor to say "aye," and those opposed, "no." But when the group is closely divided, you may need something you can count more exactly. So you can have people either raise their hands or stand up to show their vote. On particularly controversial issues, you may even want to use a secret ballot or, if your group is small, a roll call. Those two methods, of course, take the most time.

The Chairperson's Role

When you look at all the rules, the chairperson doesn't seem to have a significant job at all.

Sure, no one can speak without your permission. And no vote is official until you repeat it. But you don't really have any choice. You have to call on the person who requests the floor first. You have to repeat the vote. From the looks of things, you're not much more than a figurehead.

What's more, you should not make motions or participate in the group's debate. You're not even supposed to vote, unless your vote would either create or break a tie. You can't do anything that would seem to be taking sides, because the members trust you to be impartial.

However, the chairperson doesn't have to be only a figurehead.

The Speaker of the House of Representatives, for example, is one of the most powerful officials in our government. Similarly, the chairman of the board is usually the most influential person in a corporation. Yet these people operate under parliamentary procedure. So where does their power come from?

Partly from the nature of their organization. As president of your chapter of the League of Women Voters, for instance, you may have the authority to appoint people to committees without asking the other members for approval.

But your effectiveness as chairperson also comes from your own personality, your rapport with your group, and your ability to use the rules. Look at it this way: Your organization elected you as chairperson because the members respect your leadership qualities. The members expect you to be more than a figurehead.

When a Meeting Bogs Down

Early in the 1970s, a city council in California used to find its meetings stretching way beyond midnight every week. One problem was that the nine members were bitterly split, voting five to four on nearly every issue. Moreover, one councilman on the minority side, who knew Robert's Rules to a T, would constantly bring up a whole series of parliamentary points to delay the proceedings. Even though the points were basically meaningless, action had to be taken on them.

For instance the councilman would offer an amendment that he knew would never pass. He'd call for adjournment. Or he'd raise a point of personal privilege to protest that his seat was uncomfortable.

What made the situation worse was that the mayor was new to the job and didn't know how to stop these tactics. But the mayor quickly brushed up on the rules. The next time the councilman tried one of his delaying tactics, the mayor simply declared, "Your motion is out of order."

The councilman promptly appealed the ruling. The mayor called for a show of hands, and his ruling was upheld. The councilman then asked for the floor again and made another motion. Keeping calm, the mayor repeated, "Your motion is out of order." When the councilman tried a third time, the mayor looked at him sternly. "If you keep up these delaying tactics," he said, "I am not going to recognize you. So I would advise you not to request the floor unless you have something solid to contribute."

As chairperson, you have the right and the authority to stop the kind of obstructionism that this city council faced. You can refuse to recognize a speaker, and you can rule that person out of order.

In this case in California, the mayor was effective because he stayed calm and firm. Further, he was also careful to be fair to the councilman. He gave a warning about what he was going to do. Yet he still gave the councilman a chance to bring up serious motions.

Often, though, what will drag your meetings on won't be anything that's done on purpose. Instead the members may simply get caught up in debate without realizing it.

You can't use your position as chairperson to cut off discussion arbitrarily. But you can speed things up. It takes sensitivity to the dynamics of your group.

You have to feel pretty sure that the members have basically exhausted what they want to say and are just repeating themselves. You also have to feel that they've reached consensus.

At that point you can ask if they're ready for a vote. Or, if there's no motion on the floor, you can ask if someone wants to make a motion.

When you do this, don't be pushy. You're trying to prompt the group to move, not tell them what to do. Wait until someone finishes speaking, and ask calmly, "Is the group ready for a vote?" Usually that alone will be enough to make the members stop and think. If not, you can try a little more reasoning: "It's almost ten-thirty, and we still have several more items on the agenda. I'd like to bring this to a vote soon, if you're ready."

If your meetings constantly run long, you might want to change some of the rules. This is the kind of issue you can take a stand on, even as chairperson. You can suggest that the group set limits on the length of speeches. Another idea is to adopt a faster method of voting.

When a Meeting Ends Too Soon

On the other hand, you may face the opposite problem from that of the California city council. Someone may move to adjourn before everything's been voted on. What can you do?

Well, it's part of your job to make sure that no important business is left dangling at adjournment. Even if there's already been a vote to adjourn, the vote isn't official until you announce it. So you should let the group know where things stand.

The best way to handle this situation is simply to start with a statement: "Before we vote on adjourning, I'd like to remind you of a couple of items that are still left on the agenda. . . ."

Then pause, and see if anyone responds on his or her own initiative. If not, you can try some gentle prompting: "Do you want to withdraw the motion to adjourn, so we can discuss these other items before we go?"

You might have to be more forceful if there's something really urgent. Sheila Dale, for instance, realized that her little theater group was about to adjourn without having voted on next season's plays. This was the third time the group had ignored the issue, even though it was on the agenda, and there were only two more meetings scheduled before the summer break. As president of the group, Sheila decided she'd better act now. So she said:

"You know, we've put off choosing next season's plays for over a month now, and it's almost June. If we don't do it soon, it's just going to be too late. We won't have any plays for next year. So what if we just make a decision now? Or at least narrow it down to five or six choices?"

When things get to such a point, don't simply announce the problem. Make a concrete suggestion as to what the group should do. This is what Sheila did, and it worked for her.

When a Meeting Gets Too Fired Up

This can be one of the hardest situations to handle. If a controversial topic is under discussion and the whole group is getting excited, you may have trouble getting people to listen to you. You can try shouting over them, of course, or pounding your gavel. But a much better tactic is what James Coffey did when he was chairing a union meeting:

The union officers were in another room negotiating a new contract with the company management, and many of the union members were getting impatient. In particular, one faction was trying to get the union to set a deadline for a strike. As the meeting grew more heated, James was afraid that the other union members would get caught up in strike fever. But he didn't want a vote yet. He wanted to give the negotiators more time.

What he needed, he decided, was a way to cool everyone down.

As soon as there was a brief lull, he broke in. He had to speak loud to be heard, but he kept his voice calm. "I'd like to call for a half-hour recess," he declared.

The announcement was such a surprise that most people stopped talking to hear why James wanted the recess.

"I expect some news on the negotiations," he went on, "so I'd like to take a recess to go find out what's happening." Then he immediately proposed the action he wanted the group to take: "Would someone offer a motion for a recess?"

Not everyone agreed with him, of course. But the request was so reasonable that most people couldn't argue. The motion for a recess passed.

Naturally many members used the break to rally support for a strike. Others, however, spent the time unwinding, drinking coffee, and chatting about other things—just as James expected. By the time the meeting reconvened, passions had died down. The group finally voted to delay any strike vote.

When You Want to Get a Motion Passed—or Stopped

As we've said, you can't participate in any debates or favor any sides when you're the chairperson. Still, you can use many of the tactics we've just shown to move your organization to vote the way you want.

For example, when debate is running on endlessly, you can prompt the members to vote—if you think they're inclined to vote the way you'd like. If, on the other hand, you fear the decision will go the wrong way, you can suggest a postponement. In both cases point out how late the hour is, how long the discussion has been going on, and how much else is left on the agenda—points that are factual and reasonable. Don't give your position on which way the group should vote.

In the same vein, when you announce the business that is

left over at adjournment, you can either suggest that the group take action now—or say nothing about action.

There's also another kind of tactic you can use when someone makes a motion that is phrased improperly. If you think a change in the wording would help get the motion passed—and you want to see it pass—you can offer a better way to phrase it. That is perfectly within your power as chairperson. But use some diplomacy when you do so. You're making a suggestion, not giving an order. You might say something like: "Did you want to postpone it to a particular time?"

(By the way, you are not allowed to do the opposite—to suggest ways of wording a motion improperly if you want to see it fail.)

Depending on the rules of your organization, you may also be able to bring up topics that aren't on the agenda. Again, you can't urge a vote one way or the other on the topic, but you can explain the issue and the reasons for discussing it. Maybe there's a deadline coming up. Or maybe a lot of people have mentioned it to you. This would come probably under the heading of new business on the agenda.

When You're Not the Chairperson

Obviously, you can join in discussions wholeheartedly when you're not the chairperson. You can use the skills of persuasion—sincerity, knowledge, empathy, and enthusiasm—that we discussed earlier to help your cause. In addition, there are other approaches you can try when you want to get a group to vote your way.

For one thing, you can urge the chairperson to take some of the steps we mentioned earlier. When someone is using the kind of delaying tactics that the California councilman used, for instance, you may raise a point of order. Or, if debate is going on and on, you can call the question, which means to ask for a vote.

Of course, you don't have to be as impartial as the chairperson must be. But you will accomplish more by being fair and reasonable. After all, those are the qualities that the other members respect in the chairperson, and they'll respect those traits in you. Besides, you may want to be the chairperson yourself someday, so why not create the right impression from the start?

A particularly good example of how reasonableness and fairness can be effective is shown in using a motion to postpone when you want to defeat a measure. Here's how it works:

The homeowners' association that Sandra belonged to was planning to spend five hundred dollars on its annual party. Sandra opposed the motion, because she thought the amount was far too high. However, she knew the measure had enough votes to pass. There didn't seem to be any way she could change anyone's mind right away.

Sandra moved to postpone the motion until the group's next meeting.

"This proposal just came on the agenda at the last meeting," she pointed out. "I'd like some more time to think about it. Maybe there's a way we can keep the cost down. There wouldn't be any problem arranging the party if we delayed voting for one more meeting, would there?"

The way Sandra put it, it was hard for anyone to object. Even people who would never vote no outright would agree to postpone. After all, she was only asking for some time to study the issue. She wasn't ending all hope of passing the measure. And she was considerate enough to ask if a delay would cause any problems. In essence, she was appealing to the group's sense of fair play.

Of course, this tactic doesn't completely solve the problem for Sandra or you. You still will have to deal with the question the next time the motion comes up. But it does buy you time to gain support for your thinking.

Practice Activities

Do you think you're ready to chair your next meeting? Here's some preparatory work that will help you. Decide how you would handle the following parliamentary situations. We have provided some suggestions, but don't read them until you have come up with your own ideas.

1. You are chairing a meeting of the board of directors of your condominium owners association. You would like the group to vote to repair the roof of your building and you want to act soon, before the rainy season starts. But the issue is not on the agenda. How can you proceed effectively?
2. Somehow, your club meetings always run late. It's your first session as chairman. How can you speed things up?
3. As a member of the school board, you are annoyed at the way another member is always raising petty issues of parliamentary procedure. The president, however, never seems to do anything to stop this practice. What can you do?

1. You can't actually endorse the idea of repairing the roof. But what you can do is raise the subject—and tell why you're bringing it up. The reasons for raising the topic will actually be the same reasons for supporting a motion to take action—but that's okay, as long as you put it factually, not in a partisan way.

You might say: "I'd like to suggest another topic we ought to consider. As many of us know—those of us who keep buckets in our living rooms to catch the water—the roof leaks in many places. Several people have asked me about repairing it. Since winter is coming, I'd like to talk about it now and reach a decision soon."

Using the touch of humor (the buckets) will help keep your speech from appearing too opinionated; so will your statement that other people have asked you to raise the topic.

2. You'd probably better bring up this problem at the start of the meeting. Suggest some action for the group to take:

"There are a couple of ways we could try to shorten our meetings. Let me mention them, and see if any of you want to make a motion to implement them. First, we could set some rules limiting debate—maybe each person can speak for no more than ten minutes on any motion. Or we can allow no more than an hour for the entire discussion on each motion. In addition to that I'd like to amend our bylaws to allow voice votes. As it stands now, all votes have to be by roll call, and that takes much too long. Would anyone like to move these motions, or do you have other ideas?''

3. For starters study up on Robert's Rules—and bring a copy to your next meeting.

Don't protest the first few motions that the board member makes. Every member has the right to make a reasonable number of motions. But as soon as he starts to repeat himself or raise several frivolous motions in a row, call for a point of order. Keep your voice calm and reasonable. Don't accuse him personally. Just cite the rules and the facts.

Robert's Rules of Order

From highest to lowest priority

TYPE	NEEDS SECOND	MAY BE DEBATED	MAY BE AMENDED	TYPE OF VOTE	MAY INTERRUPT SPEAKER
PRIVILEGED					
Fix time of next meeting	yes	A	yes	majority	no
Adjourn	yes	no	no	majority	no
Take a recess	yes	A	B	majority	no
Question of privilege (comfort of the group, etc.)	no	no	no	C	yes
Call for orders of the day (to keep to the agenda)	no	no	no	no vote	yes
INCIDENTAL (no particular order of priority among themselves)					
Point of order (request to enforce the rules)	no	no	no	C	yes
Appeal ruling of the chair	yes	D	no	majority, E	yes
Parliamentary inquiry (question of parliamentary procedure)	no	no	no	no vote	yes

Robert's Rules of Order

				G	
Withdraw motion (F)	no	no	no		no
Suspend the rules (temporarily change the order of business)	yes	no	no	2/3	no
Object to consideration	no	no	no	2/3	yes
SUBSIDIARY					
Lay on the table (postpone till later)	yes	no	no	majority	no
Previous question (vote on the pending motion)	yes	no	no	2/3	no
Limit debate	yes	no	yes	2/3	no
Postpone to a certain time	yes	yes	yes	majority	no
Refer to committee	yes	yes	yes	majority	no
Amend	yes	H	yes	majority	no
Postpone indefinitely	yes	yes	no	majority	no
MAIN OR UNCLASSIFIED (no particular order of priority among themselves)					
Take up from the table	yes	no	no	majority	no
Reconsider (I)	yes	H	no	majority	yes
Rescind	yes	yes	yes	J	no
MAIN MOTION	yes	yes	yes	majority	no

Notes:

A—This can be debated unless another motion is before the group.

B—Only the length of the recess may be amended.

C—The chair decides, but a majority may overrule.

D—This may be debated unless it relates to a violation of rules or to indecorum, or if the original motion that the ruling was on was undebatable.

E—A tie vote upholds the chair's ruling.

F—Only the person who made the original motion may withdraw it.

G—No vote is needed if no one objects. But if there is an objection, a majority vote is needed.

H—This may be debated only if the original motion was debatable.

I —Only a person who voted on the prevailing side may move to reconsider, and the motion must be made on the same day the original vote was taken or the next day of the same session. These votes may not be reconsidered: adjourn, call for the orders of the day, lay on the table, point of order, question of privilege, recess, refer to committee (if the committee has already taken up the issue), suspend the rules, take from the table. Also, affirmative votes may not be reconsidered on motions to object to consideration, request leave to withdraw a motion, or rescind. A negative vote to postpone indefinitely may not be reconsidered either.

J —A majority vote is enough if notice was given at a previous meeting that this vote would take place. Without such notice, a 2/3 vote is needed.

Even with this chart, we can't mention every rule for every situation. But this should cover most types of motions you run into.

CHAPTER 15
Good Speech When You Run for Election

Campaigning for office has sometimes required silence rather than speeches. For instance, in Russia more than a century ago, candidates vying for the office of chief of a band of Cossacks would gather at a set time and stand before the voters without uttering a sound. Ballots would then be cast by having the voters toss their fur hats at the candidates of their choice. That candidate who was pelted (so to speak) with the largest number of fur hats would be declared the winner.

Historical advance soon brought improvements. In the America of the early twentieth century, Mark Twain observed that he could always tell a political speech was in the offing when local stores would have a much-increased sale of eggs. Obviously, by that time, candidates found speech so essential for winning office that they willingly risked barrages of eggs for the sake of addressing voters.

Whimsy aside, it would be almost impossible for you to run for any kind of office today without having to make at least a few speeches. You would need to give speeches whether you ran for office as head of your school board or PTA, county or town supervisor, city council member, legislator, or president of a college or school club. Of course, the better the speeches you give, the greater your chance of winning.

Basic Factors in Campaign Speaking: Key Message and Image

Most decisive of all factors in your speeches to win elections are the combined key message and key image you convey. By key message, we mean the heart of what you propose to accomplish after you are elected. Key image represents the essence of your character and background as portrayed to the voters. Considering and treating them in combination is important, because voters today don't separate what a candidate will do in office from how they view that candidate as a person. In fact, voters often judge what the candidate might do in office by how they see the candidate's personality. Carelessness with message and image can destroy the effectiveness of all other campaign efforts.

AN EFFECTIVE KEY MESSAGE. Presenting the right message can go far to guarantee success. For instance, in *How to Win Votes; The Politics of 1980,* Edward N. Costikyan points out that one of the most surprising election outcomes of the present era was the adoption of Proposition 13, which provided for drastic cuts in local property taxes—first in California in 1978, and later in other states that adopted similar antitax measures. When Proposition 13 was first raised in California, Costikyan notes, it was viewed as "a crackpot idea that had no chance." But its energetic backing by a political amateur and ordinary citizen, Howard Jarvis, eventually saw it carried by a state-wide margin of almost two-to-one. The governor of California, Jerry Brown, at that point gave the measure his approval and support. Clearly Jarvis had hit upon a dramatically correct key message—and one that will be reinforced by his image as just an ordinary person trying to get along.

Similarly, in the Carter–Reagan TV debate just days before the 1980 Presidential election, Ronald Reagan summed up his approach in what shortly proved to be a devastating key message: "Ask yourself, 'Are you better off than you were four years ago?' '' He also buttressed his key message about a fresh start and optimism in contrast to the frustrations of the prior four years with a wholesome, modest, reassuring personal image. Once, when asked how people view him, he said: "Would you laugh if I told you I think, maybe, they see themselves and that I'm one of them? I've never been able to detach myself or think that I, somehow, am apart from them."

Another version of Reagan's key message of optimism: "I want to put America back on the road to greatness, to establish her as the world's number-one power, to cut government spending, and to strengthen moral values in the family and community."

While election predictions showed that Jimmy Carter and Ronald Reagan would draw almost equal proportions of votes, later analysis revealed why the actual results were not extremely close. It was found that, in the last four days before the election, as many as 20 percent of the registered voters had a major change of mind about whom to vote for or whether to vote. Most of them changed in a way that went against President Carter. These last-minute shifts led to Reagan's victory with 51 percent of the popular vote to Carter's 41 percent.

If possible, sum up your key message with a short, catchy slogan or theme that is often spoken and displayed in your campaign. One used by Reagan, for instance, was "A Time to Come Together." Four years before, Carter had found it effective to run under the rubric "Time for a Change." A slogan that hinged entirely on a winning image was the one used for President Eisenhower's campaigns that used his nickname, "I like Ike." Strong, simple slogans you might use in campaigning for local office might include these:

"Back to Basics—No-Frills Education!" (for possible use in running for the school board or a PTA post); and

"More for Minorities!" (which could apply to a campaign for any kind of civic-group or governmental office).

An Effective Key Image in Running for Election

The key image you present when running for election crystallizes the reaction of voters to you. Positive characteristics of the image you convey by the manner in which you give a speech are: intelligence, integrity, understanding of issues and ideas, ability to think clearly and reach the right decisions, and credibility.

Don't hesitate to invite people to look up to you for values, ethical standards, and a sense of direction. You can surely recall former Presidents, Vice-Presidents, cabinet officers, and other high officials who would be unable to ask people to look up to them today. They contrast with "Honest Abe" Lincoln, who invited the voters, "With malice toward none, with charity for all, with firmness in the right as God gives us to see the right, let us finish the work we are in. . . ."

Ronald Reagan in 1980 worked hard to create an image of an American dedicated to traditional values of family and church, as we have noted. Candidate John Anderson, in the same election, hammered at the theme of independence, another traditional American value. Ronald Reagan in 1982 urged voters to "Stay the Course."

Don't indulge in character assassination, vendetta, or sarcasm. Refrain from an observation like, "If only my opponent realized how badly informed he sounds. . . ." It would highlight your ungenerous trait of ridiculing more than your opponent's ignorance, and would tarnish your image rather than elevate it.

Adlai Stevenson had the right idea in 1952 (even though he did not win the election) when as Presidential candidate on the Democratic ticket, he declared: "I hope that we Democrats, win or lose, can campaign not as a crusade to exterminate the opposing party, but as a great opportunity to educate and elevate a people whose destiny is leadership."

Any relevant experience you've had should surely be emphasized in your key image. Point it out even in brief remarks you're asked to make, and in handbills about your candidacy. Mention it in your talks. In running for school board, as an example, you might say something like this: "A remedial reading program is now working very well in our elementary grades. Everyone agrees that it does. As chairman of the citizens committee on improvement in the schools two years ago, I worked hard to have this program developed and adopted."

A candidate for a suburban town council might say: "As secretary of the Zoning Board of Appeals, I have become thoroughly familiar with the entire question of town development, a vital matter for our community. As far as I am able to tell, no other candidate has anything like this background for guiding our community to higher income while preserving its character as a fine place to live."

Endorsements can certainly contribute to your image. Consider seeking endorsements from prominent individuals whose reputation can enhance your own. Many familiar instances on the national scene illustrate how this can work. Some years ago, Harry S Truman endorsed Adlai Stevenson, and Dwight Eisenhower endorsed Richard Nixon. More recently, Ted Kennedy gave his endorsement to Jimmy Carter, while Gerald Ford endorsed Ronald Reagan.

Essentials of Good Speech in Campaigns

Elements of your key message and key image in running for office have been treated first because they can prove decisive. But the impact of these vital elements can be increased substantially by effectively handling additional factors of good speech in your election campaigns. Let us look at these additional factors now.

Your Basic Speech and Its Major Parts

Candidates for even the highest offices usually have a basic speech that they give on most occasions, being careful to modify it as appropriate and to give a different speech when really necessary. Giving much the same basic speech repeatedly can have distinct advantages. It enables you to present what you've found to be the strongest appeals of your position time and again. It also lets you use repeatedly what you've found to be the most effective techniques for delivery of these ringing phrases

A basic campaign speech of yours should be developed in the ways we recommended for any effective speech in earlier chapters. In addition, you might add the following features or emphases, which are particularly effective in campaign speeches. These are presented for each of the three main parts of any good speech—beginning, middle, and end.

BEGINNING. Follow what is nearly universal political wisdom by opening your basic speech with a statement that's as convincing and sincere as you can make it. This passage should always have the aim of identifying you with the specific people you're addressing. Give an emotional sense of the most impressive things you have in common with them. But be sure also to thank their leaders and your host courteously and by name (by nickname, if appropriate).

Then state your key message and image in an arresting and lively way. For example, Calvin Coolidge won election as President of the United States back in the business boom of the 1920s by running as a traditional Republican leader. Sounding a conservative keynote in starting his addresses, he would often say, "I am for economy. After that, I am for more economy."

As another example, a candidate for the school board could remark in beginning a basic speech: "My platform calls for a new kind of three R's in our school. I back not just the old-fashioned three R's of reading, writing, and 'rithmetic, but three more. My three new R's call for reform, restoration, and renewal. I call for *reform* of excess spending in administration. I call for *restoration* of in-service training to help develop our teachers. And I call for *renewal* of recognition for serious scholastic achievement by our children."

Follow promptly by highlighting your key image, summing up your qualification for office. As an illustration, a candidate for the state legislature might say in a basic speech: "I have proven experience in knowing how to benefit our community in practical ways. You probably know my record as village supervisor. You probably know what my record as supervisor includes. It includes completion of our new recreation center. It includes increased sanitation services. It includes introduction of our monthly Grievance Night office hours at the Village Hall.''

MIDDLE. In the longer, middle part of your basic speech, take special care to be as convincing and interesting as you can. This is the part of your address in which you make your main points, summarizing your entire platform as a candidate. It is here that you will want to dramatize the problems that need to be solved. You will want to portray the solutions you propose, in ways that are both exciting and convincing. You'll show the feasibility of your proposals, possibly because they have succeeded in other instances you briefly document. If figures are needed to prove a point, you'll give the most vivid, conclusive data you have. People cannot follow detailed statistical information. In all ways, you'll make this middle heart of your speech hard-hitting, full, well reasoned, lively, and vigorous.

END. As you go into the end of your speech, rise to a climax of intensity. Here you sum up your strongest ammunition. Use your central theme or slogan as almost the very last thing you say, so that it can be remembered. Possibly the ideal example of this is the famous ending of Patrick Henry's address: ''. . . but as for me, give me liberty or give me death!'' Your conclusion probably won't be as epochal as this. But in its own way it can be moving and memorable. Then, smoothly and swiftly, ask for the votes and the support of your listeners, and thank them for their kind attention.

Proceeding in these ways should arm you with a good basic speech for campaigning. And if you are open-minded and have occasion to give it several times, then you will surely discover more ways to make it even better. Some of these ways will be your own ideas. Others will suggest themselves when you see the ways in which your audiences react.

Effective Language for Your Campaign Speeches

CONCRETE AND SPECIFIC WORDING. For effective language in campaign speeches, it's especially important for you to try to use wording that is specific and concrete. Avoid euphemisms, for instance. Don't use "disadvantaged"; say "poor." Again, don't say "terminated" when you mean "fired." Don't say "a real challenge" for what's actually "a tough problem."

Applying concrete terms will help you guard against vagueness. You won't say, "We badly need town improvements." Instead, you'll declare: "We need storm drains to end the flooding on Grand Street. We must have a stoplight on Main at Market. And the Community Center needs to be enlarged by one third because it's terribly overcrowded."

Being concrete in your wording will lead you to use words that show organized thinking, such as "for example," "in consequence," "as shown by," and "therefore."

KEEP PHRASING SIMPLE AND DIRECT. Keep your phrasing as well as your wording simple and direct. Don't make the mistake of talking over the heads of your audience. This was sometimes done back in the 1950s by that otherwise widely admired Presidential candidate. Adlai Stevenson. In one of his campaign speeches, for example, he said: "The victory to be won mocks the pretensions of individual acumen. Victory is a citadel guarded by the walls of ignorance, which do not fall before the politicians' imprecations."

Governor Stevenson might better have stated this more simply and directly as follows: "Winning the Presidency challenges our best efforts. We cannot win merely by catchwords and slogans. We can and will win the election by overcoming the ignorance of many voters."

You can often make your sentences more simple and direct by casting them in the grammatical form of the active voice instead of the passive voice. For example, it sounds fuzzy to say, "It is considered essential for the teenagers in the ghetto to be visited." You could have more impact on your audiences if you said instead, in the active voice: "I shall visit our ghettos and talk with teenagers."

Use humor that's in good taste when it seems right to do so. A witty remark or joke can relax and enliven your listeners. For instance, a candidate who has seriously criticized the costs and delays of excessive bureaucracy in government agencies might strike a lively, lighter note by saying something like this: "Bureaucratic growth has gone so far that it's even created what I call the 'five-A' position. That's a job for which citizens now are paying. The job title for it is: Administrative Assistant to the Assistant Administrator of Administration. Let's find out what that employee does—if anything."

Often, grouping ideas or phrases in threes proves rhetorically impressive. For instance, in one of his most widely remembered addresses of the Depression years of the 1930s, President Franklin D. Roosevelt stated: "One third of this nation is *ill-housed, ill-clothed, ill-fed*." And the famous oration by Marc Antony in Shakespeare's *Julius Caesar* begins, "*Friends, Romans, countrymen*, lend me your ears."

To the extent that you can, you might subtly vary your diction and word choice to fit different audiences you may be addressing—among them, perhaps, miners, factory workers, or college professors. Be careful in using slang. You might use it in talking to audiences for whom it sounds completely natural. Even then, though, draw on slang with restraint. Careless use of slang before an audience can seem crude and condescending to the audience.

PHRASE YOUR APPEALS TO IDENTIFY WITH YOUR AUDIENCE.

We've already observed how important it is to identify yourself as closely as possible with your audience right at the start of your basic campaign speeches. Later in your speech, try to phrase your appeals so that they strongly sound this same note of identification with your listeners.

Observations of heartfelt humility can strike such a note of identification. For instance, Abraham Lincoln won the devoted support of the common people with such statements as, "God must have loved poor people, because he made so many of them."

Inspirational appeals often express strong audience identification. This was the case with a 1960 speech by John F. Kennedy, when he said: "My call is to the young in heart, regardless of age—to the stout in spirit, regardless of party." On another occasion, he similarly called for idealistic participation in his Administration by saying: "Now the trumpet sounds again . . . to struggle against the common enemies of man: tyranny, poverty, disease, and war. . . . Will you join me in that historic effort? . . . Ask not what your country can do for you, but what you can do for your country."

A few decades earlier, Franklin D. Roosevelt had similarly appealed to a sense of identification by saying: "Let all here assembled consider ourselves prophets of a new order of competence and courage. Let us go forward together."

You should find it easy and natural to identify yourself with your audiences as a candidate for local office. In running for school board, you might say: "Your children as well as mine will benefit from our recent windfall in tax income by getting better textbooks and more after-school activities." A city-council candidate could emphasize, "Inflation is destroying our hard-earned savings, as you and I know from our own personal experience. Elect me and I'll carry out your mandate to lighten the load of our tax burden."

Adapt Your Basic Speech to Your Audiences

Adapt not only the language but the things emphasized in your basic speech to each audience you address. Get or analyze background information about an audience in advance. Take into account their ages, their education, their attitudes and values. Consider how well-informed or ill-informed they may be on the issues you will discuss. Prepare to adjust to whether they're mainly people with business backgrounds, students, social-service professionals, senior citizens, or a group otherwise likely to share distinctive interests.

Your basic speech would have elements of appeal for all such diverse groups to whom you'll be speaking. In adapting for different audiences, you would naturally stress those elements most attractive to each group. For business people, as an example, you would emphasize actions you propose in order to realize sound fiscal management. Or, before senior citizens, you might stress measures you back for lowering their costs and increasing community services for them.

In a New York city campaign, to illustrate further, former State Attorney General Louis J. Lefkowitz stressed different issues before different audiences. At one opening campaign rally, he declared: "The basic issue of this campaign is one-party rule and the corruption and incompetence that go with it." To another audience, he stated: "The real issue is whether the city is to become solvent or go broke."

Handling Other Important Assets: Your Knowledge, Your Strength of Character

KNOW THE ISSUES. Knowing the issues and their background will prove valuable assets when building and running your campaign. Samuel Johnson once remarked, "Knowledge is of two kinds. We know a subject ourselves, or we know where we can find information about it." Knowledge of the first kind is preferable when you run for election. When you're conversing or holding question-and-answer sessions after an address, it's better for you to know the answers and the facts at first hand than to admit you'll have to go find out.

Senator William Fulbright illustrated this when running for reelection in the 1960s. "In the Cuban missile crisis last October," he said, "the United States proved to the Soviet Union that a policy of aggression involved unacceptable risks." And he went on to give enough key facts to be completely convincing.

In a local election, you might show your close knowledge of the situation in running for school board by saying something like this: "Parents and teachers of our high school youngsters are profoundly disturbed over the increasing vandalism in the cafeteria. Few connect this to an apparent major cause that I would correct if elected: that vandalism began three months ago, when physical education and sports activities were sharply cut back. We must reverse this trend. Sports programs will benefit all of us.''

Get and keep informed by wide reading and conversation. Broaden your perspective by listening to people with all points of view. Incorporate the best of what you learn into your own platform and speeches. Once other people know you're interested in their ideas and discoveries, they'll go out of their way to feed you information. Learn and continue to learn as actively as possible. It will pay off on election day.

SHOW STRONG CHARACTER BY HOLDING TO YOUR POSITION. Once you've identified your general stand before the voting public, show strength of character by holding to your position even if unexpected events can be seen as undercutting your views. It's all right to show reasonable flexibility, but not basic reversal. Changing your stand completely won't work. It will annoy the voters.

In 1948, President Harry S Truman held to his view of the office despite dwindling popular support. He persisted in holding his ground: "The President is responsible for the administration of his office. And that means for the administration of the entire executive branch. It is not the business of Congress to run the agencies of government for the President.

"Unless this principle is observed, it is impossible to have orderly government. The legislative power will ooze into the executive offices and influence and corrupt the decisions of the executive branch. It will warp and twist policies. . . . It is the duty of the President to say firmly and flatly, 'No, you can't do it,' . . . if I may be so bold as to say that.''

Truman kept on saying it and finally won the election in a last-minute upset.

Not only in this but in all other ways, convey strength of character to your public when you run for election. Showing the kind of character that people respect probably counts as much as any other one element in your campaign when you run for election.

Your chances for victory are better now than they were before you read this chapter. And if you don't succeed, it's not doomsday; you can try and try again. There are many winners in many offices who were not winners the first time.

Honest Abe Lincoln of Illinois said of losers: "Be like the child who stubbed his toe badly and said he was too old to cry, but it hurt too much to laugh."

Adlai Stevenson, also of Illinois, after his 1952 defeat, consoled himself with: "I have great faith in the American people. As to their wisdom—well, Coca-Cola still outsells champagne." (In 1956, again a loser, Stevenson quoted Abe Lincoln: ". . . too old to cry. . . .")

And if you win, temper your success by giving some thought to the good and modest speech of Woodrow Wilson after his election victory in 1916, when he said: "I'll watch myself carefully during my term of office to see whether I'm growing . . . or swelling."

Practice Activities

You're familiar now with the diverse elements involved in speaking well when you run for election. Here are some practice activities on which you might want to sharpen your skills before confronting the real thing. Try these situations, using what's been said in this chapter for guidance.

1. OUTLINE A VOLUNTEER SERVICES TALK.

You're running for the office of director of volunteer services in your local hospital. Plan a ten-minute talk to the association of hospital volunteers telling them why they should vote for you. Use the outline: beginning, middle, and end.

I. *Beginning*

I have worked as a volunteer in Alderidge Community Hospital for two years, and am asking for your support now in running for Director of Volunteer Operations.

II. *Middle*

My program calls for increasing patient services by adding:

       (a) Bedside hair-dressing and barber services.
       (b) Bedside distribution of books and magazines.
       (c) Baby-sitting services for visitors' children.

III. *End*

I ask you to vote for me because I'm experienced in working with patients, and want to improve hospital services by introducing additional patient services to increase patients' overall comfort at little expense to the hospital.

2. PHRASE YOUR REPLY TO A SERIOUS CHARGE.

In a political race, your opponent calls you an "unthinking reactionary with one foot in the last century." Reply to this statement and show how you'd overcome this type of personal attack.

Does your answer sound rational? Cool and well thought out? Have you used words like "reasoned," "carefully evaluated," "documentation"? Undoubtedly you'll come across with intelligence and thoughtfulness in contrast to your opponent's name-calling. You've earned points for image.

CHAPTER 16

Debate—Great Sport for Renowned Speakers of Tomorrow

Can you say what Lyndon Johnson, Richard Nixon, Hubert Humphrey, Jane Pauley, and Laurence H. Tribe have in common?

Johnson and Nixon were once Presidents of the United States; Johnson, Humphrey, and Nixon were Vice-Presidents. Pauley has been a correspondent on the *Today* show on TV. Tribe is a professor at Harvard Law School and the foremost expert on constitutional law in the country. But all five share an important trait:

They all participated in organized debate either in high school or college.

Interschool debate can be one of the best ways to develop your speaking skills. More than that, it can help you become aware of world events, learn how to research and organize your thoughts, and feel at ease in speaking before an audience. It can lead to success, not only in your schoolwork but throughout your life.

Does that sound too good to be true?

Well, consider the story of Judy, a friend of one of the authors. Judy describes herself in the days before she started debating in high school back in 1966 as "so shy that I couldn't even call up a movie theater to find out what time the show started." But by the end of the school year Judy was winning speech tournaments throughout Los Angeles. She went on to become a newspaper reporter and magazine writer—interviewing all kinds of people from politicians to sports stars to corporate executives.

Jane Pauley has said that her high school debating experience increased her self-confidence. In an interview in the March 1979 issue of *Mademoiselle* magazine, she recalled: "[My older sister was] impressive from babyhood. My being good in debates was the first thing we both did that I did better than she."

And Professor Tribe of Harvard says: "Without debate, I wouldn't have had any sense of the range of social and political issues open to me in terms of a career. I certainly wouldn't be a law professor but for debate. It also gave me a great deal of confidence, and taught me how to organize and research."

Do you want more proof? A study of *Who's Who in America* showed that people who had debated were five times as likely to be listed as were other college graduates, according to the book *How to Debate* by Harrison Boyd Summers, Forest Livings Whan, and Thomas Andrew Rousse.

In other words, participating in interschool debate can be a major first step on your road to success.

And in this chapter, we'll show you how to take that step. First, we'll tell you briefly how organized debate works. Then we'll give you valuable tips for preparing your debate case and presenting it effectively.

The Rules of the Game

The most basic way to define a debate is perhaps as a discussion in which two people or two teams take opposing sides of an issue and try to persuade their listeners to support one side or the other.

In fact, you've probably heard the word "debate" used to describe all sorts of situations—from arguments between friends to the television debates in recent Presidential elections. But what we're talking about in this chapter is more specific. If you participate in organized debate through your school, you'll be speaking in an established situation that follows a formal set of procedures.

The rules we'll discuss in this chapter are those of the National Forensic League, because it is one of the leading groups for student debaters in the U.S. At times you may find yourself in non-NFL debates, where some of the rules on time limits or order of speaking, for instance, don't apply. Still, the basic techniques and advice we'll be discussing will help you win an audience to your point of view no matter what the conditions of the debate.

Of course, in this short chapter we can't give you all the rules that could possibly apply even just to an NFL debate. We've summarized the most important rules in the following two charts (current as this is written).

Basic Rules of Debate

1. The question under debate is stated in the form of a resolution: "Resolved, that..."
2. The *affirmative* team is the one in favor of the resolution, and the *negative* team opposes it.
3. Each team has two speakers, and each person speaks twice. In addition, every person cross-examines a member of the other team once.
4. The first four speeches are the *constructive* speeches, where the teams concentrate on introducing their cases. Each is followed by a *cross-examination*. In the next four speeches, the *rebuttals*, the emphasis is on knocking down the opposing case. No new points may be brought up in the rebuttals.
5. Each constructive speech is eight minutes, each cross-examination is three minutes, and each rebuttal is four minutes.
6. The affirmative carries the burden of proof for the resolution. But both sides must prove their cases and back up what they say.
7. The affirmative must have a plan for improving the way things are now and carrying out the resolution.

Order of Speaking in Debate

1st affirmative constructive
cross-examination by either negative

1st negative constructive
cross-examination by either affirmative
2d affirmative constructive
cross-examination by the other negative
2d negative constructive
cross-examination by the other affirmative
(break period)
1st negative rebuttal
1st affirmative rebuttal
2d negative rebuttal
2d affirmative rebuttal

If you want more information—on debate or on other types of public-speaking contests—the NFL is a good organization to write to. Its address is 114 Watson, Ripon, Wisconsin 54971.

Do you start to feel as though debate is nothing but a long series of rules? It really isn't. All these lists will soon become second nature to you.

And beyond the specific step-by-step rules, there really are only two main ideas you need to remember:

- Make sure your reasoning is sound, logical, and doesn't leave any holes.
- Make sure you have evidence to back up everything you say.

There's one more general piece of advice. You may find this one hard to believe:

- Ninety percent of a debate is taken up in preparation and planning.

Sure, debate requires thinking on the spot. Most of your speeches can't be written out in advance. You can't know exactly what the other team members will say or just how they will attack what you say.

But you can be prepared. If you've organized a strong case, thought carefully about all the arguments the other side could possibly raise, and gathered enough evidence to support your points, you can be ready to handle anything that comes up during the actual debate.

Know What Your Words Mean

Before you can start to talk with anybody, you and your opponents must mean the same things when you use the same words. In debate, the first affirmative constructive speaker defines the important terms of the resolution at the beginning of the speech. The first negative then accepts or rejects the definition.

It sounds pretty simple, and it can be a key to the whole debate.

Judy, the author's friend we mentioned, remembers watching one unusual debate on whether the U.S. should increase foreign aid. She was startled when the affirmative team defined foreign aid as including weapons. Usually, foreign aid is carefully separated from military assistance. But what amazed Judy even more was that the negative team simply accepted the definition. Without realizing it, that team had just destroyed a major part of its own case.

Later, a negative speaker tried to claim that the affirmative's plan wouldn't work because foreign aid needs to be backed up with weapons. The affirmative promptly shot down that argument by pointing out that weapons were included in its definition—which the negative team had accepted.

Actually, both teams were at fault in that debate. If you're the affirmative, you should stick with the most generally accepted definitions. Don't try to win your case by twisting the meaning of the resolution. If you're the negative, you can't assume that the affirmative will always use those generally accepted definitions.

Then what can you do if you're the negative and you're faced with a definition you consider unfair?

It's not a good idea to reject the definition outright. The debate will only turn into an argument over what some dictionary tells us. Instead point out to the audience just what the affirmative is doing:

"Frankly, we're surprised to see the affirmative include weapons in the definition of foreign aid. From their research on the topic, the affirmative speakers must know that weapons are always put in a separate category. When nations talk about foreign aid, they mean food, technology, manufacturing and farming equipment, money, and other forms of humanitarian assistance—not military assistance. But, since that's the definition the affirmative wants, we're not going to get into an argument over it.''

You'll gain instant credit for being generous enough to go along with the affirmative's unfair tactic. And you might even be able to shame the affirmative into changing its definition.

Of course, don't forget to revise any parts of your case that the unexpected definition may affect.

Organizing Your Case: The Constructive Speeches

Take a look at any debate resolution—for instance, the NFL topic that was recently debated: ''Resolved, that the federal government should initiate and enforce safety guarantees on consumer goods.''

Since you've defined your terms, you know what the resolution says. But what does it really mean?

In essence, any debate resolution calls for changing the way things are now (or, in debate jargon, changing the status quo).

So if you're the affirmative, you have to prove three basic issues: You have to show what's wrong with the status quo. You have to have a plan that will right those wrongs. And you have to show that your plan won't lead to any worse results. To win the debate, you must prove all three points.

On the other hand, if you're the negative, you can win by knocking down only one of those three affirmative points. You can prove that things are fine the way they are. Or, you can agree that the status quo should be changed, but prove that the affirmative's plan wouldn't do any good. Or, you can show that the affirmative's plan, while it might do some good, would lead to much more harm. Of course, you can also try to attack the affirmative on all three sides.

There's a fourth general technique, too, that either side can use: the matter of alternatives. The affirmative can attempt to prove that there are no better alternatives than its plan for changing the status quo. The negative can come up with a counterplan.

And those, basically, are the lines of strategy you'll use in every debate.

To prove each of your general topics, you should have one major point and two or three subpoints. (You probably won't have time for more.) For example, say you're debating the affirmative side of the resolution on consumer safety. You have to show first of all why the status quo needs to be changed.

Your main point may be that without government guarantees, many products appearing in the marketplace today aren't safe. As your first subpoint, to emphasize that this is an important problem, you may want to show how many serious injuries result from unsafe merchandise. For your second subpoint, you may want to prove that when the government doesn't oversee things, companies don't take enough care themselves to make sure products are safe. Your third subpoint may be that consumers on their own can't recognize until too late that the goods they buy are harmful.

Usually it's good strategy to put your strongest subpoint last, to leave your listeners with the most effective impact. Give your second-strongest subpoint first, so you can catch your audience's attention. However, it's most important that the points follow logically.

There are two good rules of thumb to keep in mind when setting up your case:

- Never prove more than you have to.
- Never try to prove something that goes against logic, commonly accepted values, or your audience's deep-seated beliefs.

In the case of consumer-product safety just about everyone will agree that having safe products is a good idea. If you're the affirmative, don't waste time trying to prove it. If you're the negative, don't create a bad relationship with your audience by trying to disprove it.

On the other hand the idea that government should play a strong role in making sure products are safe is not such a commonly accepted idea. It's not an impossible position to uphold—you're not trying to maintain that 2 plus 2 equal 5. But, if you're the affirmative, you're going to have to be sensitive to the controversy that your case may provoke. Address it directly:

"Of course, there are times when it's not a good idea for the government to intervene in the marketplace. There is a legitimate concern about too much government regulation stifling the rights of a business to make its own decisions. But we're not advocating that sort of control. What we're talking about is control in a single, specific area: public safety and health. We give our government the authority to protect us against attack by other people by operating police departments and armed forces. Well, isn't it just as important to make sure our bodies are safe from attack by dangerous products?"

You don't have to take on the burden of proving that all government intervention is good. You only have to show that it's beneficial in the case of consumer-product safety.

You're going to be raising a lot of points in your constructive speeches, and you don't want anything to be missed. So it's a good idea to follow the old chiché: Tell the audience what you're going to say. Say it. Then summarize what you've just said.

In other words, at the beginning of your speech, briefly outline the main points you're going to raise, in the order you plan to discuss them. The typical way to do this is to say: "My partner and I will show that. . . ." Then go on with your case. When you're done, repeat the main points again. To have the most impact, say your main points in short, simple, clear sentences.

On the Spot: The Rebuttals

The nice thing about a constructive speech, of course, is that you can prepare it in advance. Unfortunately that's only half the debate—or less. It's the on-the-spot attack and defense—mainly in the rebuttals—that really determine whether you win or lose. And rebuttals are the hardest part of all.

Mark Andrews's first high school debate was typical. He felt pretty confident as he sat down after giving his first affirmative constructive speech. But then the negative team began its attack—and, Mark said, "I just froze. My whole case, which I'd thought was so perfectly prepared, seemed to be falling apart. I couldn't even take notes fast enough to keep up with what the negative was saying, so how could I have enough time to think of arguments to counter them? I really began to panic."

It's understandable why Mark, or any other debater, would feel panicky. However, the situation is not really as bad as it may seem. You can actually plan most of your rebuttals ahead of time, just as you plan your constructive speeches.

For instance, if you're the negative team, you know that the affirmative is going to have to prove why the status quo is no good. So, put yourself in that team's place well before the debate and try to think of all the reasons they might come up with. Work on that side of the question just as hard as you work on your own case. Once you've put the affirmative side together, of course, go back and plot out your defense.

In fact if you're going to be debating throughout the year and following NFL rules, you will have to prepare both affirmative and negative cases anyway. Teams in NFL tournaments always switch off, taking one side in one contest and the other side in the next round.

Sure, it's always possible you'll face a team that's come up with a surprise argument you hadn't predicted. And you can never know beforehand exactly what an affirmative team's plan will be. Still, if you've researched the issue thoroughly, there aren't too many ways you can be surprised. There are only a limited number of good arguments on any debate topic and a limited number of logical plans for correcting any problem. After just a few debate tournaments, Judy recalls, she and her partner developed a shorthand for the types of arguments they kept running across most frequently. This enabled them to make notes easily during their debates.

There are two main theories of rebuttal.

One theory follows the classic rule that you should never

concede anything to the opposition. Therefore, you should attack every single point the other team brings up—even if a point is minor, even if your attack is weak. By the same token, you should defend yourself against every single argument raised against your case.

The advantage of this theory is that you don't give your opponents any victories by default. You don't give them the chance to claim that the points you've ignored are enough to win their case. But the disadvantage is that you have to use up some of your limited time on minor points. You may find yourself without enough time for the main issues.

So, the second theory advises you to concentrate your attack on the big points. The idea is that you can knock out your opponents' case by devastating two or three of its key underpinnings, even if you do leave a few weak points still standing.

Which strategy is better? Even expert debaters disagree. It probably depends on your own personal style, as well as the particular question you're debating. The important thing is for the two teams to meet head-on on the important issues.

There is also some good, general advice that applies no matter which theory you follow:

- Your main techniques are to show either that the other team's reasoning doesn't follow logically, or that the team hasn't backed up its claims with enough evidence. You can also counterpunch by proving a point of your own that directly contradicts the other team's case.
- It's all right to ridicule the opposing side a little. But don't speak sarcastically. For instance, you can say: "Does the negative really believe that big manufacturers are so humanitarian that they always have the interests of the public at heart?"
  But don't say:
  "I guess the negative just wants to *trust* everybody. Maybe they would have trusted the makers of thalidomide."
- Even when you're accepting one of your opponents' points, never say you're "admitting" or "conceding." Use the word "agree."
- If your adversaries raise a long string of trivial questions in an effort to get you to waste time in answering, don't fall

into their trap. Tell the audience exactly what's going on—and then ignore the questions.

- Try to answer your opponents' points in the order in which they bring them up. But if the other team emphasizes an issue you don't want to emphasize, take it up at the very beginning of your next speech. Dispose of it quickly. In that way—you hope—the judges and the audience will pay it less attention.
- As much as possible, relate what you're saying directly to what the other team said. Refer specifically to the point you're refuting: "Despite the negative's claims about too much bureaucracy, experience shows that. . . ."
- Finally, remember the old saying: The best defense is a good offense.

Question and Answer: Cross-examination

The style of cross-examination is very different from any of the other speeches in a debate. It's the only part of the debate in which you and someone from the opposite team actually speak directly with one another. And there's a set way in which to conduct it.

The idea is not to build your case or present new points, if you're the one doing the questioning. Instead home in on something the other side has said. Pounce on an incorrect statement or a claim that's not backed up by evidence. Force the other person to clarify an assertion that isn't clear. Then, in your later speeches, you can use any of the information you got from cross-examination to build your case further. It's best to focus on just one issue at a time rather than ask a series of unrelated questions about several different things.

Whoever is asking the questions is in charge. You can waste time if you want. You can interrupt the answers. The other person must reply to your questions, even if he or she doesn't see how they're relevant. In fact, the best cross-examination starts with questions that seem unimportant or innocent. It slowly forces the other team to follow a certain line toward admitting something that team doesn't want to admit. For instance:

Q—You're advocating a new kind of government agency to protect consumers. Is that basically correct?

A—Yes.

Q—Would one of the functions of this new agency be to protect the public from false and deceptive advertising?

A—Well, that's part of it. It would also—

Q—Let's just take it one step at a time. So that would be part of it. Okay. Would another function be to establish mandatory safety standards governing the design, construction, contents, performance, and labeling of consumer products?

A—What are you quoting from?

Q—Just answer the question, please. Would that be one of the functions?

A—Well, yes.

Q—All right. How about developing standards on the composition, quality, nutrition, and safety of food? Would that also be a function?

A—It could be.

Q—Those functions I've just described are some of the functions of the Federal Trade Commission, the Consumer Product Safety Commission, and the Food and Drug Administration. I've taken the descriptions straight out of the Federal Regulatory Directory published by the government. Now tell me, if we already have three agencies carrying out those very functions, what do we need your new agency for?

However, the questioner has to be fair. You can't ask a complex question and then insist on a "yes" or "no" answer. You shouldn't comment on the replies either. And the answerer can refuse to answer any question that is unfair or tricky. "When did you stop beating your wife?" is not fair play in debating.

A Few Words About Evidence

Just saying that unsafe products are sold in the marketplace is not going to convince your audience. You have to have the evidence to back up what you say.

We don't have the space here to discuss how to find and organize your evidence. You can get that kind of help from your librarian and debating coach. What we do want to talk about is using your evidence.

Basically, there are three main types: statistics, examples, and quotations from subject-matter experts. You should use at least two pieces of evidence to back up each point you make.

Quotations from subject-matter experts are probably the weakest type. After all, just about every issue of controversy has experts on both sides. You don't want to fall into a rut of debating whether "our expert is better than your expert." So, limit yourself in quoting from well-known authorities.

Statistics can be strong proof, but be careful of the ways they can be manipulated. For instance, look at the following results of an imaginary poll that asked people how good a job they thought the President was doing:

Excellent	15 percent
Good	20 percent
Fair	30 percent
Poor	20 percent
Terrible	15 percent

Two different teams could interpret this poll to prove almost anything they wanted. You could say, "A full sixty-five percent thought the President was doing only fair or worse." Or you could say, "Fully sixty-five percent thought the President was doing fair to excellent."

In short, make sure your evidence backs up your point as directly as possible. And never take quotations or statistics out of context in order to twist their meaning.

If you have a particularly striking piece of evidence, it can become an effective way to begin or end a speech. For instance, a high school senior in New York used a personal example to begin his second affirmative constructive speech in the spring of 1980, when the NFL topic was: "Resolved, that the United States should significantly change its foreign trade policy." Here's how he did it:

"I'd like to tell you about George, a good friend of mine. For ten years, George worked on the assembly line at a plant that manufactured TV sets. He was saving up to put his two children through college and he was paying off the mortgage on his home.

"But after ten years, George was suddenly thrown out of work. The assembly line shut down. The TVs George was making couldn't compete with the imports from Japan."

Bob, the high school senior, said that every time he used that introduction, "The audience seemed to sit up and take notice. I could tell that they paid close attention to the rest of my speech after that."

Being on Stage

Debate is a lot like the other forms of speaking we've talked about in this book. So the advice we've given on eye contact, gestures, and projecting your voice, for instance, apply here as well. However, because debate has a specific structure, there are a few extra things you should know.

You'll be standing when you give your speeches, probably at a lectern. Don't lean on the lectern. Stand just behind it and a bit to the side. Even during cross-examination, look at the audience.

One problem many debaters have comes from holding their notes and evidence cards. The best practice is to leave them on the lectern. If you must hold them, use only one hand and let that hand rest at your side. When you need to glance at a card, raise your hand to chest height. With only one hand needed for cards, you can use the other to gesture. While speaking, don't twist, bend, or otherwise play with the cards. Also, wait until you're finished speaking before taking your papers up from the lectern.

Most likely there will be a timekeeper in the front row of

the audience to signal you when your time is finished and at other important points. There's no need to acknowledge these signals by smiling or nodding. What if you run out of time while you're still in the middle of a sentence? Of course you can finish your thought—but that doesn't mean dragging your sentence out for an extra five minutes to throw in a few more points. To end smoothly, without letting the audience know you've run out of time, you can say something like: "In our next speech, my partner will show just how this works."

How formal you should be really depends on the circumstances. In high school debates you generally won't refer to the other side by name. Instead say, "the first affirmative speaker." More advanced debaters may call each other Mr. or Ms. So-and-So. Since so much of your speaking will be off-the-cuff, you're not expected to be beautifully eloquent, and a little casualness is all right too.

There are rules of common courtesy you should follow while the other team is speaking. No doubt you will have to take notes, look through your files, or talk with your partner. But do it quietly. Don't laugh or make any other distracting noises.

Part of a Team

When debating involves teams you have to coordinate your efforts with your partner. For instance, you probably won't have enough time in your first constructive speech to present your whole case. So you have to figure out how to divide the case between the two constructive speeches. It's usually a good idea to put as much as possible in the first speech, since you'll probably need more time in the second to answer your opponents' arguments. The second speaker can briefly remind the audience of what his or her partner already said. Just make sure you don't split any main points between the two speeches.

Because there are two of you, you can take advantage of your different styles and personalities. One of you may use a clearly earnest approach, while the other concentrates on attack.

One team member may not be as good a speaker as the other or may have more trouble thinking on the spot. That person should speak first, since the first constructive speech can be planned more fully in advance than the second speech. Besides, it's usually a good technique to end with a more forceful speaker whose words will stay with the audience.

Practice Activities

Let's say the topic is the resolution on consumer safety that we've already mentioned. You're about to give the second affirmative constructive speech. Your partner has already shown what's wrong with the status quo and outlined your proposal for changing things. Now, according to the way you've set things up, you are supposed to show how your proposal would improve the situation.

But meanwhile the first negative has given her constructive speech. She has claimed that there's already too much government bureaucracy, and no new agency is needed to protect consumers. In addition she has come up with some statistics about accidents resulting from use of dangerous products that dispute your statistics.

What should you do now in your second affirmative speech? Should you answer the negative's points first, or finish introducing your case? How should you handle the argument over statistics?

(Of course we haven't given you enough information to write out an entire constructive speech—and we don't expect you to. The important thing here is to think about your strategy, not prepare the actual arguments.)

When you think you've figured out what to do, take a look at some possible answers below. Then switch sides. Try to plot out how you would refute the answers we've given.

Suggested Solutions

Remember, the constructive speeches are your only chance to bring up new points. If you don't finish outlining your case now, you can't do it in the rebuttals. So you'd better concentrate on that.

However, you don't want to let the negative's comments get by unanswered. When you organized your case, you should have planned to allow yourself a few minutes in this speech for answering charges by the negative.

The best way to handle this is probably to open your speech with the most striking piece of evidence you have to counter one of the negative's arguments. Then you can say something like: "That's only one of the fallacies in the negative case. I'll get back to their other points later in my speech. But first I'll show you just how our plan will work."

As for the negative speaker's statistics: Think about them. Did she misinterpret anything? Just how clear is the point her figures make? Do they really back up what she's saying? As we've said, it's easy to manipulate numbers. If there's any doubt about the way the speaker used her statistics, that doubt can make a good opener for your speech. On the other hand, if she seems on solid ground, don't get caught up in the issue. It's only a minor point. You might say: "Whether ten people are injured or ten thousand people, that's still too many. Consumers need the protection that only a government agency can give."

CHAPTER 17
Speechwriting for Professionals—Practical Techniques

For major political leaders and high-ranking business executives today, the work needed to conduct necessary research and to write the many speeches they give could occupy large blocks of their very expensive time. Mainly for this reason, speechwriting for political and corporate leaders has emerged in the last fifty years as a distinct professional specialty.

Another reason is illustrated by an incident involving President Lyndon B. Johnson. Once, after he had happened to give an extemporaneous speech over national TV, a friend who'd been impressed urged him to do all his addresses that way.

"Never again," Johnson is reported to have said. "It's too dangerous to speak without a script."

Professional speechwriting has tended to develop in the business world along with the rise of the field of public relations, and in politics along with growth in specialized techniques for running campaigns, taking opinion polls, and making maximum political use of communications media. The larger and more settled sector of speechwriting is the corporate variety. This chapter deals primarily with corporate speechwriting, highlighting practical techniques in the field and outlining especially notable issues and themes used in it today.

The speechwriters serving a large corporation are usually part of the in-house public relations staff of the firm or are provided by an outside public relations consulting agency retained by the corporation. Some firms assign speechwriting and related responsibilities to a department called public affairs, which carries on work connected with public relations and government relations. However, speechwriting as a corporate service functions in much the same way, regardless of the organizational forms through which it may be provided.

Incidentally, speechwriting can prove to be an attractive and fascinating profession. An able writer often collaborates with powerful and influential individuals. Subtle treatment of important, sometimes lofty, ideas may be required. Speechwriting can also be lucrative. Free-lance corporate speechwriters can earn amounts ranging up to one hundred fifty dollars per minute of the finished speech. Staff writers within a corporation can have incomes as high as thirty to seventy thousand dollars a year.

Obviously, it is not a specialty in which you can give full expression to your own ideas. But your ideas still have a substantial place in the work. You are hired to use your ideas to take the words of a client and mold them, shape them, and put them in the best light.

How the Speechwriter Typically Helps Develop a Speech

Let's quickly examine the process by which a corporate speechwriter typically helps develop a speech. Most often, the writer works with an executive on an ongoing basis, for the process works best when writer and speaker are congenial and know how to work together. Also, the writer usually has a trusted, continuing connection with the firm so that full advantage can be taken of the research capabilities and staff of experts within the company.

The speechwriter begins, generally, by listening. As the CEO (Chief Executive Officer) or other executive talks, the writer studies the executive's natural diction, speech rhythms, vocabulary, gestures, and other speaking traits. The writer's ear must attune itself to the speaker. Otherwise, the speaker will have to adapt his speech to the text, and this can result in clumsiness. The writer must also listen for the speaker's general frame of ideas and knowledge, since the speaker might be embarrassed if questioned on unfamiliar ideas and facts.

Early in the process, a good deal of research is in order, since the speaker's point of view must be supported by facts. Another reason for doing research is to learn the prevailing trends of thought on the subject of the speech. A speaker should not get caught espousing ideas that have been discredited.

Research will involve trips to the library and to bookstores plus a great deal of reading in magazines, newspapers, and books. Many speechwriting units will have available to them the services of at least one competent researcher. Other good sources of information are experts within the company and outside, such as government officials. Most companies will have lobbyists in Washington or they will belong to a trade association that has one or more lobbyists on its staff. Lobbyists can be valuable for information on legislative and executive matters.

The speechwriter will ingest this information. The next task is to do what he or she was hired to do—work magic on a body of information. It is precisely this ability that separates the writer from the researcher. The draft will then be passed around among the writer's colleagues for comments, criticisms, and editing.

Very often, there will be a session with the legal department to check any passages that might prove problematic.

At this point it is time to submit the near-final speech to the speaker. In some cases, such a draft will be accepted as is. In other cases, the speaker and other staff members will go at it with heavy revisions. If changes are demanded, the writer will often make them, but changes may also be made by others.

For delivery of the talk, the writer may become director and producer of the speech as well. If there is time, especially with an inexperienced speaker, it is best to have a session with the speaker in which he reads the text aloud. The writer should listen for awkwardness and improve the text as required to overcome the awkwardness. He will be alert to any hint that the speaker doesn't understand an idea and coach him so as to make the delivery as smooth as possible. If there are any slides or other audiovisual aids planned for the presentation, there should certainly be rehearsal in using them. As noted earlier, there's nothing more embarrassing than having a speaker talk about the wrong slide or fumble while discussing a chart.

Use Daring to Make News

Several years ago two communications professors, Donald Shields and John Cragan, set out to turn the world of political speechwriting upside down. They spent months searching newspapers and magazines for statements on about twenty public issues. Each quotation they selected had to conform to one of three strong positions on one of the issues. For example, in foreign affairs, they used cold-war, neo-isolationist, and power politics as their standards. After transferring these positions to index cards, they asked natives of Peoria, Illinois, to rank the cards in order of agreement and importance. After feeding all the quotations and the rankings into a computer, they were able to have speeches written by the computer that would please all kinds of audiences as well as speeches that would appeal to everyone and offend no one. These computer-generated speeches used the language of the quotations, complete with adverbs and adjectives.

The intent of the two men was satirical, but their experiment produced disheartening results. Instead of exposing the lack of substance of standard political speeches—which their computer was able to emulate with great skill—they found themselves pursued by candidates for a variety of offices who wanted to have the machine write inoffensive speeches for them.

In politics, where more and more politicians seem to win office by offending as few people as possible, this may be appropriate. In business, however, there may on occasion be reasons to avoid the safe speech and go for the controversial, newsworthy approach.

A study by Opinion Research Corporation found that despite all the work, skill, thought, planning, and time that go into executive speeches, only about one fourth measure up as really good.

Speechwriters might keep this in mind as they watch their work ironed out, distilled, and pasteurized by committees of lawyers, board members, and less-than-expert advisors. Many of these people have a stake in playing it safe. Others seem habitually unable to be direct in any situation. Thus, even when companies want to make news, they sabotage themselves by pulling their punches.

A good news-making speech, one which puts a speaker and his company into the public eye, is one that has a touch of daring, humor, and some style.

Qualities of a Good Speech Developed by a Speechwriter

Let's consider some important qualities of a good speech as developed by a speechwriter. One view of poor speeches or speech material developed by beginners is expressed by a top writer at a multinational bank with headquarters in New York City. She distinguished between those applicants for speechwriting jobs who write term papers and those who write speeches.

"A term paper," she says, "is something people read because they *have* to, not because they *want* to."

When people apply for jobs at the bank, all too often they hand in term papers as samples of their speechwriting.

"They write up their research in clear prose, but they lose me after the first paragraph," says this speechwriter. "It comes out deadly dull despite all the hard work that went into it. There's no humor, no memorable phrasing. They flee from taking positions of any kind."

When you read an effective speech, it may seem, on the surface, to be simple, repetitive, and somewhat naïve. It may score points rather crudely. It may not read like a great document, but it may be a great speech.

All those qualities that make the speech seem somewhat

sophomoric on reading can be effective in getting major points across convincingly. You may say to yourself, if he said it once, he must have said it a hundred times. But if he said it a hundred times, you remembered it.

It sometimes helps to tie an important idea to a memorable phrase, something which people will take note of because it strikes them on a deeper level than their immediate level of consciousness.

This could be poetic. Take this one from a Carter energy message: "[We are] dangerously dependent on a thin line of oil tankers stretched halfway around the earth." It combines alliteration with imagery.

One trick employed by many professionals is to take a phrase people are already likely to know and use it in a new and novel way.

You may know the phrase "separate but equal." This was the rationale for segregation of schools in the South. It was held that as long as the schools were equal, there was nothing wrong with assigning white children to certain schools, and black to others.

In writing a speech on the inherent unfairness of regulating banks while allowing nonbank financial institutions to function as banks without any regulation, a speechwriter used the phrase "separate but unequal." It may strike you as a cheapening of an emotion-charged issue, but the fact is that when the phrase was used before audiences of congressmen and regulators, it was dynamite.

Using Elements of Suspense and Surprise

If you can think ahead of your audience for the sake of surprise, you will often succeed. Many benefits are to be gained from a little scheming and brainstorming. Speechwriting is strategy as well as wordsmithing. You might think of holding back some of your best material until late in your speech and using it to throw a late knockout punch.

One of the best examples of this comes once again from the world of banking.

When New York City was in dire financial trouble a number of years ago, the Senate Banking Committee held hearings to decide whether the federal government should guarantee loans by private banks to the ailing city. At the time, the private banks were being criticized for extending loans to poor countries so they could pay their oil bills with the result that the banks' liquidity was in jeopardy. The press harped only on the fact that the banks had made these loans out of greed to gather in the high interest rates that were available.

What the press omitted was the fact that most of these loans had been guaranteed by individual governments or by world lending authorities.

The speechwriters decided, in the interests of drama, to hold back this bit of information until their speaker was challenged on the point by one of the senators. It was a calculated risk. If the question was never asked, the point would never be made.

Sure enough, however, the chairman of the committee asked how the banks could lend billions to poor countries with little hope of repayment and yet deny aid to New York City.

The answer came back—because those loans were guaranteed. The point was made and made big.

Elements on Which the Speechwriter Is Expert

Addresses tend to turn out well if the seasoned speechwriter is given full freedom on elements in which he is expert.

Suppose you're an experienced speechwriter. One element on which you're the expert is adapting new material to the natural style of a speaker. There may be times as an outside writer when you must write without ever meeting the speaker. You will simply be given an order and told to execute it. In this case you have no choice, but you might try to secure copies of the client's other speeches and perhaps a tape recording of the client's voice.

It is always best, however, if you can meet the client and observe and listen. Watch the client for any signs of discomfort or lack of ease. Listen for the words he uses most often. Try to establish his fluency not just with language but with ideas.

It is imperative that you avoid giving him material outside his normal range of thought, and words outside his style of delivery.

A New York speechwriter tells of a time when as a free-lancer he actually persuaded a client to make an entirely different kind of speech than what was ordered.

The original order was for a prepared text with jokes to introduce an after-dinner program. It quickly became obvious as the writer listened to the client that this approach was inappropriate.

"I told him he didn't need a speechwriter. I could have charged him seventy-five dollars an hour for my time, but he wasn't the kind of person who works well from a text. Instead I advised him to work on some notes he could refer to during his speech. What he had to do wasn't really a speech at all as much as performing as master of ceremonies. He was better off winging it than giving a speech."

As a professional speechwriter, you are selling experience and judgment. You are the expert on certain key elements, and you should act like an expert.

For instance, someone may order a forty-five-minute after-dinner speech with lots of figures. You might ask the client, "Do you want to put everybody to sleep?"

Or someone may insist that you water down a speech that is intended to make a major news announcement. You might respond, "Do you want press coverage, or don't you?" You are the experienced writer and must give your clients the benefit of your experience.

After a text is complete, try to go over it with the speaker. It is common sense to realize that your words are going to be affected by the person who says them aloud. The full weight of those words is unpredictable until you hear them spoken by the person who will be delivering them.

Listen for any clumsiness. If the client's breathing pattern cannot support your sentences, change them to enable him to speak them easily. You want the client to be familiar with what you've done, and if any revisions have to be made, make them yourself whenever possible.

Be alert to the client's understanding of the content. If the emphasis used in reading aloud is wrong, there is a chance he doesn't understand the point of what you've written. It can be embarrassing to hear a speaker reading a text stumbling over an idea he doesn't fully understand.

What else can go wrong if the client reads your text without adequate preparation? One executive received a speech from a trusted writer at the last minute and went before his audience. In the middle of the speech, the writer had included a joke. The speaker read the joke and found it so funny that he cracked up with laughter and could not continue.

So far we have been dealing with you as the expert. But your client is an expert too. He pays the bills and that qualifies him as an expert on lots of things. If he wants something, all your exhortations to the contrary will not change his mind. You must recognize where your responsibility ends and live with it.

A warning: You can't turn a bad speaker into a silver-tongued orator overnight, and even though business executives speak in public fairly often, they tend to be pretty bad at it. Thus a bad speech is not usually the speechwriter's fault.

Don't be surprised if the text you hear given from the dais is unrecognizable as the one you wrote. There are two reasons why this might be true. One is that your text may have been homogenized and pasteurized by a committee before the final draft was complete. The client has had the last word in deciding how he wishes to conduct his business.

The other reason is that he may just butcher it with his phrasing, his emphasis, and so forth. You wrote the speech to perfection for his voice, but he refused to rehearse with you.

You're a pro. Don't go to pieces over it.

On the other hand, a great speaker can lift your text above itself. One speechwriter tells of having once done an assignment for Carl Stokes, once mayor of Cleveland and now a broadcaster. Her reaction to Stokes's speech was rapturous. Chances are you will have good experiences as well as bad.

Research Tips for Speechwriters

The heart of any speech may well be the research that goes into it. You want to know the facts, even if it suits your purposes to bend them a little.

There may be times when the facts dictate something other than the conclusion you want to give. You may want to deliver an upbeat message when the data you have gathered call for doom and gloom.

Either way, you need the best you can get so that the facts can be used artfully. You will develop your own methods, but here are a few tips.

Many big companies maintain libraries of their own that will help you greatly. It pays as well to do your own clipping and ordering for the library. Don't be afraid to call outside your company to appropriate sources in government and industry for further information.

Facts can be interpreted in as many ways as there are people who know them. Even figures can be confused, bent, or obfuscated. Try to get second and third opinions. Interview people in your company and outside, if possible.

One widespread impression is that *Time* magazine can be a valuable source of information, in particular for statistics. *Time* researchers are known for the quality of their fact-checking. Other excellent business sources are *Fortune, Business Week,* and trade magazines.

Use articles and company reports. If you have trouble with pronunciation of a foreign name, call the embassy of the country or person in question. If your company has a lobbyist, call him for information about what the government is doing.

If you are part of a team, help the other members of the team. In many speechwriting departments, camaraderie is of a high order. Ask others for old speeches, not for duplication but for verifying policy.

Research will help you establish what the policy of your company is on various issues. Brainstorm for anecdotes. Call colleagues and ask for whatever they have on the subject you are researching.

Get second opinions. One banker told his speechwriter that Shanghai was becoming *the* center for Asian finance, but someone at the Treasury Department told him it was absurd. What about Singapore? What about Hong Kong? In short, check and recheck.

Key Business Issues and Themes

Most speechwriters are employed by big business. After making soundings in the business community, we have discovered a number of issues and themes that promise to figure more and more in the speeches of business people in this decade. These key concepts and slogans are as follows.

DEMOCRATIC WAY OF LIFE—The assumption is that conducting business is a freedom more basic than any others, that without it, freedom of religion and freedom of the press will soon disappear.

NO SUCH THING AS A FREE LUNCH—Even three-martini lunches are not free. When a business person writes off a business lunch, the taxpayer picks up the tab. This is an all-purpose saying that can be used by conservatives or liberals.

SOCIAL BENEFITS OF BUSINESS—Profits for business may lift the rest of the country along with corporate dividends.

PRIVACY—The right to privacy is an inalienable right. When business champions privacy, it may really want to keep the books outside the scrutiny of the IRS and the SEC.

SELF-REGULATION—Government regulation, according to business gospel, may cost more and be less effective than the restraint imposed by sound business practice.

PAPERWORK—Regulated industries often point to the amount of time, money, and manpower they devote to complying with government regulations. This drag on their resources may sap economic vigor.

INTERNATIONAL MARKETPLACE GOVERNED BY OUT-OF-DATE LOCAL REGULATION—Business progresses so quickly that government regulation may distort the marketplace. Government is always in the position of fighting the last war.

INFORMATION KNOWS NO STATE OR NATIONAL BOUNDARIES—There has been an electronic revolution in business, particularly in finance. The transfer of money for investment can now follow the line of greatest profit, no matter where, and irrespective of state or national boundaries.

CAPITAL FORMATION—The process of building up resources to pay for new plants and equipment. This process may be a major focus of the debate on economic policy.

You can expect to see these buzzwords and themes again and again in business literature. There is a remarkable degree of agreement among people in business that government is the villain.

Occasionally you will see a dissenting opinion that blames management. It helps to examine both sides, although you may usually need to argue in favor of the company line.

Practice Activities

1. As you read newspapers and magazines, consider how you can be alert to adding to key issues and themes. For example, there is a complaint that *dumping* of foreign steel on the American market at less than cost of manufacture is killing the American steel industry. So "dumping in the American market" could go on your list. Start such a list. Keep it current. Start a clipping file for each topic on your list. This file will become a major source of information for the speeches you write.

2. Develop skill in analyzing both sides of an issue for treatment in speeches. For example, the big manufacturers' position on recall of shoddy merchandise often blames slipshod workmanship by assembly-line workers. The manufacturers blame the unions for making it impossible to fire lax

workers. At least one major industrialist, however, claims that every instance of major recall of merchandise, particularly automobiles, really reflects failures of design, management, or quality control—all management faults.

3. Make a list of familiar phrases such as "separate but equal" and try to transform them into provocative new ones. For example, "life, liberty, and the pursuit of profits," or "happiness is a warm bank account."

CHAPTER 18

For Executives: Shaping and Giving Major Addresses and Interviews

Speaking ability represents an increasingly important skill for an executive today. "Throughout the business community," business columnist Philip H. Dougherty wrote recently in *The New York Times,* "there is new emphasis on the need for executives to operate well on their feet, to handle themselves capably before audiences, and to speak articulately."

Outlined in this chapter are important actions that executives can take to improve their major addresses. The chapter treats, as well, the most important strategies to apply in speaking situations that are crucial for an executive—interviews with the press, including interviews on sudden emergencies for network TV.

Working with Speechwriters to Best Advantage

Much of an executive's prowess in giving major addresses can hinge on getting the best results from work with the company's speechwriting services. As noted in the previous chapter, corporations typically provide such services as part of an in-house public relations department, or through an outside public relations agency retained by the firm.

The experts with whom you may work should provide all the knowledge needed to give your address adequate professional quality. But you can make your addresses far more than just adequate by taking certain initiatives with your speechwriting team. (These initiatives will be discussed shortly.)

On that team would probably be two speechwriters—one who assists you regularly, and another who serves as backup when the first is unavailable. You would probably also often confer with the manager of these speechwriters. A congenial and time-saving working relationship is very likely to grow among these members of the team and the executive they serve.

Generating the Basic Idea for Your Address

Feel free to originate the basic idea for your talk, even though your speechwriting aides probably can suggest a number of good possibilities. Thinking about the assignment before you meet with the aides should lead to two or three ideas from which you can choose on further reflection. A main advantage of generating your own basic idea is that it tends to give the talk a distinctive originality and personal identity.

As one example, Walter B. Wriston decided on courage and the importance of risk-taking as the basic idea for one of his many major addresses. Wriston is the chairman and chief executive of Citicorp, which developed under his leadership into America's second-largest bank. Drawing on his personal background, Wriston recounted in the speech how his grandmother had journeyed West in a covered-wagon train with other pioneers, and how they had gone on to reach their destination even after half the party had been killed in Indian attacks.

Courage of that high order, Wriston declared, has since degenerated and now appears to have been replaced by a widespread attitude of "Be nice, feel guilty, and play safe."

In his speech Wriston went on to state his basic idea with the denunciation, "If there was ever a prescription for producing a dismal future, that has to be it."

A similarly stirring but different basic idea was expressed by Cornell C. Maier in a recent address before a chamber of commerce meeting. Maier is the chairman and chief executive of one of the country's largest aluminum producers, Kaiser Aluminum and Chemical Corporation. In his talk on "The New American Revolution," Maier said of the revolution of the 1980s that its first step "is the most important—to reestablish our identity, our pride, and our determination." He went on: "We must raise, not lower, our national expectations. Raise, not lower, our standard of living. Raise, not lower, our determination to succeed." He called for "a new approach, a revolutionary change, in the way all segments of our society work together."

In emphasizing that business in particular must shoulder social responsibilities with other groups, Maier said: "It is no longer true, if it ever was, that the business of business is only profits. . . . Business has to be involved in helping solve the broader social issues which do not affect our businesses in a direct sense but which do affect the social, political, or economic atmosphere that surrounds our employees, our shareholders, our customers, or the communities in which we operate."

To his audience of fellow business leaders, he declared, "You and I must be involved in solving the problems of minority unemployment, crime, housing, health, energy, inflation, and education—to name only a few." He added, "Business can't solve these problems by itself, but it can solve them through creative partnerships with government, educators, labor leaders, special interest groups, activists, and interested citizens."

As these examples suggest, you should be imaginative and open-minded in considering possible basic ideas at the start. Thus, it is best to begin by originating several alternative ideas to think over and talk about with associates and aides

Framing General Plans in the First Conference on Your Talk

Some time before your address is due to be given, you and your speechwriting aides should hold a first conference on the talk. At that session you'll be able to start discussing back and forth and settling on a basic idea for the address that you're excited about. If you have not thought about the talk beforehand, that first conference will be much less effective.

Many other useful steps can be taken at the conference. For example, you will all analyze where your address fits into the sequence both of the meeting at which you'll speak and of the company statements and moves that are anticipated for that general period of time.

Other facets of the speech on which you'll be able to reach initial understandings are such matters as the kind and content of visual aids you may use, details of the time and the place and the meeting-room arrangements, and general plans for publicity and publication.

Reacting to Initial and Revised Outlines of Your Talk

An initial outline of the talk will be prepared by your speechwriter, and this outline will be one of the main results of the first conference. This outline and the revised outlines that will inevitably be conceived may consist of highlights of passages or sections, each given in a few lines or words, interspersed with descriptive highlights. This type of summary outline gives something of the flavor and style of the talk as well as a structural identification of major parts of the talk.

It's at this outline stage that you can most easily make major changes in the coverage of the talk. Don't feel you must hold to the sequence or form of the talk as you first envisioned it. As with a blueprint, an outline gives you the chance to develop and improve a design in advance. It's easy at the outline stage to add or cut content for better coverage, timeliness, or flow.

Shifts in the first outline would generally be followed by the first revised outline with the changes worked in smoothly. One or more revised outlines can then be checked through by you and your aides until all the main parts appear to have been worked out well.

Polishing the First Draft and Revised Drafts

From a final outline your speechwriting team would develop the first draft of the talk. Go over the draft mainly to check how its translation from outline to fully worded form carries out what you want to convey in the address. Mark a copy of it with any changes you think are needed to bring it close to the mark you have in mind.

Next would come a second draft incorporating changes you have made and changes you have approved after suggestions by your speechwriters. A corrected copy of the second draft would enable you and your aides to seek clearances from higher management in your company. Approvals, or "sign-offs," you might want to get could include those provided by the firm's legal counsel, or by engineers checking on technical accuracy, and possibly those required from other company functions particularly affected by the speech, perhaps marketing or personnel.

After clearances and incorporation of resulting changes, your speechwriters may want to review visual aids with you, if you're using them. If so, the writers would develop and review with you any sketches or actual samples of possible aids, such as slides or flip-chart sheets. As you direct and they advise, they would go on developing the visuals into final form. They would also double-check the running time of the talk (with visuals, if used) at about this stage, and would work out with you any cuts or additions needed.

On one or more of the drafts, be sure to polish the language to fit your preferences and style, as well as the precise meanings you intend to convey. You might want to read through the talk aloud in private. In addition, once you feel comfortable with it, recite it into a tape recorder. After listening to the tape, polish the wording further as needed to give the talk the flow and flavor that will stamp it as your speech.

Giving Your Personal Touch to the Copy for Actual Delivery

Your speechwriting team would next supply you with a clean copy of the speech text for you to use in actually delivering the address. As we discussed in an earlier chapter, you might want this delivery copy made up on small, loose-leaf sheets that are perhaps 5 by 8 inches or 6 by 9 inches in size. The sheets can in turn be bound into a compact binder that you can hold easily or slip into a jacket pocket.

Basic directions and notes on such matters as (PAUSE) or (LAUGHTER) or emphasis on important words or phrases, indicated by underlining, would very likely be typed in on this delivery copy by your speechwriters. If slides or other visual aids are to accompany the talk, this copy would also show cues for each visual: Slide 3—PROFITS, *ON* . . . Slide 3—*OFF.* The copy might also carry notes about elements of a visual for you to point out.

Go through the talk in at least two or three private sessions with this copy. Put in any additional notations you will want for gestures and movements. As needed, smooth out the wording with changes you mark until all the phrasing feels completely natural to you. Adjust the pauses, the humor, the emphasis, the use and cues of any visual aids. When you have finished making these adjustments, you will know that everything is just the way you want it.

Adjustments and touch-ups like these give the address the stamp of your own personal thought and style. They help make the talk smoothly professional. They also help make the talk come alive with your own sense of interest and commitment.

Perfect Your Technique in Rehearsals

If you can, take enough time to rehearse the talk with your speechwriting aides or with a speech coach listening and watching to suggest improvements. Run through the address once or twice with full presentation of any visual aids you include. You must become thoroughly familiar with every aspect of your talk.

Conduct a dress rehearsal in the actual hall and with all the actual equipment and visuals that you'll use for the talk, if at all possible. Do this with a speech coach assisting and watching to advise. But if that cannot be done, at least try to check over the room and equipment with an aide in advance in order to have a fair idea of what you'll run into.

With careful preparation like this, you can't miss. Your address should be at the least a thoroughly competent job. At best, a knockout.

Elements of Good Speaking to Remember

For your actual delivery, be sure to remember to use those elements most essential for effectiveness, as we explained in an earlier chapter. First, keep eye contact with your listeners as much as possible all through your talk.

Be completely natural in your manner. This means being natural not only in your words but also in stance, gestures, movements, and facial expressions.

Let your voice be natural, not at all forced. But make certain to deepen it somewhat, and to speak slowly. These actions give it richness, carrying power, and strength of conviction.

For Interviews: Be Ready, Be Positive, Be Brief, Keep Cool

Most of the press or broadcast interviews you will schedule as an executive will provide time for some planning. Other interviews may come up without warning and have you confronting lights and microphones before TV cameras. Here are key points of advice on how to speak effectively in either kind of interview.

A press or broadcast interview for which you can prepare represents a cross between an address you would give from a complete text and an impromptu talk of the kind we described earlier. In getting set for such an interview, you and your speechwriting team can pull together past talks and other material for you to digest as background. Your speechwriters may draft short statements answering questions the interviewer is likely to ask. You can have these and key facts and figures in note form on cards or on a clipboard. It could be helpful for you to do some rehearsing, working with a speechwriting or public relations aide and recording the practice interviews on tape for checking.

For any possible surprise interviews by broadcasters or newspaper reporters, you must train yourself to stay in a constant state of readiness. Have in mind what you might say for each major kind of emergency news involving your company that may come up: a shipping accident, plant catastrophe, labor strike, public demonstration, or other sensational incident.

Specifically, be ready to comment briefly on each type of trouble but have at hand good ways of then switching to related positive facts about your firm. For example, in the event of a shipping or plant accident, be ready to supply information on how much your company spends on accident prevention and safety—for employees as well as the public— how good your company's safety record has been, and what emergency teams or other facilities are provided by it to prevent and deal with accidents.

Especially if you're being interviewed for TV news, say first the most important thing in favor of your company. And preface it by stating, for example, "Here is the most important fact of all." Mentioning this unmistakably at the beginning and at least once more early in the interview will give TV tape editors and news reporters the opportunity to recognize and include your statement in the report.

In addition, keep your "most important" statement brief— perhaps two short sentences, taking no more than about twenty seconds to say, repeating it verbatim the second time. If any of the interview is eventually put on the air, it would include this central statement justifying your position. Similarly, in print, reporters and headline writers would tend to treat your central statement with some respect.

You should of course go on after your opening "most important" statement to give further reasons, evidence, and explanations as time and need permit.

Don't be stampeded even if the story represents fast-breaking news. You will almost always be able to phone back in a few minutes if you are called for a statement to be recorded immediately over the telephone. You can have the interviewer and camera operator of an on-the-scene, mobile TV news unit get back to you for another two-minute take with their microphone and camera. By the way, before a TV news camera zooms in on you, put away anything shiny you may have on, like a piece of jewelry or a pocket pen and pencil. Shiny things sometimes flash irritatingly under TV lights.

Above all, under no circumstances should you let broadcast interviewers make you express anger if they try to put you on the defensive. The trick is to turn the tables on a hostile interviewer, making that person appear the villain to viewers or listeners. You do this by keeping calm and confident, and by smiling and continuing to look the interviewer directly in the eye. You may also say, politely and firmly, things like:

"Don't you think that's a loaded question? I'd like to restate it and answer as follows. . . ."

"Pardon me, but you are getting the facts wrong. The truth is this. . . ." Make such an observation as soon as a misstatement is made. Interrupt in a polite way rather than let it stand unchallenged.

Remaining constructive and level-headed when being needled by an interviewer can prove difficult. You may want to set up some practice sessions with a speechwriting aide to develop this ability. Your aide will know how to be as caustic as interviewers can be.

In the nation's capital, Vada Ward Marcantonio is a former actress who coaches government and business leaders in public appearances. NBC regularly sends its own broadcasters to her for training. She has also trained many members of Congress as well as business leaders, including a former head of the American Gas Association. He consulted her in preparing to testify before Congress on the question of deregulation of natural gas.

"Appearing before Congress can be rough," Ms. Marcantonio has said in discussing stressful interviews. "Congressional questioners can be so insulting." To prepare her clients for such ordeals, she explains ways in which they can control their anger and then gives them practice by asking them sarcastic, stinging questions like ones they may soon face. "Anger shows in your face and body language," she observes, "and unless you are extremely adept, you lose your audience. I tell my students just to consider their adversary uninformed and to try to maintain the attitude that you are giving them information."

Training sessions like hers to prepare prominent individuals to act effectively in the stress of situations like TV or Congressional grillings have become increasingly popular in the business world. You may want to take a training course like this. Firms that have put many of their top management people through such programs include Lockheed, Adolph Coors Company, Allstate Insurance, and Standard Oil Company of California. Gulf Oil has provided such training for some 2,000 of its managers, down to levels including refinery heads and ship captains.

This training is expensive, though, according to a *Business Week* article of 1981. Hill and Knowlton, the nation's largest public relations agency, offers a full-day seminar for five executives for a fee of five to ten thousand dollars. In Dallas, Texas, CommuniCorp provides a two-and-a-half-day course attended by eight executives for a fee of $12,500. Lilyan Wilder, a New York City consultant, charges fees which start at $1,000 per student for six hours of training.

Experience in varied settings can give you helpful practice in handling such hostile, high-stress situations. Speaking before community groups may provide experience in answering acrimonious questioners, particularly in the question-and-answer sessions following a talk or panel discussion. Debating experience in school or college also helps develop poise and resourcefulness in the face of opposition and pressure.

Good Speech Shapes Individual Fortunes

Learning to speak well in an emergency or just in the normal course of business meetings takes much energy and work, but the effort involved tends to be handsomely rewarded. The really able speaker in business normally pulls far ahead of otherwise comparable peers who can't speak well.

Countless people fit this description. Linda Wachner, for example, became president of a major cosmetics house, Max Factor, when she was only thirty-two years old. She was the youngest woman president of a Fortune 500 company. Initially, she came to prominence in the job she took when just out of college. She went to work for a retailing firm, Associated Merchandising Corporation.

"I was there a very short time when at the spur of the moment I had to run a meeting," she says. "Well, I'm not nervous at all when I speak to people, so the meeting went very well."

So did her subsequent meteoric career. And with increasingly effective powers of speech, you should move into larger career horizons yourself.

INDEX

MONEY TALKS!
How to get it and How to keep it!